Wakefield Press

An Indigenous South

An Indigenous South

German Writers on Colonial South Australia

Edited by
Peter Monteath and Matthew P. Fitzpatrick

Wakefield Press
16 Rose Street
Mile End
South Australia 5031
www.wakefieldpress.com.au

First published 2024

Copyright in this collection © Peter Monteath and Matthew P. Fitzpatrick, 2024
Copyright in individual chapters remains with the respective author

All rights reserved. This book is copyright. Apart from
any fair dealing for the purposes of private study, research,
criticism or review, as permitted under the Copyright Act,
no part may be reproduced without written permission.
Enquiries should be addressed to the publisher.

Cover and text designed by Michael Deves, Wakefield Press

ISBN 978 1 92304 235 3

A catalogue record for this book is available from the National Library of Australia

Wakefield Press thanks Coriole Vineyards for continued support

Contents

Acknowledgements	*vii*
Foreword by Dennis O'Brien	*ix*
Matthew P. Fitzpatrick and Peter Monteath, 'Einheimisch': German (Mis)Understandings of Indigenous Australians	*1*

Sojourners and Immigrants

Hermann Koeler, 'Some Notes on the Natives on the East Coast of Gulf St. Vincent in South Australia, 1837 and 1838'	*23*
Dirk Meinerts Hahn, 'On the Savages, or Natives, in South Australia'	*41*
Friedrich Gerstäcker, *Australia*	*49*
Gustav Listemann, 'On the Natives'	*66*
Emil Jung, 'The Murray Estuary and Its Inhabitants'	*76*

Missionaries

Christian Gottlob Teichelmann, 'Letters, Diaries and Reports'	*91*
Clamor Wilhelm Schürmann, 'Letters and Diary'	*115*
Samuel Gottlieb Klose, 'Letter to Dresden'	*143*
Heinrich August Eduard Meyer, 'Manners and Customs of the Aborigines of the Encounter Bay Tribe, South Australia'	*147*
Carl Strehlow, 'The Aborigines of Central Australia'	*160*

Geographers and Naturalists

Hans Hermann Behr, 'On the Aborigines of Adelaide Based on His Own Observations during His Stay There'	*173*
Wilhelm von Blandowski, 'On the Aborigines of Australia'	*184*
Charles Wilhelmi, 'Manners and Customs of the Port Lincoln Natives in Australia'	*193*
Georg von Neumayer, 'On the Intellectual and Moral Characteristics of the Natives of Australia'	*222*

Anthropologists and Ethnographers

Wilhelm Krause, 'Anthropological Journey to Australia'	*243*
Erhard Eylmann, 'Journey to Point McLeay'	*250*
Leonhard Adam, 'On the Customs and Law of Some Australian Tribes: Personal First-hand Accounts from Two Natives'	*263*
Index	*279*

Cultural Notification

Readers of this volume are warned that it contains many terms, descriptions, concepts and images which are highly insensitive and offensive. These would not now be acceptable. The language reflects the original authors' attitudes and the explicitly racist assumptions of the period in which the items were written. The editors wish to make clear that these are rightly considered highly inappropriate today.

Readers should also be aware that, in some Aboriginal and Torres Strait Islander communities, use of the names of people who are now deceased may cause distress, particularly to the relatives and descendants of these people. This book includes the names of deceased Indigenous people.

Instances of the removal of passages on the grounds of cultural sensitivity are indicated in the text through the use of square brackets. Elsewhere, the use of ellipses shows where text has been edited to remove thematically irrelevant material.

Acknowledgements

This book was enabled by research funding provided by the Yitpi Foundation, which promotes the study of the culture of Indigenous people in Australia. It has also benefitted from the Australian Research Council's Future Fellowship scheme (FT210100448 – Strategic Friendship: Anglo-German Cooperation in the Asia-Pacific Region). Along the way it has profited from the dedicated research support provided by Lisa Mudge and Charissa Kurda; Lisa also took on the task of preparing the index.

We thank Dennis O'Brien for his advice on the texts considered for publication here, as well as for his thoughtful Foreword. Also to be thanked are the archivists of the Lutheran Archives in Adelaide who were generous with their time and expertise, above all Rachel Kuchel, Angela Schilling and Ben Hollister. As on numerous previous occasions, thanks are due to Lois Zweck for her assistance with archival materials, and to both Lois and Lee Kersten for their kind permission to make use of earlier translations of works included here. Greg and Christine Lockwood provided invaluable advice on German missionaries. Once again, we are indebted to Michael Bollen and Wakefield Press for their commitment to publishing work on South Australian history. In Germany, thanks are due to Dr Stephanie Walda-Mandel of the Overseas Museum in Bremen for her time and expertise.

Finally, we thank all eleven translators, both those whose previously published work has been included here, and those whose work was specifically commissioned for this volume. In alphabetical order they are: Heidi Brasse, Lothar Brasse, Lee Kersten, Marcus Krieg, Thomas Kruckemeyer, Greg Lockwood, Erich Meier, Peter Monteath, Geoff Noller, Aileen Ohlendorf, Harald Ohlendorf, Lois Zweck.

Foreword
by Dennis O'Brien

Ngai Nari Dennis Kartameru O'Brien Ngai Kaurna Narungga Meyu. My name is Dennis O'Brien and I am a Kaurna and Narungga man, first born son of my family.

This work is important to Aboriginal peoples in Australia. More needs to be written about the historical events and views of early colonisation / invasion of our countries.

Some of the language in this book can be confronting for Aboriginal people and non-Aboriginal people alike, but this needs to be seen. Racist words are nothing new to Aboriginal people in Australia, these all have an origin. This book helps to show these origins. Understanding the history of this country is understanding why the use of pejorative terms like 'monkey' for our Aboriginal people is so offensive, as are others too numerous to mention. Such things go beyond 'just words'. As this book shows, our people were treated like this for a hundred plus years, described as 'primitive', 'less evolved', in line with social Darwinian theories. Most Aboriginal people have little doubt that these ideas led to the excuses for land occupation and the cultural genocide of our people.

We are survivors. We are still here, and we are becoming stronger again through our cultural and linguistic revival. Today Kaurna people work with people who had connections with the German missionaries that came to Adelaide as part of our own Kaurna language revival and have made close connections. Teichelmann and Schürmann, two Lutheran German missionaries from Dresden, documented just over three thousand Kaurna words and a thirty-page grammar. I have no doubt that they would have had a good rapport with the Kaurna people to do this.

Many of my people have mixed feelings about early missionaries, colonists and anthropologists. In one way they are happy that culture, language and history were documented, but in another rightfully angry for the reasons it was documented in the first place.

However, our people acknowledge that not everyone that interacted with our people in the early days of colonisation and invasion was determined to destroy our lives, culture and language.

I think it is also important to mention here that the British as well as other European nations that colonised parts on the world, including the Americas in 1492 onwards, were well aware of the effects of smallpox, massacres, assimilation and the seizure of land from Indigenous people well before they landed in Australia in 1788. I think the argument of ignorance or that non-Indigenous people didn't know what they were doing at the time does not hold here.

I appreciate as an Aboriginal person the chance to read and then 'write back' in this publication.

Matthew P. Fitzpatrick and Peter Monteath, 'Einheimisch': German (Mis)Understandings of Indigenous Australians

This book was not merely created in Tarndanya/Adelaide. It also reflects the entangled Indigenous and European histories of this place. The city's European name commemorates the German royal Adelheid von Sachsen-Meiningen, who was later known as Queen Adelaide of the United Kingdom and Hanover. The land upon which this city has been built, however, is Tarndanya, the name given to the area by the Kaurna Miyurna, the custodians and traditional owners of the land whose culture and language marked the region for the twenty millennia before it was effaced by the European settlers who built upon it a European-style city.

This was not a mutually agreed upon change. As one sympathetic author has written, 'No attempts were ever made to negotiate with the Kaurna for the voluntary transfer of their lands.'[1] Instead, without reference to the interests or views of Indigenous people, 'the colonisers, in the form of the South Australian colonisation commissioners ... attempted to mobilise the resources of the law in order to ensure that Aboriginal rights in land would never be respected.'[2] Consequently, not only the Kaurna people but all of South Australia's Indigenous peoples saw their country knitted together with other British settler colonies to become part of the nation-state of Australia. Even those Aboriginal nations living beyond the bounds of settlement were declared subjects of the British Crown, with their law deliberately set aside as 'too "savage" to be recognised'.[3] Meanwhile,

Matthew Moorhouse, the man appointed South Australia's Protector of Aborigines, was also the author of 'South Australia's most devastating single massacre of Indigenous people on official record'.[4]

Unsettling South Australia and 'Anglobalisation'

In the twenty-first century, the enormity of these events is well understood by South Australia's First Nations peoples but is still sinking into the historical thinking of its non-Indigenous settler population. As histories reassessing South Australia's frontier history emerge, difficult facts about the processes and the extent of dispossession have come more clearly into view. Even as much official business across South Australia today begins with a version of the affirmation '*ngandlu tampinthi ngadlu Kaurna yartangka tikanthi*',[5] it still remains difficult to summon up a mental picture of the grave historical realities that sit behind these words. Walking along North Terrace or through Rundle Mall in central Adelaide, the shape and rhythms of Kaurna country prior to the long process of dispossession have become increasingly difficult to imagine. Less than two hundred years ago, however, the entire state of South Australia was unmistakably Indigenous.

Prior to formal colonisation there had been numerous contacts between Indigenous and non-Indigenous people, particularly along the South Australian coast. Most infamously, this 'pre-colonial' history includes that of the whalers and stolen Indigenous women living on *Karta Pintingga*, the 'Island of the Dead' (Kangaroo Island).[6] Apart from such footholds, however, the land and the ways that it was lived on reflected the beliefs and way of life of the Kaurna, Ngarrindjeri, Ngadjuri and other Indigenous peoples who had lived in the region for tens of thousands of years. These First Nations had carefully managed the land in accordance with their lore and law, which, in what is today's greater Adelaide region, saw fire-managed grasses attracting herd animals like kangaroos that could be hunted. Well-watered scrublands encouraged the growth of edible plants, which in turn encouraged the proliferation of nutritionally valuable birds and reptiles. Unlike the bushfire-prone wilderness of uncleared wattles and eucalypts that grew after dispossession, the surrounds of pre-settlement Tarndanya were often described in the early years of colonisation as a resembling a well grassed and cared-for park.[7]

Wresting this territory from Indigenous people entailed violence, most shockingly physical violence such as the murder of Aboriginal people by pastoralists,[8] but also violence to land management practices and the cosmological and epistemological frameworks within which Aboriginal people had lived for millennia.[9] This destruction, however, was unevenly distributed across the state. In areas further from coastal and riparian European settlements, language and firm ties to Country and culture survived, and Indigenous people gained valuable time to adapt to new circumstances. In urban areas, however, the rapid and comprehensive processes of colonisation and forced assimilation made preserving language and culture more difficult. The retrieval of these has required painstaking work by the First Nations people of the twentieth and twenty-first centuries.[10] In a bitter irony, the Indigenous record was so effectively obscured in South Australia that the process of reclaiming culture and of epistemological decolonisation has required a careful reading of the records left by settler-colonists against the grain, because some of these colonists, particularly missionaries and anthropologists, had assiduously recorded their encounters and understandings (but also misunderstandings) of local people, language and culture in great detail to aid the work of colonisation. Deep immersion in colonial materials, that is, has proved itself indispensable to the processes of cultural reconstruction.[11] It is hoped that the current volume will further assist in this process.

Like the British queen after whom Adelaide was named, many of South Australia's missionaries, anthropologists and settlers were German in origin. This basic but often overlooked fact adds an often-hidden complexity to histories of Australian colonisation that have traditionally focused on the central role of Britain and its empire, a one-dimensional view of the past enthusiastically labelled 'Anglobalisation' by one historian.[12] Peeling back this image of South

Australia as simply another British colony in a predominantly British colonial world has required a deep engagement with the myriad other settler populations that came to Australia prior to World War One. Some of this recovery work has already been done, and there is now a clearly emerging record of the role played by Germans,[13] alongside others such as Chinese and Afghan settlers in the early years of South Australia.[14] As Peter Monteath, Mary-Anne Gale, Peter Mühlhäusler, Bill Edwards, Pauline Payne, Philip Jones and others have made clear,[15] not only were Germans thick on the ground in the early years of South Australia's colonisation, these Germans had very different experiences. As in the case of the British, Germans settlers cannot be simply seen as a homogenous group. Indeed, not all of their interactions with one another were harmonious. 'Old Lutheran' dissenters fleeing changes to Prussian religious practices, for example, held little in common with the small but influential wave of urban liberals who deserted the German states after the revolutions of 1848. Meanwhile, the German missionaries sent to South Australia were often viewed with aloof disdain by visiting German anthropologists who considered themselves to be dispassionate men of science, unlike the men of the cloth they sometimes visited.

Missing, however, from this picture of a more multicultural understanding of settler colonialism beyond 'Anglobalisation' is a third crucial dimension, namely the connections between this history of non-British colonisation and the history of South Australia's frontier encounters and entanglements with First Nations peoples.[16] It is this missing but integral element of South Australia's colonial history that this book addresses. Here too, enormous differences between the Germans who flocked to South Australia can be quickly spotted. Missionaries such as Clamor Wilhelm Schürmann and Christian Gottlob Teichelmann immersed themselves in the language and culture of the Indigenous people to whom they ministered as a prelude to their work of translating the Bible and its message into locally intelligible terms and concepts.[17] The methods and motivations of these missionaries were often utterly incompatible with those of the steady trickle of German anthropologists who came to South Australia seeking to confirm their racist belief that Indigenous people were an anthropologically valuable population of 'primitive' humans. For others who were in Adelaide only briefly, such as the globe-trotting Friedrich Gerstäcker, the Indigenous people encountered in South Australia were simply some of the dozens of colonised peoples that might be fleetingly encountered and written about while travelling the world.[18]

Far from an exhaustive collection, this book seeks to recover the full variety of these early and varied German impressions, many of which appear here in English for the first time. The views of early colonial life this book presents are not merely of antiquarian value but broaden the evidentiary base for the historical study of colonialism in South Australia. Beyond this, the book also offers up these early German impressions as a resource for the First Nations of South Australia engaged in the important work of cultural restoration, enabling them to view their communities through the (admittedly distorted) lens of non-English speaking Europeans during the earliest period of colonisation. These sources lay bare once again both how the damage done to community and culture by colonialism unfolded, and what attempts were made by some to mitigate this damage. It also offers potential source materials for communities who are investigating and launching native title and statutory land claims.[19] Often such claims rely on a capacity to demonstrate a continued connection with land, and those preparing such claims have rightly turned to some of the earliest accounts of colonisation to do so.[20] As efforts elsewhere in Australia have demonstrated, translating non-English works from the early colonial period has proved to be often an important preliminary step for addressing the history of dispossession and alleviating its continuation into the present.[21]

Histories of Where and for Whom?
Despite its potential interest and utility for Indigenous and non-Indigenous readers, it is important that this book not be mistaken

for an incontestable history of the First Nations of South Australia. Instead, it is primarily a collection of representations (and misrepresentations) of Indigenous people and their lives by German migrants, scientists, missionaries and sojourners, the majority of whom had very little contact with or understanding of those they were describing. Although some of these descriptions were garnered through long periods of interaction and the gradual accumulation of linguistic and cultural competence resulting in elaborate and extremely systematised descriptions, others were almost offhanded and marginal comments that offer little more than a set of prejudicial assumptions within larger works devoted to other concerns.

To be clear, many of the descriptions documented here are shockingly racist, so racist that reprinting them can only be justified by the fact that far too often the virulent racism that permeated colonial Australia has been diluted or hidden from view. This attempt to gloss over uncomfortable elements of the past has been the result of either an effort to preserve a heroic narrative of benign European colonisation, or a concern that to draw attention to and study racism might be confused with endorsing it. Regrettably, however, it is only by studying the colonial past in its raw and ugly complexity, with attention to the specific contexts within which racism operated and the structures that it served, that we can we approach the localised 'truth-telling about our history' called for by the Indigenous authors of the 2017 'Uluru Statement from the Heart' as a step towards improving intercommunal relations in Australia.[22] Failing to present this painful evidence of past racism, which extended well beyond the British population of colonial Australia, would make the historical mistreatment of Indigenous Australians somehow inexplicable, even unbelievable, if all that remained of the historical record of frontier interactions were the cordial encounters and entanglements that this collection also in part evinces.

Shifting to the German dimension of this book, a secondary contribution that might be expected from a source collection devoted to the specifically German complexion of frontier interactions with Indigenous Australians relates to the ongoing question of the continuities that some historians have drawn between colonial racism and the racially based foundations of later Nazi genocide.[23] Colonial racism and colonial violence, whether in Australia or in one of Germany's overseas colonies, gain their significance, according to these historians, through the ostensible 'boomerang effect' that this violence had in Europe.[24] Attempts to draw such lines of continuity and causality have proved extremely controversial, however, and should be approached with caution. There are some problems, for example, with mining events on the colonial frontier to serve as a prelude to later European events. Doing so might well suggest that the acts of Germans in the colonies are somehow best understood as programmatic harbingers of the 'real' event to come in Europe, rather than as fundamentally important objects of study in their own right. That is not to dismiss tangential links between these disparate histories outright.[25] Indeed, discussions and descriptions of Indigenous Australians, particularly those of late colonial period anthropologists such as Hermann Klaatsch, might well have found a later echo in the racial 'science' of the Nazi period. Certainly, the search for links between Imperial German anthropology and Nazism's underlying biological racism continues, for better or worse, to be a productive field of inquiry for researchers.[26]

Nonetheless, this attempt to find a historical lineage for the Holocaust in colonial events (which in the past has underwritten an ahistorical notion of a uniquely German racist – even genocidal – historical trajectory)[27] has been sidestepped in this volume in favour of a more concentrated, site-specific portrait of the South Australian frontier and the Germans' role in a broader colonial milieu that, enabled by a racist colonial imaginary, collectively dispossessed the region's First Nations. To do otherwise would be to risk instrumentalising the history of the South Australian frontier and the Germans' role in it as a mere window through which to view Germany's history. It would be a great disservice to Indigenous Australians, bordering on a second dispossession of their past, if the German sources reproduced here were simply deployed to serve intrinsically German debates, in search of a tortured line of racism that somehow led from Adelaide to Auschwitz. Far more urgent for this project is the Australian experience of colonial relations and the modes of thought that both facilitated and critiqued violence and dispossession.

The firm context of this book, therefore, is the experience and nature of settler colonialism in Australia, itself a fraught enough field of research in which firm lines of historiographical difference have been drawn. As a settler colony where migrating waves of Europeans (and non-Europeans) came to live on the lands of First Nations in satellite European settlements intended to become towns and then cities, South Australia shares a number of attributes with other settler sites established with similar expectations. Several historians, most notably Patrick Wolfe and Lorenzo Veracini, have argued that not only did a logic of displacement and dispossession underwrite such settler colonies, but that such colonies were intrinsically eliminatory and even tacitly genocidal in their expectations and plans for the Indigenous peoples whose lands they settled.[28] This totalising picture of settler colonialism has not, however, met with universal acceptance. Shino Kinoshi, for example, has rightly pointed out that settler colonial studies in the vein of Wolfe and Veracini 'leave little space for Indigenous (or even "settler") agency.'[29] Miranda Johnson too has persuasively argued that 'settler colonialism obliges us to demonstrate a *singular* logic' that ultimately flattens complex historical terrain,[30] while Tim Rowse has convincingly insisted that the emphasis on the putatively 'eliminationist logic' posited by settler colonial studies overlooks the multiplicity of ways in which settler-colonialists approached Indigenous peoples in differing contexts, and, importantly, how Indigenous peoples engaged with and actively responded to this.[31] It is the desire to capture this type of complexity that underpins this book. While the Indigenous people represented in the following sources rarely have the opportunity to speak directly for themselves without being ventriloquised by their European interlocutors, it is clear that while colonial changes affected – indeed destroyed – many Indigenous lives, so too the ways in which First Nations peoples engaged with colonial structures demonstrated a capacity for innovative, strategic and even empowering adaptation to radically altered circumstances. A careful reading of some of the sources here, particularly those composed by Germans who were more than passing observers, offers a strong sense of the multiplicity of ways in which frontier interactions unfolded.

German Settlers, Sojourners and Missionaries

As has been mentioned, the sources presented in this book reflect not only the complexities of colonisation and frontier relations, but also the variegation within the German population that settled in South Australia. While the colony's German history has primarily been associated with the persecuted 'Old Lutherans' from the regions of Silesia, Brandenburg and Posen who sought refuge in a 'paradise of dissent' from 1838,[32] in reality the story of German migration has many strands. Religious persecution in Prussia might have fuelled the first wave, but it was liberal convictions that prompted another a decade later in the wake of the 'failed' revolutions that had occurred in the German states.[33] Over time, the push factors that persuaded Germans to leave their many states – or from 1871 the unified German Reich – multiplied. Foremost among them were economic factors, with migration reflecting the course of German economic fortunes and misfortunes throughout the remainder of the nineteenth century and into the twentieth. These factors also largely dictated the dispersal of German populations throughout the colony of South Australia and – especially in the wake of the Gold Rushes of the early 1850s – to other parts of Australia. In this way Germans across time became deeply implicated in the broader expansion of European settlement in all directions, from the initial precarious foothold on Kaurna land through to the neighbouring lands of the Peramangk and Ngarrindjeri, and ultimately to all parts of the territory claimed by Britain for its colony.

The complexity of the motivations leading to travel to the Antipodes is reflected in the authors gathered here. The early Lutherans made the long voyage to Australia with no plans to return to their homeland; their intention was to transplant as faithfully as possible their rural Prussian communities to territory they had been given to understand – or preferred to assume – was unoccupied and therefore ripe for 'settlement' and agricultural or pastoral exploitation. Other Germans imagined the replication in an urban setting of the existences to which they had been accustomed in the towns and cities of German Europe, whether as artisans and craftsmen or in pursuit of liberal professions in medicine, law or journalism. While these settlers may have envisaged staying in Australia forever, not all who had planned on permanent relocation – such as Gustav Listemann and his family – found the colony to their liking. In returning to his homeland, the disappointed Listemann wrote a bitter account of his experiences in South Australia, warning his countrymen against repeating his mistake.

So too, not all Germans who arrived in Adelaide had any intention of staying. In an age of incipient globalisation facilitated by massive advances in the technology of international travel, there were growing proportions of short-term visitors among those who sailed south. Their motivations ranged from scientific curiosity to professional obligation, and they, too, are very well represented in this collection. The early sojourns of a ship's doctor, Hermann Koeler, and the ship's captain, Dirk Meinerts Hahn, were sufficiently long to enable the collection of detailed observations derived from sustained contact with the country and its Indigenous population. Neither traveller intended to make his future in Australia, yet both were committed to intermediary roles and to relaying their experiences to their compatriots.

For many travellers like Friedrich Gerstäcker, frontier encounters were at best fleeting, with the impressions gleaned from them as much the product of prevailing preconceptions and prejudices as of empirically grounded observation. Remarkably, other Germans like Reinhold von Anrep-Elmpt even claimed not to have come across

'Einheimisch'

Indigenous people in South Australia at all. In June 1880, the Baltic German would state that during his exhaustive travels across South Australia 'natives were no longer present,' or at best found 'here and there by accident; forlorn, cast out and mistreated.' They had, he argued, already fallen victim to the avarice and violence of the colonisers, despite the greatly vaunted humanitarian hue and cry of the period:

> The fact remains that the rightful population of the country not only finds itself in the process of extinction, but is already partially extinct, and that the conduct of the invaders, who monopolise the land with gunpowder violence and atrocities of the most dire barbarism against the original inhabitants can only be compared to that of wild animals.[34]

Perhaps the furthest from such fleeting glimpses of Aboriginal life was the experience of missionaries, whose observations are well represented here. It was not just the integration of a kind of amateur anthropology into the missionary project but also the sheer scale of German missionary endeavour in Australia that explains this heavy representation. As Regina Ganter has pointed out, until the outbreak of the First World War, 'practically half of the missions in Australia were staffed with German speakers'.[35] South Australia was no different.

By the nature of their work, the missionaries experienced prolonged close contact with Indigenous communities and were correspondingly well positioned to write in great detail about the Indigenous people they had lived alongside. This kind of sustained contact presented opportunities to learn languages and become steeped in the cultures and belief systems of those among whom they lived. It was, moreover, a necessary precondition for the achievement of the missionaries' proselytising brief. Though they had no formal anthropological training, they dutifully followed the injunction 'that the researcher be familiar with his flock and walk among the natives as a human being among other human beings who had souls, religion and language'.[36]

That is not to suggest that the missionaries' anthropological interests and endeavours were only ever a means to an end. In some cases, at least, individual missionaries became engrossed in the study of the people among whom they lived but found that their enthusiasm was not shared by those who had sent them into the field. Johannes Reuther, for example, having sent a collection of Aboriginal lore from his Bethesda mission at Killalpaninna in the Lake Eyre basin to the President of the Lutheran Synod in Adelaide, received the terse response:

> 'If, instead of the thick wads of "liar legends" and fables that you have concocted – and which are of no use to anybody – who is going to put money into getting them printed? – if you were to let us have brief monthly reports, then you would be fulfilling your duty, satisfying us, and doing something useful.'[37]

In a similar vein, the most prolific of the missionary anthropologists, Carl Strehlow, on sending the first volume of his study of the Arrernte people to the mission authorities in Adelaide, was chided:

> 'My heartfelt thanks for sending me your work on the Aranda. It is a wonderful document of German diligence. However, the material which you have put into written form is the most worthless imaginable. Almost everything is chaff, with hardly a grain of moral value here and there. In truth, it must have cost not a little self-denial on your part to write down these insipid legends which can be of interest only to an ethnographer. I do not doubt the historical value of your collection as the sole monument of a tribe which will vanish from this earth.'[38]

German Anthropologists and their Discipline

That anthropologists proved more interested in such records than missionary authorities is clear, and many anthropologists were keen to make contact with missionaries when they travelled to South Australia to record their own observations of Indigenous people. Here too, however, there was a clear divergence in approaches, both between anthropologists and missionaries, and among various anthropologists.

Indeed, it is questionable whether it is meaningful to speak of a 'German' anthropological tradition at all to explain the attitudes of German-speaking anthropologists towards Indigenous Australians. Only from 1871 was there a unified German state, and even after that time there were anthropologists, trained and untrained alike, who hailed from other German-speaking parts of Europe outside the Reich. There is certainly no simple genealogy of German anthropology that would allow the anthropologists presented in this collection to be placed on a single line of development from the nineteenth century and into the twentieth. Similarly, German anthropology did not develop in a national vacuum. Like other scientific disciplines, it was fertilised by and itself gave crucial impetus to Anglophone, Francophone and other anthropological traditions. Its practitioners worked, networked, studied and corresponded with colleagues from other parts of the world.[39]

Nonetheless, it is possible to identify some recurring themes that suggest that there might be some merit in the loose concept of 'German' anthropology. One of the common threads, visible in a number of contributions to this collection, is the schematic distinction between *Naturvölker* and *Kulturvölker*, that is between 'natural' peoples and 'peoples of culture'. In the minds of some proponents of this taxonomy, generally attributed to the eighteenth century German philosopher Gottfried Herder, the words invoked a division of humankind into two distinct groups. By the 1840s, just as German interest in Australia was rising, it was a taxonomy that was being circulated widely among Germans.[40] When combined with the complementary intellectual tradition of racism of German intellectuals like Immanuel Kant and Georg Wilhelm Friedrich Hegel,[41] the distinction readily lent itself to assumptions that certain 'races' were superior to others, and in the minds of many precisely that assumption was made and applied during the age of empire, with often fateful results. For those inspired by Herder, however, the distinction did not necessarily dictate a hard and fast racial hierarchy. Rather, for these anthropologists, who developed a cultural chauvinism of their own, the study of a putative *Naturvolk* (as they assumed Indigenous Australians to be) was thought to offer a window into a paradise lost and a form of natural nobility which had evaporated with the onset of civilisation and the alienation of humans from the natural world. By the end of the nineteenth century it was in remote parts of South Australia (and its Northern Territory) that the prospects of observing Indigenous people in a 'natural' state seemed to anthropologists still possible, with these regions comparatively less affected by the inexorable march of European colonisation.

While the fraught binary of *Naturvölker* and *Kulturvölker* was widely applied, Germans also recognised that such a coarse distinction did not do justice to the great variety of human beings across the globe. Some, like Erhard Eylmann, viewed the terms as representing the extremes of a spectrum or continuum, with an almost endless variety lay in between. Eylmann was also sceptical of the myth of Indigenous populations untouched by outside influences. 'Strictly speaking', he concluded after crossing the Australian continent twice, 'we can speak only of *Kultur-* and *Halbkulturvölker*; in reality there are no pure *Naturvölker*'.[42]

With these assumptions in mind, it has been tempting for some to read the history of German anthropology backwards from the Third Reich and assume that in the nineteenth century German anthropologists must have understood the differences among peoples in similarly biological terms. As the writings here show, that would be a mistake. There were multiple German anthropological understandings of human difference, and until the turn of the century many of these foregrounded cultural differences. For many, variegation among humans was understood as a function of differences in the historical and environmental circumstances in which they had been established and developed.[43] Much German anthropology was thus characterised by an attention to the 'historical particularism' of each *Volk*,[44] above all as it was manifested in language and culture. This particularist, Herderian understanding stressed a process of diffusion, of cultures spreading beyond their points of origin and thereby influencing the development of others. While this theory of diffusionism is commonly associated elsewhere with Franz Boas,[45] in the Australian context, it was represented by Fritz Graebner, who developed the theory of the culture circle, *Kulturkreis*.[46]

Crucially, however, this notional acceptance of a common humanity did not mean that in a settler colonial context such as Australia Germans took a sanguine view of the encounter between a *Naturvolk* and a *Kulturvolk*. On the contrary, with notable exceptions such as Carl Strehlow, German observers of frontier encounters in Australia wholly subscribed to the 'doomed race theory' and drew the conclusion that the demise of the Indigenous population was simply a matter of time. Many of the authors represented in this collection recorded the devastating impacts of the settler colonial violence they witnessed and expressed a sympathy for its Indigenous victims, yet they did so while sharing the assumption of an ultimately genocidal conclusion to colonisation. In fact, like other anthropologists elsewhere, their activities were driven at least in part by a commitment to 'salvage anthropology,' the attempt to preserve a cultural record of Indigenous Australia while there was still time left to compile it.

The drive to engage in anthropological activity could manifest in various ways and reflected the differing traditions that the discipline encompassed. The German word '*Anthropologie*' carries a different connotation to the English term 'anthropology', focusing on physical anthropology, which in practice meant the study of the physical attributes of peoples, whether on the basis of living subjects or of human remains. It is a branch of anthropology represented most obviously in this volume through the work of the Berlin craniologist Wilhelm Krause. According to the physical anthropologists, the best way to understand the great variety of humanity was to collect and study the physical manifestations of it, particularly through – as in Krause's case – the collection of human skulls.

German anthropology was, however, also known as '*Völkerkunde*', '*Ethnographie*' or '*Ethnologie*', that is, cultural or social anthropology. Unlike the British and then Anglo-Australian anthropologists, who focused their attention on studies of society and kinship, the primary interest of German ethnologists was culture and language. Their goal was to seek to enter and understand the mental world of the people they observed. To achieve it, these German anthropologists, like German missionaries, sought to learn Indigenous languages, viewed as crucial portals into the mental world of their interlocutors. Only with a knowledge of languages, they assumed, would it be possible to understand systems of culture and belief rapidly disappearing under colonial pressures.

Other developments in the realm of high politics similarly impacted the development of German anthropology in Australia, with stark consequences for the ways in which it engaged with Indigenous Australia. Throughout the nineteenth century Germans in Australia were viewed favourably by British authorities; their contributions to colonisation were valued and encouraged. Those cordial relations facilitated the pursuit of anthropological and missionary activities by Germans. The eventual souring of Anglo-German relations, however, reverberated in the colonies, making collaborative undertakings more difficult and prejudicing the work of Germans.

The nadir came with the outbreak of World War One. The severe rupture it caused is best illustrated by the fate of two of the anthropologists. The above-mentioned Fritz Graebner, champion of the theory of diffusionism, happened to be in Australia to attend an anthropological conference at the crucial moment in August 1914. He was interned for the duration of the war. Meanwhile in Europe, Leonhard Adam, whose anthropological interests might otherwise have led him to other parts of the globe, found himself conducting anthropological studies involving Indigenous Australians in a POW camp outside Berlin.

The scale of the rupture caused by the war and the damaged relations both before and following it are difficult to assess. Through the 1920s there remained a German anthropological interest in Australia, and even during the Nazi period a significant anthropological expedition to North-west Australia – the Frobenius expedition – was staged. By that time, however, German anthropology had utterly capitulated to the advocates of biological racism. As

Andre Gingrich notes, the work of men like the future Nazi physical anthropologist and eugenicist Eugen Fischer, who had trained as an anthropologist in Germany's colonies, 'made an intellectual contribution to the rise of racist ideologies by making these ideologies look more respectable'.[47]

Conclusion

The Germans who wrote about the First Nations people of South Australia did so from a wide range of positions. Some of them were settlers, others were physical anthropologists seeking to verify their pseudo-scientific theories of biological racism. Others still came to South Australia with the objective of Christianising Indigenous people after having sought to understand the particularities of their language and culture. Many, however, were simply passing through as travellers, leaving only a careless impression of a fleeting visit. Together, however, they were instrumental in shaping understandings of Australia's First Nations peoples in the German speaking world and in Australia itself. Despite their accounts' numerous inaccuracies, misunderstandings and in some cases clear disregard or contempt for Indigenous peoples, it is because of the often-forgotten influence of their views that they require study if the effects of such frontier encounters are to be understood.

The record of these Germans and their interactions with Indigenous peoples represents an important and rarely glimpsed part of the history of European colonialism in South Australia that lies beyond the better-known experience of British subjects. Their impressions of Indigenous life make the racial complexion of frontier relations in South Australia more intelligible and illustrate the full range of responses to colonial era encounters and entanglements. The chapters of this book reveal both the reasoning that motivated the search for avenues of intercommunal understanding and the callous indifference and offhanded racism of those who, in the name of Europeanisation and civilisation, assumed the historical necessity of the demise of those who had lived in Southern Australia since time immemorial.

An Indigenous South

Notes

1. Geoffrey H. Manning, *A Colonial Experience 1838–1910* (Adelaide, Gillingham Printers, 2001), 75–76.
2. Bain Atwood, 'Returning to the Past: The South Australian Colonisation Commission, the Colonial Office and Aboriginal Title', *Journal of Legal History*, 34(1), 2013, 82.
3. Damen Ward, 'Constructing British Authority in Australasia: Charles Cooper and the Legal Status of Aborigines in the South Australian Supreme Court, c. 1840–60', *Journal of Imperial and Commonwealth History* 34(4), 2006, 496.
4. Amanda Nettelbeck, 'Colonial Protection and the Intimacies of Indigenous Governance', *History Australia*, 14(1), 2017, 38.
5. 'We acknowledge we live on Kaurna land.'
6. Rebe Taylor, *Unearthed: The Aboriginal Tasmanians of Kangaroo Island* (Adelaide: Wakefield Press, 2002).
7. Bill Gammage, 'The Adelaide District in 1836', in Robert Foster and Paul Sendziuk (eds.), *Turning Points; Chapters in South Australian History* (Adelaide, Wakefield Press, 2012), 7–23; Paul Sendziuk and Robert Foster, *A History of South Australia* (Cambridge, Cambridge University Press, 2017), 1–8.
8. Robert Foster, Rick Hosking and Amanda Nettelbeck, *Fatal Collisions: the South Australian Frontier and the Violence of Memory* (Adelaide, Wakefield Press, 2001).
9. For attempts to address this in approaches to Indigenous history, see Karen Martin–Booran Mirraboopa, 'Ways of Knowing, Being and Doing: A Theoretical Framework and Methods for Indigenous and Indigenist Re-search', *Journal of Australian Studies*, 27(76), 2003, 203–214; Aileen Moreton-Robinson, 'Towards an Australian Indigenous Women's Standpoint Theory', *Australian Feminist Studies*, 28(78), 2013, 331–347.
10. Lewis O'Brien, Irene Watson, 'In Conversation with Uncle Lewis: Bushfires, Weather-Makers, Collective Management', *AlterNative*, 10(5), 2014, 450–461.
11. Rob Amery, 'The First Lutheran Missionaries in South Australia and their contribution to Kaurna language reclamation', *Journal of Friends of Lutheran Archives*, 2000, 30–58.
12. Niall Ferguson, 'British Imperialism Revisited: The Costs and Benefits of "Anglobalization"', *Historically Speaking*, 4(4), 2003, 21–27.
13. Peter Monteath (ed.), *Germans and Their Descendants in South Australia* (Adelaide, Wakefield Press, 2011).
14. See for example Carmel Pascale, 'Chinese immigration restriction and the pursuit of nationalist ideals in colonial South Australia', *Journal of the Historical Society of South Australia*, 44, 2016, 89–101; Katharine Bartsch, 'Building identity in the colonial city: the case of the Adelaide Mosque', *Contemporary Islam*, 9, 2015, 247–270.
15. Peter Monteath (ed.), *Germans and Their Descendants in South Australia.*
16. For recent histories of Indigenous interactions with European settlers see for example Skye Krichauff, 'Mullawirraburka and Kadlitpinna: How and Why Influential Individuals Facilitated Amicable Cross-Cultural Relations in the Adelaide District, 1836-1840', *History Australia*, 18(2), 2021, 342–369. For South Asians in colonial Australia and their interactions with Indigenous peoples, see Samia Khatun, *Australianama: The South Asian Odyssey in Australia* (Brisbane, University of Queensland Press, 2018).
17. Rob Amery, 'Four Dresdeners in South Australia in the early-mid nineteenth century: a lasting legacy for Kaurna, Ngarrindjeri and Barngarla peoples', *Zeitschrift für Australienstudien*, 26, 2012, 47–65.
18. Friedrich Gerstäcker (P. Monteath ed.), *Australia: A German Traveller in the Age of Gold* (Adelaide, Wakefield Press, 2016).

19 Nicolas Peterson and Anna Kenny, 'The German-Language Tradition of Ethnography in Australia', in Nicolas Peterson and Anna Kenny (eds.), *German Ethnography in Australia* (Canberra, ANU Press, 2017), 3.
20 ibid.
21 For Western Australia, Peterson and Kenny cite translations of work by Andreas Lommel and Helmut Petri. See too Kim Akerman (ed.) and Margaret Pawsey (trans.). *Cologne to the Kimberley: Studies of Aboriginal life in northwest Australia by five German scholars in the first half of the 20th century* (Perth, Hesperian Press, 2015).
22 'Uluru Statement from the Heart', in Shireen Morris (ed.), *A Rightful Place: A Roadmap to Recognition* (Melbourne, Black Inc, 2017), 3.
23 For a recent overview of a long debate, see Thomas Kühne, 'Colonialism and the Holocaust: Continuities, Causations, and Complexities', *Journal of Genocide Research*, 15(3), 2013, 339–362.
24 For an exploration of the idea of a 'boomerang effect', see A. Dirk Moses 'Hannah Arendt, Imperialisms and the Holocaust' in Mohammad Salama, Volker Max Langbehn (eds.), *German Colonialism: Race, the Holocaust, and Postwar Germany* (New York, Columbia University Press, 2011), 72–92.
25 See for example the important work by Michael Rothberg, *Multidirectional Memory: Remembering the Holocaust in the Age of Decolonization* (Stanford, Stanford University Press, 2009).
26 Angela Zimmerman, *Anthropology and Antihumanism in Imperial Germany* (Chicago, University of Chicago Press, 2001); H. Glenn Penny and Matti Bunzl, (eds.), *Worldly Provincialism: German Anthropology in the Age of Empire* (Ann Arbor, University of Michigan Press, 2010); Matthew P. Fitzpatrick, 'Indigenous Australians and German Anthropology in the Era of "Decolonization"', *Historical Journal*, 63(3), 2020, 686–709. See too the special issue of *Anthropological Forum*, 27(3), 2017.
27 On this question see Matthew P Fitzpatrick, 'The Pre-History of the Holocaust? The Sonderweg and Historikerstreit Debates and the Abject Colonial Past', *Central European History*, 41(3), 2008, 477–503.
28 Patrick Wolfe, 'Settler Colonialism and the Elimination of the Native', *Journal of Genocide Research*, 8(4), 2006, 387–409; Lorenzo Veracini, *Settler Colonialism: A Theoretical Overview* (Basingstoke, Palgrave Macmillan, 2010).
29 Shino Kinoshi, 'First Nations Scholars, Settler Colonial Studies, and Indigenous History', *Australian Historical Studies*, 50 (3), 2019, 285–304.
30 Miranda Johnson, 'Writing Indigenous Histories Now', *Australian Historical Studies* 45(3), 2014, 317.
31 Tim Rowse, 'Indigenous Heterogeneity', *Australian Historical Studies*, 45(3), 2014, 297–310.
32 David A. Gerber, 'The Pathos of Exile: Old Lutheran Refugees in the United States and South Australia', *Comparative Studies in Society and History*, 26(3), 1984, 498–522; David Hilliard, 'Unorthodox Christianity in South Australia: Was South Australia Really a Paradise of Dissent?' *History Australia*, 2(2), 2005, 38:1–38:10.
33 Gerhard Fischer, '"A great independent Australian Reich and nation": Carl Muecke and the 'forty-eighters of the German-Australian community of South Australia', *Journal of Australian Studies*, 13(25), 1989, 85–100.
34 Reinhold von Anrep-Elmpt, *Australien: Eine Reise durch den ganzen Welttheil*, Band II (Leipzig, Wilhelm Friedrich Verlag, 1886), 253, 259.
35 Regina Ganter, 'German Missionaries in Australia – A Web-Directory of Intercultural Encounters' Accessed 22 February 2022. http://missionaries.griffith.edu.au/.
36 Walter Veit, 'In Search of Carl Strehlow: Lutheran Missionary and Australian Anthropologist', in *From Berlin to the Burdekin*, edited by J. Tampke and D. Walker (Kensington, UNSW Press, 2017), 110.

37 Kaibel, letter to J. G. Reuther, 18 February 1904, translated and cited by L. Hercus and K. McCaul, 'Otto Siebert: The Missionary-Ethnographer', in *The Struggle for Souls and Science. Constructing the Fifth Continent: German Missionaries and Scientists in Australia*, edited by W. Veit (Alice Springs' Strehlow Research Centre, 2004), 36.
38 Walter Veit, *'Arbeiter im Weinberg' oder 'Der ungebildete Missionar'? Die nicht-theologische Bildung der Missionare* (Berlin, Berliner Gesellschaft für Missionsgeschichte, 2005), 38.
39 Heather Ellis and Ulrike Kirchberger (eds.), *Anglo-German Scholarly Networks in the Long Nineteenth Century* (Leiden: Brill, 2014).
40 Anne Löchte, *Johann Gottfried Herder: Kulturtheorie und Humanitätsidee der 'Ideen', 'Humanitätsbriefe' und 'Adrastea'* (Würzburg, Königshausen und Neumann, 2005), 100.
41 Matthew P Fitzpatrick 'Race' in Kirsten McKenzie (ed.) *A Cultural History of Western Empires in the Age of Empire* (New York, Bloomsbury, 2019), 176–181.
42 Erhard Eylmann, *Die Eingeborenen der Kolonie Südaustralien* (Berlin, Dietrich Reimer, 1908), 60.
43 Anna Kenny, *The Aranda's Pepa: An Introduction to Carl Strehlow's Masterpiece* Die Aranda-und Loritja-Stämme in Zentral-Australien *(1907–1920)* (Canberra, ANU Press, 2013), 52.
44 Diane Austin-Broos, 'Of kinships and other things: T.G.H. Strehlow in Central Australia', in Nicolas Peterson and Anna Kenny (eds.), *German Ethnography in Australia* (Canberra: ANU Press, 2017), 238.
45 Franz Boas, 'The Diffusion of Cultural Traits', *Social Research*, 4(3), 1937, 286–295.
46 Fritz Graebner, 'Zur Kulturgeschichte der Melville-Insel', *Ethnologica* 2(1), 1913, 1–13.
47 Gingrich, 'The German-Speaking Countries', 112.

Sojourners and Immigrants

Hermann Koeler, 'Some Notes on the Natives on the East Coast of Gulf St. Vincent in South Australia, 1837 and 1838'

Hermann Koeler, a ship's doctor born in Celle in 1813, spent just over six months in South Australia from October 1837 to April 1838. Apart from his medical training, which allowed him to travel widely through the world as a ship's doctor, little is known about him.

The ship which brought him to Adelaide, the Solway, *was chartered by the South Australian Company to bring immigrants and supplies to the newly-founded colony. From Hamburg and via London it made its way to Kingscote on Kangaroo Island with some fifty German emigrants on board. Most were delivered to Kangaroo Island, but Koeler travelled on via the cutter* William *to arrive at Glenelg in Holdfast Bay on 21 October. It is likely that Koeler's stay in South Australia was longer than anticipated, because the Solway was wrecked in a storm near the whaling station in Encounter Bay on 21 December – fortunately with no loss of life – giving Koeler the opportunity to expand his observations. For much of his stay in Adelaide it seems that he occupied a reed hut at Glenelg, while also taking the opportunity to travel through the infant colony to satisfy his curiosity. He finally departed Adelaide on 22 April 1838, bound for Tasmania.*

In the following decade Koeler continued to travel widely, setting foot on five continents, in all probability financing his travels by continuing to work as a ship's doctor. Apart from his writings on South Australia, he also published a book on the people and language of the coast of Guinea, published in 1848, and in the following year a book on temperature measurements in the Atlantic.

Koeler's key contact in Germany was the esteemed geographer Carl Ritter. It was Ritter who introduced Koeler's observations of South Australia to a German readership. A founding member of the Geographical Society of Berlin (Gesellschaft für Erdkunde zu Berlin), and a seminal figure in the development of the discipline of geography, Ritter made two presentations of Koeler's work at separate meetings of the Society, the first in July 1841, and the second a couple of years later, in May 1843. The observations were published in the Society's monthly journal.*

Source:
Extracts from Hermann Koeler, 'Einige Notizen über die Eingeborenen an der Ostküste des St. Vincent-Golfs, Süd-Australien; 1837 und 1838', *Monatsberichte über die Verhandlungen der Gesellschaft für Erdkunde zu Berlin*, 1842, 42–57; 1844, 33–75.
Translation: Lois Zweck.

Part One

The following notes focus principally and primarily on observations of those among the natives [...] who customarily reside in the vicinity of the [...] main settlement Adelaide Town, and the neighbouring Holdfast Bay and Port Adelaide. I cannot refrain from emphasising this distinction, since, despite the small extent of the designated district and in spite of the great correspondence and similarity among its inhabitants in general, there are differences to be found here and there in individual customs and traditions, and indeed even not inconsiderable deviations in their dialect, their character and even in their physique.–

If one wishes to subsume them under one of the commonly accepted human races, these South Australians (whom one could call the *Adelaide tribe*) have to – like all the original inhabitants of the mainland of New Holland and Van Diemen's Land – be counted among the Ethiopians. And if this entire race occupies the lowest rung of the

---

* *Further reading:* Peter Mühlhäusler (ed.), *Hermann Koeler's Adelaide: Observations on the Language and Culture of South Australia by the First German Visitor,* Australian Humanities Press, Adelaide, 2006.

human race in both physical and intellectual aspects, then these South Australians in turn represent the lowest of them all, and in some ways are backward even in comparison with other New Hollanders.

As far as physique is concerned, they are in general only of moderate build (the women can mostly be called small), although individuals among them are of a stature which is considered impressive even among Europeans. The colour of their skin is a brownish black (with a deceptive similarity to the facial colour of some species of ape), which manifests itself as a yellowish brown in new-born children and in early youth in general, and only darkens with the years, a change due to the effects of the sun and to a small degree also presumably to dirt, the neglect of skin hygiene. But, as with all blacks, the inner surfaces of the hands and feet remain strikingly lighter in colour, darker only in the furrows, although this naturally becomes less noticeable on the soles of the feet, because of the greater amount of dirt and the bark-like thickening of the outer skin. Their hair colour is without exception black, turning grey in old age together with the hair on the cheeks and chin, and thus forming a strange contrast with the skin colour. The downy hair of the children is always brown and proliferated so long and luxuriantly that the back of a 5–6 year-old boy, seen from the side and with the sun shining directly on it, has – to put it bluntly – a pelt-like appearance and is reminiscent of the fur of a young donkey; the early, brownish downy beard often contrasts in a ridiculous manner with the small size and youth of the subject. The growth of hair on the back, chest, and the front and back surfaces of the upper thigh of the men is usually very thick and is also very curly. The growth of beard on the cheeks, lips and chin is mostly very thick, and in colour always black, like the hair on the head, and where hair is lacking, it seems in the majority of cases that the lack of hair is caused by it being torn out, a practice which individuals submit themselves to according to whim. Some individuals have also deigned to amuse the English by having themselves shaved. The hair on the head does not ever grow very long, not even in the case of the women, among whom I never saw hair longer than touching the shoulders at most. The hair is often frizzy and curly, but never woolly like that of the African Negro. In spite of that, one cannot classify the South Australians as members of any race other than the Ethiopian. When the hair is straight, it is not soft and supple like that of the Malays, but mostly shaggy and rough, and stands out stiffly, which no doubt is caused for the most part by their lack of cleanliness in contrast to the cleanliness of the Malays.

The eyes, which are deep-seated and are protected by thick bushy eye-brows, are brown or grey; the white of the eyes has a reddish yellow tinge, as is normally exhibited among the *ferae* [wild beasts] or as a pathological condition with some illnesses. The look of the eyes is lively and fleeting but changes according to the emotions, as it does everywhere, as a mirror of the spirit. The nose is usually very broad and flat, the mouth is large and stands out clearly against the dark colour of the face, with its beautiful white teeth and red tongue. Instead of a sharp cutting edge the incisors have such a broad surface that they look as though they have been filed down, an assumption which is inadmissible in view of the fact that they are equal in height to that of the other teeth, and of the lack of any trace of such an obviously intrusive operation, as well as of any instruments appropriate for the execution of such an operation.

Concerning the form of the head, although the forehead is mostly low, the nose flat, and the jaws, the cheekbone and the eyebrow-arches of the frontal bone are all protruding; the expression of the face and the skull is not as animal-like as that of some African nations, because the angle of the profile is not so small. Some physiognomies, namely those of the children, are attractive because of their unmistakable expression of innocence, friendliness, trust and a certain intellectual activity, just as some of the men take on a special character through their wild boldness and proud impervious earnestness. In other and indeed the majority of cases, the ugliness of the physiognomy, accentuated by savagery, deceitful cunning and intellectual lifelessness, and even more by artifices or by the overall impression of their whole figure, is truly repellent. The neck is without exception short, and indeed to such a conspicuous degree that one may be inclined to assume they have only six cervical vertebrae, as is occasionally observed in families with an inherited disposition to apoplexy. I have sometimes found the earlobes curved outwards and upwards to a significant degree, particularly among the children, without being in a position to explain this anomaly satisfactorily. As a supposition, which I do not however wish to give any particular weight, I would like to cite the way that small children are carried by their mothers, attached to their backs in a kangaroo skin, as a possible cause. The newborn infants are suspended between the back of their mother and the kangaroo skin, with the face turned sideways in such a way that only the head projects, and as its relative size leaves the ears unprotected by the shoulders, they must be mechanically forced upwards in this way.

As the bones of the skull tend in general to be thicker among all peoples which go bare-headed, and as they are above all firmer and harder among those who expose their heads to frequent acts of violence – among the Botocuden and other South American peoples for example, who aim for the head with their sticks in a fight, or among the African negroes, who are accustomed to striking one another on the body with powerful blows of the head, like steers (and this is the reason why slave overseers are accustomed to direct the blows of their canes not at the head but rather at the more sensitive shin-bone), or finally, to mention an example closer to hand, among the Irish, whose fights are also aimed at the head. So the same cause leads to the same effect among the South Australians too, and their skull bones are extraordinarily thick and firm. The blows of their clubs, which would break the skull of any white man, usually only stun them and only lacerate the soft flesh, and on the whole the head is the least vulnerable part of the body. The rib cage of the men is high and well-rounded; the arms and upper thighs, like the whole body, are mostly very muscular; hands and feet universally very small, so that handcuffs which have been applied to individuals because of acts of violence committed against whites, can be slipped off without difficulty. The skin of the soles of the feet is cracked and thickened to such a degree that it looks like bark and allows them to run over the sharpest pebbles or glass fragments without suffering. The toes, which have never been confined by any footwear, have a mobility and flexibility like that of the fingers, and they therefore also fulfil many of the same functions. If anything is to be picked up from the ground – a piece of glass, a small stone, a spear or a bird which has been hit by a spear, a kangaroo skin, or a knife, which they often make use of now – the South Australian will only on rare occasions stoop to pick it up; his toes save him this trouble. The relatively thin, unsightly calves – even of the strongest men – are undoubtedly caused by constantly sitting cross-legged. But the legs of the women, particularly the lower thighs, are repulsively thin and stick-like; the women's bodies are on the whole very lean and disfigured even more by the breasts which hang like empty pouches. Even in full flower they scarcely deserve the name of the 'fairer sex', and in old age they become a terrible sight because of their wrinkles and their mummy-like shrinking, an impression which can only be made more repellent by their good-natured, friendly grinning.

Among the children and young people, the knee joint protrudes to such a degree because of the usual thinness of the upper and lower thighs that it seems to be enlarged by a pathological swelling.

In general the children have such bloated fat stomachs that it serves the youngest, who often stumble and fall because they are still unsteady on their feet, as a sort of cushion when they fall, warding off the blow from the head; and because the ground is constantly very dusty in the dry season, the stomach is often decorated in a ridiculous fashion by a big patch of dust in the vicinity of the navel. The same corpulent stomach occurs also among the men, but less obviously, and is presumably dependent on the food supply, which is at some times more abundant or more scanty, more nourishing or meagre; for as a rule a South Australian does not stop eating until he has consumed all that he can get, and only very rarely can he restrain himself and put something aside for another occasion; after that he is accustomed to not making another move until forced into it by hunger. Because the backbone of the children has not yet taken on the beautiful curved form of later years, but tends to be bent outwards, the outline of the figure of a small savage who is sitting cross-legged has a sack-like appearance, in that the backbone curves to the same degree at the back as the bloated stomach does at the front. The children of other peoples have in common with the young South Australians the pointed *nates* [buttocks], but it is especially obvious in this instance, because one otherwise – thank God – does not have such frequent occasion to observe these parts. The good impression that would be created by the powerful muscles and the individually well-constructed limbs, disappears in view of the very striking length of the lower extremities, in comparison with the short fat rump and the short neck, which spoil the overall proportions so that the South Australian, together with the other New-Hollanders as a whole, is to be seen as one of the ugliest of human races.

> Situs genitalium in mulieribus posterior cognoscitur ex urinae ut in vaccis retrorsum demissione, et ex eo quod nunquam genitalia earum conspicere liceat, quando surgentes pellibus halmaturi gigantei sese obtegunt quibus infantes dorso pendentes sibi adligare solent. Coitum quoque aliarum Novae Hollandiae plagarum Aborigines ita saepissime exercent ut viri canum instar a dorso penem in vaginam immittant mulieris, quae posterioribus corporis partibus elevatis, capite bracchiisque in humum prostrata suffulcitur.[1]

The language of such a lowly-ranked people cannot be other than limited and undeveloped. But in order to afford at least a superficial glimpse into its nature, sounds and forms, I will choose a few words from the collection which I ascertained and learned through my contact and communication with them. I am convinced that I have ascertained and grasped the correct meaning and pronunciation of these words because I have used them frequently and have repeatedly made careful enquires about them. Concerning the very small range of this glossary, I cannot refrain from making reference to the difficulties which present themselves to anyone researching the names of nouns, adjectives and verbs which designate objects, qualities and actions which cannot be perceived by the senses. In communicating with people who possess such a dearth of concepts despite their ability to comprehend ideas, one must abstract the properties of certain objects, whereby gesticulation is perhaps the only means of clarifying the ideas on both sides, and at the very least as many comparisons and combinations as possible are necessary if one wants to be certain that both sides have clearly understood one another. In the following discussion therefore, when I express certain views on the language of the South Australians based on my observations, I must at the same time remark that these views possess only a relative value, since they would perhaps have been formed differently if I had had longer and more frequent opportunities for checking and a more precise knowledge of the language, and it is indeed possible that aspects which I tend to see as deficiencies in the language will in time prove to be deficiencies in my observation.

The language of the South Australians and in particular of the Adelaide tribes contains only two numbers: komá = 1 and poleítje = 2. These two words serve in combinations for the numbers 1 to 6 in the following way: it begins kóma 1, poleítje 2, and then an addition of the words takes place, with the larger number always given first: poleítje kóma 2,1 – 3; poleítje poleítje 2,2 = 4; poleítje poleítje kóma 2,2,1 =5; poleítje poleítje poleítje 2,2,2 = 6. A number which goes beyond 6 cannot be divided into individual parts; they call everything above 6 *poleitje* but without continuing to count by twos, but rather this *poleitje* has the same sort of meaning as the *sexcenti* of the Romans, a great, enormous number, an amount that is too large to be divided into individual parts and counted.

So they say, stretching out all the fingers of one hand and one finger of the other hand *poleítje poleítje poleítje*, but then showing 7, 8 or all 10 fingers they still say just *poleítje*. In this case the multiple repetition of *poleítje* has the significance 'many', for which they now normally use the English word '*plenty*' in communication with whites. In general they possess the gift of imitation to a high degree. A little savage will imitate the conspicuous walk of any white man or the particular tone of his voice with deceptive accuracy, to the great glee of his playmates and of his elders; even old people, when they see someone writing, will ask for a piece of paper and a pencil, so they can scribble on it too. In the same way they can repeat words that they hear quickly, successfully and with an excellent memory, only distorting them a little here and there to avoid hard sounds which they cannot pronounce. Thus everyone knows the words *no, yes, bad, good, mutton, money, black man, how do you do, good morning, good day* etc, and knows how to use them correctly. So one hears them speaking of *schépeh* (ship), *birkétti (biscuit), black money* (meaning copper money), *ueipeh money* (instead of *white money* ie. silver money); and one hears everywhere the favourite call *'me very hungry'*, whereby the whining, begging tone has to serve to prevent the opposite assumption on the basis of the fat, full stomach. One letter which seems to be totally lacking, and which they cannot pronounce well in foreign words, at least not when it is used in combination with another consonant, is the *s*. All words in their language end in vowels, most in *a* or *e*, less in *o* or *i*, least in *u*. All words have the stress on the penultimate syllable; only a few nouns ending in *a* have it on the third last syllable, and a few verbs on the last. I could not detect any trace of declension or conjugation, and the verb exists only in the infinitive form. They also seem to have no idea of articles or prepositions, and with such poverty one cannot of course speak of any more specific word order, other than that the subject precedes the verb, also in interrogative sentences. In negative sentences the negation precedes the verb. Thus eg *eítju wianínni Adelaide* = I go to Adelaide, or I come from Adelaide; *eítju mollánna wianínni Adelaide* = I am not going to Adelaide, or I am not coming from Adelaide; *nínko wianínni Adelaide (?)* = you are going to or coming from Adelaide, or are you going to Ad.? or coming from Adelaide? *eítju koboló kaúeh* = I drink water; *wilia mollanno kobolo kaueh* = the bird doesn't drink water; *nínko kádleh warrawarróka* = your dog is barking; *eítju pikkenínni meíjeh ménu* = my child eats gum; *eítju panjáppi mollánna jutándeh nínko wínta* = my brother didn't break your spear. Although the language itself is not lacking in euphony (except for a certain monotony because of the constant sameness of accent), it tends to lose a lot of this because of the peculiar singing, almost weeping and whining sounding way in which it is spoken. Even in cases of passionate excitement and most rapid speech, the last syllables are lengthened in a manner which is difficult to describe, and the voice, which is anyway shrill and rough as in all tribes of savage peoples, is forced up into higher tones; a characteristic which makes an unpleasant impression because of the howling, pathetic shrieking which it produces. Minor variations, which are to be seen as dialect variants, are found among various tribes living within narrow boundaries. A totally different language, together with other customs, prevails in New South Wales and on the other side of the River Murray as a whole, as well as among the inhabitants of Van Diemen's Land (who have now been transported to a small island in Bass Strait and have already shrunk to a very small handful), and among those who are now engaged in bloody feuds with the colonists on the Swan River and at King George's Sound. It is striking that the word *pikkenínni* = 'small' and therefore also 'child' is found not only among almost all the Aborigines in New Holland which have become known by now, but also among many tribes of southern Africa. It is probably originally the Portuguese diminutive *pequenino*, from *pequeno*, and may have been passed on to the savage tribes of this continent, and then spread further as far as the southern regions, from the East Indian islands which contained – and in some cases, like Flores and Timor, still contain today – the former Portuguese colonies whose Malay inhabitants pursue intensive trepang fishery on the north coast of New Holland.

As far as proper names are concerned, they are sometimes given on the basis of obvious physical conditions, and a blind person is named *Patjútteh* (blind), another is named *Jérko* (calf); others bear in part very euphonious names whose meaning (if they had one at all) I could not ascertain. eg *Katanja, Manuto*. The majority now bear English names like *Bob, Gim, Tom, Bill, Peg, Moll, Betty, Jack, Rodney*, and apart from that the most absurd names are often repeated to a ridiculous extent so that one is compelled to add other appellations in order to avoid mistaking identities.

In response to the question about their name, one often receives the answer '*no name*', and they seem to be able to manage without them among themselves, whereby they may make use of the bulging horizontal scars on the stomach, which also serve as a genealogical register, to obtain this information in case of need.

> [*The final part of Koeler's first essay discusses the numbering system used by Kaurna people, followed by an extensive word list.*]

Part Two

Each tribe has a specific territory where it will commonly hunt first in one area and then in another, according to the movement of the birds and the kangaroos, sometimes nearer the coasts, sometimes nearer to the hills. Any intrusion into this territory on the part of another tribe leads to feuds but is tolerated under duress if the other party is too strong. Thus the Adelaide tribe had to tolerate the fact that a far greater number of hills dwellers, who are taller in stature and more savage in character than most of the coastal tribes, came down into the white settlements and laid claim to its share of *birketti*. The only trace of a legitimate will of the people, a sort of constitution, is expressed in the punishments which are at times meted out, consisting – as has already been mentioned – in spear throws which the guilty party must ward off.

Otherwise conflicts tend to be settled on the spot and without authorisation; and when one hears the screeching, howling quarrel resounding through the stillness of the forest in the evening, it usually ends in the blow of a club or the throwing of a lance as the *ultima ratio*. The only communal ceremony in which the whole tribe participates was, as far as I was able to observe, the solemnity with which three of the greatest warriors were tattooed one day. A great number of 1¼–2 inch long deep cuts, running more or less parallel to one another in each group, were made with glass splinters and sharp fragments of stone on the chest, the shoulders and the upper parts of the back.

While the blood still flowed freely, all the other warriors of the tribe had their veins cut at the wrist or elbow joint and allowed their blood to flow over the head and the body of those who had been operated on, probably with the idea of transferring to the elect the strength and courage of the whole tribe together with their blood.

The elect sat cross-legged with 3 acacia twigs in each hand, stiff with pain and unmoved by sun or rain until the bloody scab had flaked off their bodies after 4 or 5 days, and only the hair on their heads remained stuck with blood. But the granulation is allowed to protrude markedly from the wounds so that the scars bulge above the skin like the weals on the stomach. The face and the other parts of the body remain always untattooed, and in the case of the women only the afore-mentioned stomach tattooing is carried out. The greatest communal entertainment is provided by the dances, called *korróbora*, which are only held at night by the flickering light of the fire. The kangaroo skin and any other items of clothing are tossed off, and the men step forward with their *waddis* in their hands, from among the women, children and old people, who represent at one and the same time both the orchestra and the audience. Then all together they front up in rows to the crouching spectators, who strike the spears, clubs and shields against one another, keeping correct time, shouting in the one single tone as long as possible, and when they are out of breath, they hastily fill their lungs with air in order to continue the same monotonous howling a moment later. The men, however, spread their legs wide apart and move them and the lower part of the body in a manner that the muse of the dance would presumably disavow, in the meantime betraying an extraordinary agility and elasticity of the muscles. At the same time they shout, as far as the vigour of their movements permits, in a monotonous humming din, and after a few minutes, when they leap from the second position to the first and all run together in a dense mass several steps towards the spectators, they end the dance with a single high-pitched screeching shout and the raising of their *waddis*, only to start it again immediately. Everyone joins in this last shout, in jubilant rejoicing, and eager to do the same as their elders, many a lad leaps into the rows of the men, undaunted by the scornful laughter when the violent movements tire him more quickly than the others.

One afternoon I and two other whites went out in the company and under the protection of the Adelaide tribe to meet a tribe which came from the hills and was approaching the settlements of the whites for the first time. Since it was far more numerous, the savages who were our friends could not even think of putting obstacles in their way or of opposing them by force; therefore they were setting out to encounter them at some hours' distance from Adelaide in order to celebrate a peaceful and brilliant *korróbora* with them. At last we caught sight of the groups of the unknown tribe, some clustered around their fires, others occupied with games and spear-throwing. Until that point we had all moved individually, the one in silence, another shouting his loud *ku-íh* through the stillness of the woods; the one tossing his *witas* into the distance with his *midla* and then picking it up again with his toes, another prowling through the long grass and throwing his *waddi* at quail. But now they all crowded together; the women and children withdrew silently behind the little group of men, peering in anxious suspense through the evening dusk at the numerous fires, which allowed an estimate of the size of the other tribe, even though the dense smoke already shrouded the individuals. Having arrived at some distance from them, we came to a halt at a somewhat more open spot in the wood, and soon our fires were blazing too, beneath the branches of several gigantic trees. Everything was quiet on both sides; our little group was afraid of the large number of the others, and they in turn knew that among our small troop they would find some excellent warriors, and they presumably also guessed that the colonists would not tolerate them in the vicinity if they should dare to oppress the Adelaide tribe whom they had befriended. On both sides all without exception were crouching down in order to mutually exclude any idea of a hostile attack; thus they contemplated one another until finally several of the distinguished warriors on both sides, acting as parliamentarians, moved forward, still squatting in a crouching position. Slowly and cautiously they approached one another, halting frequently, each one prepared to leap up and fight at the least sign of treachery or hostility on the part of their opponents. Finally they stopped at about the middle of the intervening space separating the two parties, at some distance from one another, and came to an agreement regarding their mutual peaceful intentions and decided, as had already been expected earlier, to celebrate their meeting with a combined *korróbora*. Then the boys and young men ran to drag together dry branches, and soon the initially smouldering and smoking fire cast a bright glow up to the high trees and illuminated clearly the dark masses of savages who, still squatting, accompanied the din of their weapons with that noisy monotonous shouting which is the starting signal for each *korróbora*.

The older warriors on both sides had in the meantime made extraordinary preparations for their dance; they had stuck great numbers of snow-white cockatoo feathers in their beards and hair, so that their faces seemed to be covered by a white mask, framed by the thick matted black hair of their heads and beards. They had attached to their arms and legs basket-like plaits and bunches hurriedly made of grass and reeds, which created a rustling sound with the vehement movements of the dance. Fitted out in this way they began the *korróbora*, but with different, more grotesque poses than usual; at one moment hopping on their knees and growling in a deep voice, at another trembling in convulsive movements, then leaping about with monkey-like agility and joining in the rhythmic noise of the spectators with high shouts. When the groups had run together for one last time, each stamping his feet on the ground with raised club and ending the dance with a loud penetrating shout, the two tribes mingled with one another and distributed themselves around this or that fire. Now for the first time they became aware of the whites who had been squatting among the Adelaide tribe until now; the news of their presence spread like wildfire, and all came over to look at the strange unknown creatures; at first from a distance. But when they saw that there were only a few of them and they were unarmed, and that the other savages sat next to them, spoke with them and touched them, friendly and unafraid, then their confidence grew and curiosity drove them closer; their astonishment was visibly expressed on their faces with gathering clarity and strength. Then one took courage and touched one of the whites, and the magic spell was broken and the fear disappeared. All of them crowded around to do the same, and their amazement was expressed in peals of laughter. But, one thinks, they have just painted themselves white as we do sometimes for battle – moistens his finger, strokes it across the cheek of the white man and, lo and behold! – the colour does not come off; renewed astonishment and laughter.

Others do not want to surrender yet, they think that the clothing conceals the black parts of the *pindi miu*, and one turns back the sleeve, another rolls up the trouser-leg of the white man, and when he finds there too only white limbs, he tries to rub off the make-up; – but in vain! And again they all wonder and laugh, look silently at one another and then at the black brother from Adelaide. He justifiably adopts a knowing expression, because there are many things that he can report about these strange beings.

A circle of listeners gathers around him and glances sideways now and again at the subject of the report. Then it occurs to one to try to gain certainty regarding the hair colour; the white man raises his straw hat and reveals his blonde hair, and instantly the narrator is abandoned and all stare at the new wonder. Then they get to see a watch, and it strikes; undoubtedly it is a living animal which can speak; then a reflecting pocket mirror arouses their curiosity; each one makes faces in front of it, laughs at himself and is surprised at not being able to capture his aping double at the back of the glass.

Some time before this tribe came down from the hills, I had in a strange way made the acquaintance of two savages belonging to it. I was in the house of an acquaintance who lived at the outermost limits of the city area one day; suddenly the servant, who was busy in the garden shouted for help, since two blacks had thrown spears at him and then run away. Since one always has loaded rifles in the room and on even the shortest journey, the inhabitants of the nearby huts and tents were soon summoned by alarm shots and they tried to catch up with the fugitives. They did not run any faster than us, but just when we were about to grab them and thought we had caught them, they had already headed off in the opposite direction and were far ahead of us. As they ran they threw their spears at us and when they had discharged all of them they picked up sticks and stones without pausing and tossed them at us and our dogs. Some of the Englishmen fired shots at them without compunction but fortunately without success. Finally the younger and weaker of the two was caught; the other had no choice but to leap into the Torrens. But all the same he could no longer escape, because there were colonists standing in wait already on the other side; in order to force him to give himself up threats were made to aim at him; but then he dived under for as long as possible, but had to in the end throw away his club and dagger and climb up the river bank to surrender. When he tried to escape again, several threw themselves on him, and five of us (none of them weaklings and most of them presumably stronger than him according to a dynamometer) had great difficulty in tying him up, as he – naked and as slippery as an eel with the water – weaved and twisted among us so that it was difficult to hold him fast. His shouting had summoned a third to the scene, but he too was driven into the river, dived under for as long as possible and finally retreated behind a tree trunk which hung over the water so that he could use it as cover to come up for air.

He withstood the blows of branches and pieces of bark and clubs that were aimed at his head for a long time, since they could only strike his least vulnerable part; and lassoes, not thrown by the hand of a Spanish American, he was able to slip off. At last he was too weak to hold himself above water any longer and surrendered. All three were questioned and released immediately as it turned out that they had never seen white men before and had only thrown their spears and run away at their first sight of one; just as the poisonous snake does not attack, but wounds anyone who disturbs her in her nest of leaves and frightens her with incautious steps.

> [*At this point the medically-trained Koeler provides a section on diseases and their treatment before moving to his conclusion.*]

I will herewith close these brief and fragmentary notes in which I have strived to demonstrate several characteristics by which I have attempted to confirm the view – often challenged by uneducated and brutal European inhabitants of distant continents – that the spirit, with all its inclinations and passions, all its poetry and efforts, is the same in the educated person, who makes his own ego the subject of his studies, as in the most primitive natural man who views his surroundings with purely material eyes alone and is hardly aware of more than the lowest rung of social interaction (which is the only means permitting the individual to reach the highest level of development available to him), which knows no other goal than the maintenance of his species.

But only the heart, in its moral and in its passionate instincts, beats to the same measure across the whole human race. The understanding, while living and creating according to the same laws, moves with greater energy in one race than in another, here it soars up to a safe height which remains vertiginous and beyond reach for another; in one race it plumbs depths which are for another eternally unfathomable chaos. The lessons of history are constantly renewed and constantly reiterated, but they remain nonetheless the same truth. It shows us that the limits to the physical and intellectual power of states as of individuals are given and fixed; in that only the form changes, while the substance remains. It reveals to us not the ideal but the real greatness which man is permitted to attain; it shows us a turning point in the fate of all peoples, which occurs in each instance in the same period of development of that people. It also teaches, in constant change, that there is a 'So far and no further!' for each race and introduces each one to us at its height: but how different this is in each case! The South Australian will have disappeared before he has had an opportunity to reach his height, and history will recall him as a people which did not outlive its childhood.

Notes

1 [The genitals of women, which otherwise are not possible to be seen, may be observed as she lowers herself downwards in order to urinate, at which time she lifts the large pelts with which the women cover themselves and to which they are accustomed to tie to their backs their infants dangling. The S.A. Aborigines most frequently practise coitus in the same manner as other New Hollanders, the men enter the penis into the woman's vagina like a dog, with the rear part of her body having been elevated, and her head, supported underneath by her arms, being cast down onto the ground.]

Dirk Meinerts Hahn, 'On the Savages, or Natives, in South Australia'

Dirk Meinerts Hahn was Captain of the Zebra, which brought a human cargo of German emigrants to South Australia in 1838. The distinctive feature of the Zebra's passengers is that they were 'Old Lutherans' who had chosen to make their way to the other side of the world to escape religious persecution by the King of Prussia.

Himself the son of a ship's captain, Hahn was born in 1804 on the island of Sylt – at that time part of Denmark – and went to sea at the age of sixteen. His first major voyage, at the age of eighteen, was a trans-Atlantic crossing to the United States. Later voyages took him to Spain, Portugal, Italy, Sicily and Russia. The first of Hahn's voyages on the Zebra, to Havana, was as first mate, but on subsequent voyages he was engaged as captain. In that role he took 140 emigrants from Cuxhaven to New York. When the Zebra under Hahn's captaincy was in Hamburg in 1838, he was once more presented with the task of transporting emigrants, but this time 199 Old Lutherans from the province of Brandenburg bound for South Australia. The Zebra departed the Hamburg port of Altona – at that time under Danish administration – on 12 August and landed its passengers at Port Adelaide on the second day of the following year. It was in large part due to Hahn and his negotiating skills, brought to bear on landowners in the Mt Barker district, that the immigrants were able to lease land for the establishment of their own settlement. As an expression of their gratitude to Hahn, they named their village Hahndorf. Hahn commenced his return voyage early in the following month and would never step foot on Australian soil again before his death in 1860.

> *Source:*
> The original source is the unpublished and undated two-volume manuscript by Dirk Meinerts Hahn entitled: 'Die merkwürdigsten Begebenheiten meines Lebens'. An edited German edition relating to the voyage to South Australia of the *Zebra* was published in 1988. The extract below is from the English translation of that volume, published as: Martin Buchhorn (ed.) *Emigrants to Hahndorf: A Remarkable Voyage from Altona, Denmark to Port Adelaide, South Australia, Captain Hahn of the 'Zebra' 1838. Transcription from the original and notes on the text by Frank Rainer Hahn. Notes and commentary on sources extensively revised and expanded by Lee Kersten.* Lutheran Publishing House, Adelaide, 1989, 111–117.
> *Translation:* Lee Kersten.

The savages there are a race of humans of extremely ugly physical appearance. They go about like cattle, as naked as they came into the world. Only a few of them have a kangaroo hide slung around them to hide their nakedness. Smallpox must be common among them, as the majority of them bear its scars. Their hair is stiff and so long that it hangs down to their shoulders. They have a liking for smearing fat into their hair and dyeing it red. In fact, they do this to the whole head, using the powder produced by rubbing two stones together. This plasters the hair so that it dangles in thick clumps around their necks. Their facial features are without exception very ugly. The upper part of the body is thick and clumsy, but they have quite thin loins and legs.

They have divided themselves into small tribes (as the English call them), perhaps fifty to sixty men in each company. Each tribe has its own king. They are almost always at war with each other, generally fighting about their women. There are many more male than female natives. People think that they kill and eat the children of the

---

* *Further reading:* A.E.R. Brauer, *Under the Southern Cross. History of the Evangelical Lutheran Church of Australia,* Lutheran Publishing House, Adelaide 1956; David Schubert, *Kavel's People: From Prussia to South Australia,* Lutheran Publishing House, Adelaide 1986.

female sex at birth. A man who is looking for a wife will wear a white cockatoo feather in his hair, which means that his desire can be seen even from the distance. Each has a hole in the lower part of the nose between the nostrils, and they stick a six-inch-long thin reed through this when they are in mourning.

In spite of their being sluggish and lazy, each group still has its own burial ground to which they take their dead, sometimes a distance of some miles. They make a proper grave which they even line with kangaroo skins, and they adorn the tops of these graves with tree bark. The German missionaries there told me that they have witnessed such a funeral procession. The dead man is laid on six sticks and covered with a kangaroo skin, and at each end of the sticks there is a man who acts as bearer.

Every forty to fifty paces they stopped; each time a person charged with this particular duty went to the corpse, raised the kangaroo skin, and carefully inspected whether the dead man had not perhaps come back to life.

Their laziness extends so far that they do not even build themselves any sort of hut to protect themselves from the wind and rain. Generally sixteen to twenty of them gather near sunset, tear some branches from the trees, and lay these in a circle around the company. Then they start a fire in the middle and sleep lying around it. On the following morning each goes his way.

In spite of their brutish existence, they show a tendency to vanity; if someone gets hold of a piece of European clothing, he looks proudly at his colleagues; but as none of them has a complete suit of clothes, and they just use what they have, they often appear in absurd outfits. The most comical one that I saw was a man who was completely naked apart from a blue frock coat with bright buttons. It was astonishing to see this coat on the naked body. They are very fond of things which are brightly coloured and shiny, such as pieces of coloured glass or bright metal. If they manage to get something of this kind, they tie it to a thread and hang it around their necks. When Captain Blenkinsop's boat suffered a misfortune at the mouth of the Murray last year, his sextant was washed ashore. The savages found it and straight away broke the expensive instrument into small pieces, so that each of the participants could have a piece of it to hang around his neck as adornment.

For all that they are savages, they each have a name of their own. However, they seem to prefer the European names to their original ones and now all use names of the English kind, as for example, Jack, Tom, Jim, Pat, etc. They also have an approximate idea of their age, though only in months. Each carries a stick in which he makes an incision with a sharp stone at every new moon. He is as many months old as there are incisions in the stick. However, I doubt whether these people have so much sense that parents make this sign for their children before they are able to do so for themselves. It is very likely that the number of notches is a record of their age from about four or five on, although perhaps earlier, for their children are soon able to fend for themselves. I was amazed at the little black people, who could scarcely have been a year old to judge by their size, already running about among the old ones and playing games as children do. It is certainly not physical strength which gives them this advantage over the Europeans, indeed even over negroes in general. I ascribe it to their natural hardiness, as their body build is, as I have already said, only slight. A man whose word can be trusted told me that one morning at ten he had found a woman lying in childbirth under a tree five English miles from the town, and that at three in the afternoon he had seen the same woman in the town with her child on her back.

The female sex seems to me more advanced in the kind of knowledge they have been able to acquire than the men, who know only how to use their spears. I saw a jacket there, made solely of small opossum skins, which a female savage had made, and it was so beautifully sewn that few European women could have done the work better. If one considers the tools with which this work was done, then it is clear that it deserves even greater admiration. A thread had been made from the gut of a kangaroo. A small bone, pointed at one end, served as the needle; it had apparently not occurred to them to make a hole or eye in the blunt end, because first a hole was made with the needle, and after that the thread was drawn through separately.

Each savage, whether male or female, wears over one shoulder a net skilfully made from kangaroo gut, in which they store the spoils of their hunting. The men always have their instruments of war fastened across the net as well. These consist of a spear, that is, a long stick, one end of which resembles an arrow. Since Europeans arrived, they fix bits of glass (previously, pieces of flint) to the pointed end, and gum sharp pieces on both sides as well. There is also a small stick about three feet long, with a kangaroo tooth fastened on one side of the tip, forming a barbed hook. They fix this tooth to the upper end of the spear and are very adept at shooting with it for a distance of 60 ells [approx. 70 metres]. In addition to these weapons, they have a small cudgel of very hard wood, about two feet long, with a knob at one end, which they call 'wirri' in their language. When the spear has been thrown, then this cudgel serves as a weapon of war. They use a fourth stick, which has been smoothed down at one end, as a spade for digging roots out of the ground; it also serves as a calendar record of their age, as mentioned earlier.

I have myself seen how they instructed their children or conducted exercises with them in the use of these weapons. They had set up a round wooden disc as big as a plate, at which they then took aim. Each child was lined up with his spear, then one of the old men placed himself at a distance of about twenty paces from them and rolled the disc along diagonally in front of the children. I saw them hit the disc several times when it was moving at its fastest.

In the company of one of the missionaries I was once present when a whole crowd of these savages had gathered. A spear had been stood up against a tree in the sun, and I took it up in my hand so that I could inspect it. One of those present gave a terrible cry and sprang at me, tore the spear out of my hand, and stared at me malevolently. My companion intervened and indicated to this savage that I had only wanted to inspect the instrument, and then he immediately calmed down. He pointed to his spear, which was still new and had been propped up at the tree for the gum to dry. I pointed at the spear and then at my arm, to indicate to him that he could injure the arm with it. This made him and his comrades laugh heartily; he shook his head and came toward me, first pointing to his spear and then to his heart, and nodded at me, as if to make me realise that it would have been a better place to aim at.

These people seem to be very good-natured, at least those of them who live in the region of the Onkaparinga River. The general opinion is that they are less good-natured on the other side of the Murray. If they are not provoked, they do no one any harm. The few cases where the savages have committed murder since the English settled here, are rather to be ascribed to ignorance or folly than to viciousness. The story of Capt. Barker's murder two years before was certainly an outrage, but it was clearly not caused by bloodlust. Captain Barker was on the south side of the Murray and wanted to make a sketch of Granite Island in Encounter Bay; he was prevented from doing so from this side of the Murray by the hills jutting out from the Australian side. So he decided to swim across the river and make his observations from the opposite side. He left his companions behind, as they were not good swimmers, tied his compass to his head, reached the other shore and completed the work as planned. However, when he wanted to go back, a crowd of savages gathered around him, gazing in amazement at his compass. After Barker had fastened this to his head once more and had stepped into the river, it apparently occurred to the savages that they should take possession of this shiny object, and so they speared Barker. If he had been willing simply to hand over his compass to these savages, they would not have murdered him.

The former king of the savages on the Onkaparinga, usually called King John, has been appointed to a post in the police force by Governor Gawler and is doing an excellent job here in Adelaide. If the savages have stolen something or have committed some other such misdemeanour, the Governor just gives John a hint and he finds the miscreant – he does not return to the town until he can bring the criminal along with him.

It is almost inconceivable that these people used to live solely on kangaroo meat, as the country has never been particularly well supplied with these animals. Of course, it is true that the kangaroo retreats whenever the white man arrives anywhere. But if they were so common, then some of these animals would have been encountered on the overland journeys between Adelaide and Sydney that have already been undertaken by several Europeans. It is possible that the kangaroos have moved away right up into the interior, which has not yet been explored. The great number of skins they still own is evidence that they have hunted down many of these animals. Anyway, there are very few now in the surrounding district. It is therefore more likely that the people eat the fish which abound in the rivers. One also finds that the various tribes always stay near a river, and many mussel shells have been found on the banks of the Murray, although no mussels have actually been seen. Therefore people surmise that the savages get the mussels by diving down to the bottom of the river.

They also have their own method of fishing. They make themselves a dam in the river, high enough to let about a foot of water flow over it. When the fish get near the dam, they have to come up close to the surface of the water, and the savages are standing there, ready to spear them.

Their kangaroo hunts are also of a simple kind. If they notice one of these animals, ten or twelve men gather in a circle around the prey, and in this formation they gradually close in on it, until they are so close to the kangaroo that they can hit it with their spears. Similarly, when the savages catch the opossums that are always to be found in hollow trees, they usually hunt in pairs. One of them climbs up the tree and waits at the hole that the animal uses as an entrance, the second man lights a fire at the bottom of the tree, and then the smoke drives the animal out of its hole and they catch it.

There is another strange and shameful kind of hunt which takes place in summer, when the grass in the hills has become dry as straw. But this involves a whole tribe. They form a circle about twenty English miles in diameter, light fires around this area, and then direct the fire closer and closer in toward the centre of the circle. The long dry grass, bushes and young trees burn fiercely; all the animals living in this area flee toward the centre, where the savages then catch them. A hunt like this occurred during our stay, and the fire burned for some days; I had never before seen such a fire. It is desirable that this practice be abolished. Of course, they light quite large fires in the hills at every new moon, which has led people to conclude that they worship and pray to the moon; but this latter practice is hardly to be compared with the former one.

A number of people are now surely wondering how the savages light the fires. However, they have a simple, easy way of doing this. There are many thin sticks about two to three feet long, growing in the long grass – the English call them grass-wood. They break one of these sticks in two, put the pointed end against the blunt one, and they then rub the two pieces so skilfully between their hands that the stick is burning briskly within two minutes at the most.

There are still various things remaining to be said about the conditions reigning among these savages, but I will omit them in order to avoid going into too much tedious detail. And so I will now close with the comment that the present generation of this race of people will, in my opinion, surely never be able to be trained to be useful beings in the world.

Friedrich Gerstäcker, *Australia*

Friedrich Gerstäcker, born in Hamburg as the son of opera singers in 1816, was one of nineteenth century Germany's most prolific authors. When his complete works were published posthumously in the 1870s, they amounted to 43 volumes embracing various forms of fiction and non-fiction – including a prodigious quantity of travel writing. Among Gerstäcker's travel books was one devoted to Australia, originally published soon after he travelled around the world in the years 1849 to 1852. With financial support from the Frankfurt Parliament and the publishing firm Cotta, Gerstäcker travelled to both the Americas and then across the Pacific to Australia, before returning to Germany via Java. In Australia he sought to satisfy his curiosity about the fate of Germans who had emigrated to South Australia. In one of the great adventures of his times, after landing in Sydney Gerstäcker made his way by coach, canoe and on foot to Adelaide, which he reached in mid-1851. His book, published in 1854 under the title Australien, *reveals a keen ethnographic interest in Indigenous Australians. It records his own encounters during his travels, but it also reveals that he drew on material – in the form of a journal and annual reports – provided to him by the South Australian Protector of Aborigines Matthew Moorhouse.*

Gerstäcker was also able to consult with German missionaries, who by the time of his visit had gathered substantial experience living and working among Indigenous people.

Gerstäcker was a professional writer; he wrote to entertain as large a readership as he could find. His book highlights his own travel adventures, not least his exposure to dangers and hardships in his encounters with people and places. On the one hand it seeks to satisfy his German readership's yearning for tales of adventure set in exotic locations, while on the other it also conveys familiar images of Teutonic idylls transplanted incongruously to the Antipodes.

Below are two extracts in translation. The first is from Chapter 5, which records the author's trek from the neighbouring colony of Victoria into South Australia. Here Gerstäcker applies the techniques and tropes of the fiction-writer to conjure a sense of suspense as he encounters – and proceeds to desecrate – a burial site. The second, from Chapter 6, describes his visit to the mission school for Indigenous children originally established on the north bank of the Torrens in 1839.*

Source:
Extracts from Friedrich Gerstäcker, *Australien* J.G. Cotta'scher Verlag, Stuttgart and Tübingen, 1854, 218–227, 281–292.
Translation: Thomas Kruckemeyer.

1. March through the Murray Valley

I was by now between the two inland lakes Victoria and Bonin [Bonney] – the main abode of the mysterious bunyip – and even though several whites had predicted that I would find the blacks here rather numerous and deceitful and wicked, I had so far come across only a relatively low number, and those few had, maybe with the exception of that somewhat ambiguous throwing of the boomerang, been friendly enough toward me. Mind you, I had kept them at arm's length as much as possible and was under the impression, probably justifiably so, that the most dangerous stretch in that regard was now behind me. But I was not yet completely out of harm's way, as I was to find out soon enough.

---

* *Further reading:* Friedrich Gerstäcker, *Australia: A German Traveller in the Age of Gold*, Adelaide, edited by Peter Monteath (Adelaide, Wakefield Press, 2016); Leslie Bodi, 'Gerstaecker, Friedrich (1816–1872)', *Australian Dictionary of Biography*, National Centre of Biography, Australian National University, https://adb.anu.edu.au/biography/gerstaecker-friedrich-3604/text5593, published first in hardcopy 1972, accessed online 27 May 2022.

I had covered around five English miles that morning, when I suddenly spotted several Indians on a small hill to my left. Since they had already seen me, however, I would not allow myself to be panicked and just kept walking straight on until I saw, also to my left, the whole camp, which consisted of some thirty gunyahs or bark roofs. A bunch of white-haired old fellows sat around the fire, but they must have been informed of my approach, because before long – after they had called out to each other from one fire to the next – three young lads, armed with spears, headed toward me and, as in the past, tried to block my path. This time, however, I was not at all in the mood to be drawn into any form of conversation with them or have them move in on me again. I therefore halted my step, slipped the gun off my shoulder, cocked both barrels and motioned them in a completely unequivocal way not to come near.

They immediately stood still like a brick wall, and just one of them called out to me that all they were after was a little bit of 'smoke'. However, I declined any deal by shaking my head and, deviating a little from my previous course, made my way into the scrub to my right. The blacks, possibly somewhat baffled by such an unsympathetic refusal from a single traveller, stayed where they were. I was not at all sure that they were not going to follow me after all and took cover several times after walking a certain distance, but I could detect no sign of life and, finally, continued on my way, feeling completely safe.

Around evening, with still no road to walk on and just maintaining roughly the same course, by the banks of a small, dry creek I came upon three Indian graves which lay silently and eerily in the wilderness, shaded by a few strong gum trees.

The graves consisted of three simply piled-up mounds. Each had a small hut of saplings and brushwood erected above it, so densely covered with foliage that there seemed to be total darkness inside. The space in front of the hut showed everywhere fresh foot-prints, and when I passed in close proximity and glanced inside, I was greeted from the gloomy death mound of one of the huts by three gleaming white hemispheres, much like skulls, but far larger. They attracted my interest to such a degree that I paused, first looked inside and then all around, and felt very eager to inspect these strange items from close up.

I would have really loved to crawl in, but the entrance was extraordinarily narrow and low, because the grave, raised and covered by leaves and small twigs, occupied nearly all of the interior space. And besides – may the devil trust those black wretches – just one of them might still have followed me despite all my vigilance, and would I then, by desecrating their burial places, not have given them proper cause to attack me?

I was already turning away again, but then, aware that such an opportunity might never present itself again, I made an instant decision at least to have a look what these white items in there might mean. I quickly threw down my blanket and hunting pouch, checked the gun, felt for the knife at my side, and then, after taking a careful look around, crawled into the grave hut.

Once inside I was enveloped by a fatal odour of decay. The blacks bury their dead not very deep, and I nearly had the impression that the thick layer of leaves and brushwood lying on the mound merely covered the top of the corpse. I climbed over it without wasting any time and reached for one of those white heads, which by now appeared to be giving me a particularly gruesome smile. These were not skulls, however, but rather some form of bowl modelled from white clay and rushes, which lay upside down on the graves, their meaning not easily explained. I wished I could have taken one with me, but they were too large and too heavy to carry. And breaking off a bit of them would not have been easy either, since the rushes that had been kneaded in with the clay had turned the whole thing into one solid and tightly-bound block. Besides, I did not feel like staying in there any longer. The hut had been too tightly woven or covered in shrubs to scan even the immediate surroundings from inside. All of a sudden I had a sensation of not being able to breathe in there anymore. It was the same feeling that had once grabbed me under a huge fir tree under which I was working in California, and which, after I had barely got out, without making any further sound or breaking any of the roots we had not yet cut, suddenly crashed to the ground with terrible and irresistible force. I quickly crawled forward, and when I stuck my head out, I could have sworn I saw a black shadow just behind the nearest saltbushes. I did not even take the time to pick up the bag and blanket but instead ran straight toward that spot, where I actually did find some tracks, but no further signs of any human being. The footprints might well have been older, since the whole ground around there had been stamped on by bare feet of all sizes.

The faster I got out of there, however, the better it would seem to me to be, especially since the terrain was covered in a mass of rather dense tea scrub and so-called lignum, and the blacks, if they were indeed plotting something against me, could not have chosen a better place for it. I therefore quickly threw the blanket and the bag back over my shoulder, and, still somewhat on guard, took the gun under my arm and marched off.

During the morning I had been marching along the sandy slope of the mallee, but since then had now veered off too far to the south. As I had come across a dray track running roughly in my direction through the bush, I was now following it through wild and dense scrub. I had run out of water as well and intended to walk on until it got dark, then to light a fire and lie down beside it. Before that, however, I wanted to satisfy myself once more that I really was not being followed, and that the black shadow I had positively glimpsed was not that of a black, but a wallaby, or, if it was a black, then one who had just coincidentally been strolling in the area. I therefore left my trail, lay down behind a dense salt bush and decided to stay put there for a full hour, and if I did not notice anything suspicious, I would set off again.

However, I had hardly been lying for five minutes when, without a care in the world, one of those black scoundrels approached in my tracks, closely followed by a second one. And I was not a little surprised when one of those two turned out to be that little old shrivelled-up fellow, whose boomerang I was still carrying in my pouch, and who I had presumed to be at least twenty miles away from here. What had motivated that black Satan to follow me all this way, and why was he now creeping around here in such sneaky, stealthy fashion?

I had come into this wilderness with a truly peaceful disposition toward the blacks and had intended from the very outset to spill blood only if the worst came to the worst, and only in self-defence or in order to protect another white. Now, however, the gun was raised nearly in spite of myself, and its sight focussed, as of its own accord, on the body of the black rascal, but eventually I put it down again and decided to see how they would react once they spotted me.

They were still about a hundred paces away and approaching quickly, when, suddenly, a small flock of black cockatoos swooped screeching and whistling over the bushes and attempted to settle just where I was lying. I turned my head to look at them, and the moment they spotted me, they scattered amid ear-piercing shrieks. This had, above all, a wonderful effect on those Indians snooping around out there. I was very confident that they could not see me since I was lying behind dense, low scrub, but when I turned my head back toward them, I just caught a glimpse of them disappearing into the undergrowth to their left and right, and even though I stayed put in my position for nearly a full hour or so, I neither heard nor saw anything of them again.

There is nothing more awkward on earth than the uncertainty of finding oneself in a dangerous situation, but not being able to identify its type and cause. I would have preferred it twentyfold for these chaps to confront me head-on rather than creeping around in the bushes in that treacherous manner and spoiling that last bit of fresh air one was still breathing out here.

My initial inclination was to end the matter quickly and turn the trick they had played on me back on them. I therefore picked up their tracks in order to follow one of them, but to my surprise, instead of two, I found three tracks, of which two went off to the right and one to the left, even though I had only seen two blacks. That led me quickly to the realisation that, by following these tracks, I was exposing myself to far greater danger than if I continued on my own route. I could not hope to compete against these clever blacks where this kind of warfare was concerned.

But why were they pursuing me so doggedly? The shadow at the grave mounds had probably not been a delusion after all and, who knows, maybe they were seeking revenge for that desecration. If that were the case, then that would be far more dangerous than a mere lust for loot, because religious fanaticism has provoked people into crazy shenanigans forever and made them impervious to reason. Evening was approaching, however, and since I felt a rather urgent thirst, I resolved firstly to beat my way to the river, and then come to a decision on how I would spend the night without exposing my kidney fat to any unnecessary risk. It is a pretty damned feeling if one cannot even be sure of preserving that little bit of fat one had a hard time acquiring in the first place.

Just as it was dark, perhaps three quarters of an hour after sunset, I reached the river, chose a decent spot for camping, cooked myself a few pigeons I had shot during the day, had an excellent meal, and then turned my thoughts to what best to do now. If there had been two of us, one would have had to keep guard, while the other could have had a restful sleep and gathered strength for the coming day. That, however, was impossible here at the fire, and yet I was so fatigued that I could hardly keep my eyes open. There was absolutely no doubt that I could not lie down right here, and even though the night was very cold and inclement, I decided that I would nevertheless rather abandon the fire and squeeze in behind some bushes. Before that, however, I collected a lot of wood and stacked it in a long pile against the wind, so that the embers would keep some heat for most of the night. I then gathered my belongings and made my way down to the banks of the river and followed it for about a quarter of a mile downstream. I was pretty certain that *here* the blacks would not be following my tracks during the night, since this close to the water they would be too afraid of the devil-devil.

Without a fire, however, I myself did not want to camp near the water either, because it was terribly cold. Therefore, once I felt that

I had left my fire far enough behind, I climbed back up the bank and lay down between two saltbushes standing close together and covered with dense foliage. There it took me just a few seconds after the anxiety and exertions of that day to fall into such a deep sleep that I am convinced that, if the blacks had found me there, I would have been totally at their mercy.

When I finally awoke, I jumped up with a start, because I had dreamt around morning that I could see the blacks creeping up on me again, and the sun was already high in the sky. With daylight, however, all danger had disappeared, or at least I did not fear it anymore, and my main concern now was to go back to the fire to have a look in the soft sand whether those black scoundrels had not paid me a visit at night. I was able to congratulate myself that I had not slept at the fire – their footprints were everywhere, leading all the way up to it, and I even missed a piece of cloth which, in damp weather, I usually wrapped around the lock of my gun, and which I had taken off last night and forgotten by the fire.

As I was by now completely convinced that my pursuers did indeed have evil intentions indeed, I now slogged on again in a straight line through the lower country saltbushes and tea trees towards the sand hills, at the foot of which I had at least open terrain and could not that easily be surprised. Besides, I had to be near some station, and if I could make it there, I was more likely to be safe from my former shadows.

During that day I had a most unnerving march, where one had to be constantly alert, with the gun always at the ready, being hungry and tired on top of it – such marching is no damn good to anybody. My neck nearly twisted off from all the looking left and right and, most likely as a result of the constant stressful use of all my senses, as well as having nothing but a bit of pigface to eat for lunch, I developed such a stinging headache in the afternoon that each step felt like a knife being driven into my brain.

It might have been around three o'clock in the afternoon when I first spotted once more the dark shadow of a black slipping across my path, and this time it was in front of me. At least, the wretches were shy of creeping up on me in my tracks, and, in making a detour, they had arrived a bit too far ahead of me. But by now I was utterly sick of being stalked and surrounded by such a mob. Raising my gun in one swift action, I fired a round of lead shot in the direction where I could assume that character to be hiding amid the swaying bushes, and the shot rattled into the branches. Practically at that very moment and so fast that, after turning around by sheer chance, I had just enough time to jump aside, a spear flew past me before getting stuck in the sand only a few paces from me. It must have been thrown from a fair distance because it had already no power left. But even though the scrub in the direction where it had come from was sparse and low, I was not able to spot the enemy who had thrown that weapon.

Naturally, I did not waste any time, but reloaded quickly and then held my position, from which I had a decent view to all sides, for quite a while. At this point I was determined to singe any black hide that might show itself, but nothing came into view anymore. So I finally continued on my way, very cautiously at first, but without being molested at all from that time onward. And I took the spear with me.

In the evening I found sheep tracks and, by following them, reached a sheep station where I was at least able to have a secure night's sleep, and where I gorged myself on a quart of tea, a piece of damper and some mutton chops.

The shepherds, when I told them of my adventure, thought that it was definitely my crawling into the grave hut which had caused the blacks, and probably the relatives of the deceased, to chase me, since they might have been of the belief that I had performed some magic in there. Otherwise these tribes had been reasonably friendly toward whites in recent times. Having said that, the stories they told me straight after about all these 'friendly tribes' were not exactly in the latter's favour. It seemed that just in the last three months they had not perpetrated 'anything new', at least nothing that had become common knowledge.

For readers not familiar with the circumstances it may seem somewhat strange that the shepherds who, during the day, travel among them with their flocks, are hardly ever attacked, even if that does occasionally occur here and there. And in the past, the blacks have indeed done so, but had to find to their own cost that such people were always missed after a very short time, and that the neighbours, together with the police, were then mobilised to conduct search and revenge parties. While they always came off second best in those encounters, they got away with murdering single travellers at will without any enquiries being made. These people would usually walk from one station to another, looking for work. Nobody was expecting them where they were heading, nobody missed them where they had come from.

Nobody knew on which side of the river they were walking and cared even less. Such people mostly remained missing unless individual murders came to light by chance, often as a result of a voluntary confession by the savages themselves, who, as has been mentioned, believe in a certain kind of statute of limitation.

Incidentally, as the shepherds assured me, from here on in I had nothing to fear from my previous pursuers, because I was now entering the territory of another tribe, onto which they were not allowed to follow me. While I still found plenty of other Indians, I must not tire my readers any further, nor do I have the space to tell them how I came across a tribe doing their corroboree or dance the very next evening, and how I circumvented it in one of their own bark canoes, because the possum-hunting dogs blocked my path through the bush. Or how, later and further downstream, I met a jolly company of white labourers who, in the caves in the limestone banks on which they were meant to build a house, had literally made themselves nests to sleep in. I have already filled too many pages with blacks, and shepherds, and 'hut keepers' and must now continue on my path a little more rapidly.

[...]

II. The Adelaide District

Similarly of great interest was the acquaintance of a Mr Moorhouse, the Protector of the Adelaide Blacks, to whom I had been recommended by

Pastor Meier in Tanunda, and who most kindly not only supplied me with all desired information but also conducted me to the school of the Blacks to witness the lessons there.

The Australian Black, who by the way has the skin of the negro but not the woolly hair, but rather long hair sometimes curly and sometimes smooth, has – according to outward appearance at least – originated from a mixing of the Malayan with the Ethiopian race. Now in his original state he is the wildest, dirtiest and most treacherous being that I have found among the Indian tribes at least. At first glance he also seems to possess the least intellectual faculties, since his dwellings are the most primitive possible, his weapons simple and crudely worked, his entire clothing only – in cold weather – a rectangular blanket stitched together out of opossum skins. He does not even use a bow and arrow like almost every other tribe and knows of no higher being to whom he could pray – he only fears the devil. In spite of all that, however, I believe that there is scarcely a tribe in God's wide world who possesses a better gift of comprehension than this apparently so dull-witted savage, or one who knows better how to handle the imperfect weapons that he bears, and at the same time holds so fast with such steadfastness of character to his manners and customs, not yielding to the civilisation of the whites but only to their violence, resisting them every inch of the way.

Already at the Murray I was astonished at the enormous skill with which they cast their light, crudely worked spears, and with what assurance they found their target; then I was surprised at the ease with which they without exception grasped the English language, while the English themselves, who had already lived among them for years, had retained barely a word of their language.

Here in this school I was to find confirmed that this nation is not by any means as antipathetic to culture as one would believe at first sight and as many insist.

Their teacher was kind enough to put several of his best pupils – they were four boys and one girl – through their paces in various branches of education, and he asked me to have them read something aloud. In the New Testament that he handed me I opened by chance at the first chapter of John's Gospel and said that to the first boy. Each of them had the book in front of them and quickly found the text I had named.

'In the beginning was the word and the word was with God and the word was God', the one boy read with really great skill; the second took the second verse and so forth through the chapter. The pronunciation of all the children was excellent, and although their language lacks some of the letters of our alphabet, they had acquired the English accent perfectly, and even read with far more expression than we find in our village schools.

I asked the teacher if the children also understood what they were reading, and instead of replying he began to ask them the meaning of the chapter. I must confess I was greedy to hear from the lips of Australian Blacks an explanation of the meaning of the sentence that Faust had brooded over for so long, until in the end even the poodle became impatient. The explanation did not go smoothly, however, and I hardly think that Faust would have been satisfied with it. The children had nonetheless remembered quite well what they had been told about it some time before. 'The word' here meant Christ and was, according to the explanation, not for example a quality of the Saviour, an intellectual term, but yet another name. Just as He was called Saviour, Redeemer and Son of God, here He was called *the Word*. The Indians are children and must be led by a friendly hand over such difficult places.

In the meantime, while some were explaining the Bible texts, another one of them had picked up a slate lying in front of him and was copying a picture of a white swan hanging on the wall in front of them. Naturally he did not yet have the firmness of hand to copy the outlines sharply and accurately, but his eyes grasped every deviation of the lines faithfully, and though it was crude, anyone who saw the black's drawing could see at first glance that the picture was supposed to represent a swan – and that is more than can sometimes be said for pictures by civilised people.

The talent for mimicry on the whole seems to predominate among them, and that may be a great advantage to them in writing. I saw the copy books of several boys who had been going to school for only a few years, and in those years only for a few months, and there were a couple among them who can truthfully write better than I can myself, even if I took great pains over it. If one could only fetter both boys and girls to the school for a longer period and to a peaceful bourgeois life forever, I have not the slightest doubt that one could make everything out of them, but the innate wild spirit has too much supremacy over them and culture cannot prevail against it. The black Australian on the whole depends too much on sudden impressions, neither past nor future bother him much. Apart perhaps from the threats of the medicine man, he grasps only what the moment brings and devotes himself to it with heart and soul, and it seems to be of no account whether it turns out for good or ill. No matter how long they have been in the school or how much they have learnt, or how much progress they have made, once the thought of their old freedom, the old, wild, cheerful life in the bush enters the mind, and in a flash it is all over with civilisation. They all at once throw away European ideas and clothing, and leap with a jubilant shout back into their old, wild life, and the teachers are left behind sadly shaking their heads in despair.

The teacher also got the children to count and do sums, and in a very practical, lively and easily-grasped way, with beads strung on a series of wires in groups of ten that could be pushed back and forth.

A number of picture tables hanging on the walls and intended for school use seemed to be of the greatest interest to the little Black community in general. They consisted of little pictures of people and animals with captions, individual tables showing the whole process of cultivation from clearing the land through to harvest, others dealing with animal husbandry, hunting etc. And the children were not only able to say exactly what the picture meant but also what the caption said and what the colours were, and while some of them were explaining this, others stood around of their own accord and copied the things that interested them most.

The conclusion of this little examination was an attempt at geography, which could however only turn out most imperfectly. The map showed only the outlines of the various continents; they could of course name them all, and also show where they themselves were located in Australia, and where East and West, North and South were. Locating Sydney was much more difficult, and they had to be guided there step by step, but that too is hardly to be wondered at, since until now their only concept of the whole world had been the little stretch of land that they inhabited and the narrow strip of land surrounding it. How could they be expected to grasp and understand the enormous size and extent of the globe? But all the same, a beginning has been made there too, and they will in time gradually be led further and further towards it.

But just what has been the result up until now of all this expenditure and the attempts to civilise the black tribes? Sadly, it is only meagre; they simply do not want to allow themselves to be civilised, and all attempts with the adults ended in hopelessness. The missionaries abandoned their station in despair and realised belatedly that they had sacrificed an enormous number of souls to the evil one. According to the doctrine of various individual Christian sects, savages are still capable of attaining a certain level of bliss after death as long as they do not know any better; but once the doctrine of Christianity and the one and only God have been proclaimed to them according to God's command, if they reject it they incur the *just* punishment of subjection to the evil one and are irredeemably lost, according to the testimony of Methodists, Baptists and other –ists. It is a strange story with such doctrines: if one wanted to believe them (and anyone who does not is damned as an unbeliever), the Devil would have no better agents in the whole world than the missionaries themselves. How many thousands of souls have they already delivered into his hands in Australia in this way?

Since they could make no headway at all with the adults, they experimented with the children, who did in fact attend school punctually enough in the winter, when they received warm clothing, blankets and good food, but in summer they just as punctually flew off in all directions, returning under the influence of the old men of the tribe, hearkening to their words with innate respect.

In the case of the boys there were always a few who could be persuaded to persist for a shorter or longer time, but the girls fled irremediably as soon as they had reached a certain age and could never be retrieved. Their own customs, their own superstitions which take root too deeply in young hearts to be easily uprooted again, bear the major if not the sole blame for this. A girl is betrothed to some man when she is still quite young – often soon after birth – and until she reaches marriageable age the tribe is quite indifferent to what she does, but as soon as she reaches that age the groom demands his bride, and the tribe calls her back, while the medicine men threaten her with instant death or an insidious illness if she does not obey the command.

Such an admonition they cannot resist, and no matter how much her heart may at that moment be attached to the culture which has step by step become a habit, they throw it all away and obey the command.

The teacher told me a striking example of this. They had taken a girl into the school when she was small, and she attended regularly for four years, making significant progress. Then she went into service in the home of the missionary for two years, followed by two years in Government House. She was well kept and treated kindly everywhere and seemed to have totally forgotten the old ways and become accustomed to her new life; she liked wearing European clothes and did not have much contact with her tribe when it was located in the vicinity. But after eight years this girl – who spoke English perfectly, had adopted the Christian religion and learned everything necessary for housekeeping – threw away at the same time both her clothes and her new way of life and ran back into the bush just as God had created her, and just as she had been taken from the bush eight years earlier.

This particular case is said to have been uncommonly discouraging for all those employed in the education and civilisation of the blacks. A real obstacle which has an especially detrimental effect on their real and lasting civilisation is the fact that all savage Australian tribes are not inclined to become accustomed to permanent dwellings. Even where they have been built for them, they make no use of them, and often on the Murray I have even in bad weather seen them around a fresh Indian camp-fire, while only a few hundred steps away there are huts abandoned by whites who had lived there previously. Whether it may be superstition or God knows what that prevented them, they preferred to sleep out in the open rather than under a sheltering roof.

The protector has however come up with a novel way to guard against such relapses, which may perhaps be appropriate for a few of them at least, but whether it can in the first place pass the test of common humanity and not end up instead in some kind of European imposition of universal happiness remains to be seen.

As soon as girls or boys reach marriageable age, they are paired up and married off and then transported to Lincoln Point (as I believe the place is called), where the government gives them a certain portion of land and agricultural tools and puts up a little cottage where they are to live and cultivate their own land. But the area they are sent to is located on a peninsula and the land route is cut off by hostile Indian tribes inhabiting the intervening land. So they simply cannot return to their old life and are compelled to play the role of Europeans whether they want to or not. This is, by the way, a totally new experiment, and only the results will show how it ends up. I for my part believe it cannot end well, for such compulsion cannot exercise a good influence in the long run, and if a man wants to throw off the shackles that have been imposed on him in this way, he will find an opportunity to do so. If he does not, and if the chains hold, he will be unhappy, and then the question is, are the whites allowed to exercise such compulsion, and are they not making the Indians much more miserable than they were with their old manners and customs in the wilderness?

The children going to school here were all respectably dressed – the boys in shirts and trousers and the girls in long blue dresses – and of course they had to keep themselves clean, that is, cleaner than they were accustomed to in their original state. But the noses, the fearful noses!

Mr Moorhouse was, however, also obliging enough to entrust his journal to me for a time to look through and to make extracts – a journal on the Indians and their circumstances, kept since 1839, in which he has recorded a mass of notes on their manners and customs. Of course I did not neglect to take advantage of his kindness, and I found many highly interesting things therein.

Gustav Listemann, 'On the Natives'

The passenger ship with the most illustrious list of German passengers in the nineteenth century was the Princess Louise. *It departed Hamburg in March 1849 and arrived in Port Adelaide in August.*

The timing of the voyage was significant, because on board were a number of passengers who have been labelled 'Forty-Eighters', that is, liberals who were disenchanted with the apparent failure of the revolutionary movements in various parts of Europe – including the German states – in the years 1848–49, and who decided thereafter to start new lives on the other side of the world. Whatever the motivations were of the Princess Louise's *passengers for leaving Germany, a great number went on to make notable contributions to South Australia, some to become household names. Thus the passenger list includes the names Basedow, Büring, Kreusler, Linger, Mücke, Schomburgk and Schramm.*

The name that occurs most often on the Princess Louise's *passenger list is Listemann – altogether nine times. Pater familias was Gustav, and he was accompanied by his wife and five children, along with two family servants, also entered on the list under the name Listemann.*

Unlike some of their hardier fellow passengers, the Listemanns were not to remain in South Australia. Disappointed by what the fledgling colony had to offer them, they returned to Germany, where Gustav wrote and published an account of his experiences as a warning to those Germans who might be considering making their futures in the Antipodes. His intent, and his attitude to South Australia, are evident in his book's *title, which translates as 'My Emigration to South Australia and Return to the Fatherland: A Word of Warning and Instruction for all Contemplating Emigration'.**

Source:
Extract from: Gustav Listemann, *Meine Auswanderung nach Südaustralien und Rückkehr zum Vaterlande; ein Wort zur Warnung und Belehrung für alle Auswanderungslustige.* Hayn, Berlin, 1851, 85–95. *Translation:* Lothar Brasse, Heidi Brasse and Peter Monteath.

Dispersed among the European colonists there now live individual small tribes belonging to the race of native Papuan Negroes, and the government has taken care of them by creating numerous sections as reservations, so that they can live there unhindered. Thus a number of tribes live in the immediate proximity of Adelaide, and usually one even finds several huts of the Blackfellows, as they are called by the English, in the park located between both parts of the city. Their external appearance is repulsively ugly. The face is broad, the nose thick and lumpy, the mouth large, beset with huge snow-white teeth reminiscent of those of wild animals, the torso protruding rather strongly, whereas the arms and legs are thin and long, the whole body smeared with a fatty ochre, chalk or ash, depending on the happiness or sadness of the occasion, so that one may initially question the true colour of their skin, which on closer inspection is revealed to be black-brown. The black hair of the head and beard shines with the copious amounts of fat rubbed into it, and red or white colour is often thickly applied to the face. – In place of the elaborate tattoos of other peoples they bear on their breast, back and arms the circular scars of incisions made by a sharp shell. They clothe themselves by wrapping a mat around their body and wearing a rug or blanket, skilfully sewn together from sheep or possum skins, over their shoulders. In the vicinity of Adelaide, many wear scraps of European clothes which make them a sight to behold. I encountered a youthful beauty whose

---

* *Further reading:* Reg Butler, 'Ship Princess Louise (7Aug1849)', https://localwiki.org/adelaide-hills/Ship_Princess_Louise_%287Aug1849%29.

calico dress swept the dust half a yard behind her, and a black dandy, whose attire consisted of a white shirt, a vest, cravat with collar and white gloves, appeared to find himself as handsome as our young men in their most elegant attire. There is, by the way, a law that no native may enter the city unclothed, and any intruder of that nature will be ejected by the police in no time. Every now and again the government has a number of woollen blankets distributed among them. Their domed or vaulted dwellings are huts – wurlies – made from the branches of trees, strips of bark or reeds providing makeshift protection against the rain. They are readily constructed in a location protected from the wind, and the low entrance is always to be found on the wind-free side, that is, mostly the north-east.

Inside a fire burns through the entire night, in part to keep the insects away, but also because they fear the dark. It is for the first reason that the Aborigines have hitherto stubbornly declined to move into stone dwellings built especially for them and cannot be persuaded to even by force. For the same reason they like to change their place of abode from time to time, because the rapid increase in bugs, particularly fleas, causes insufferable torture when they remain in the same place for a prolonged period. In the hot season they do not even bother to erect their huts, and one frequently sees them camped around a fire, smoking their pipes in quiet comfort, joking and laughing in the way that children carry out all sorts of mischief. Their nourishment is very basic, comprising the little that nature offers them. Those living close to Adelaide are a bit better off, as offcuts from the abattoirs come their way, and the little offerings from the whites enable them to buy tobacco and bread. They are also more likely to have the opportunity without too much effort to earn a few pence. Whenever a rider arriving in the city is looking for someone to hold his horse for him, there will also be a Jemmy to whom he can entrust the animal with full confidence. I have also observed how the men collect branches from the tangle of timbers from the Torrens River bed at low water level; they were then sold by the women in the city for a few copper coins. Not uncommonly therefore one encounters blacks carrying a bloody mutton head or proudly looking at the bread they have just purchased. The men hunt and fish. Kangaroos have already been driven away, but possums and birds still abound. They are adept at climbing even the tallest trees and with cunning easily prise the former from their burrow; they kill the latter with their spears. On the Murray they fish with spears and nets. Apart from that, they enjoy snakes, lizards, woodworms as well as roots and herbs for their meals. It is often the poor women who solely depend on these latter food sources, as the men just leave them to fend for themselves, unless there is an abundance of food at hand. – During the day they roam around either singly or in small groups, occasionally calling out to a white man crossing their path 'give me copper,' or asking a colonist for a gift. They rarely leave empty handed, but some have taken to not handing over to the spokesperson a piece of bread, some cabbage leaves or even the leftovers of a meal until a bit of work is done, and if the black is hungry, he will certainly be persuaded to carry water, to split some wood or to make himself useful in some way. But he does not understand why he should work if he is not driven by need, and there will certainly be some great difficulties, which could not be resolved by the means hitherto attempted, in bringing the native to undertake a regular activity.

Based on my personal experiences, and from what I have learned from others about the native Australians, they do not possess the wild, bloodthirsty character attributed to them. Rather, they are receptive to friendly treatment, thankful for any help provided, keep their promises, and tend to resemble harmless but spirited children rather than dehumanised barbarians. Hundreds of whites live individually in the far-reaching country districts without fear of violent treatment on the part of the Aborigines. On the other hand, they appear resistant to the influence of civilisation, and to date all efforts to introduce civilisation to them have largely failed, whereby in their crude customs and unbridled passions they commit acts which we would normally regard as despicable. It can also not be denied that from time to time one hears of bloody deeds they have perpetrated on whites, but one is surely going too far to reckon them among the lowest and depraved classes of humankind on that basis. As countless examples have shown, the natives are not lacking in powers of comprehension, and in particular they are reputed to have outstanding memories. To date they have received little of value from civilisation, so why should they be well-disposed towards it? Their burdens are often driven by need and custom, and as far as the violent actions they have perpetrated on settlers are concerned, in most cases the guilt must lie on the side of the whites rather than the coloureds, because the former not uncommonly treat them with atrocious roughness, thereby provoking revenge.

According to statements made by people who have lived in the vicinity of natives over a longer period, although the latter are spread over a large part of the country, they have a striking resemblance to each other; their habits, customs and activities also are largely the same, and individual differences are caused only by local circumstances.

The natives are divided into loose tribes, which have often already been reduced to the small number of 20 members. The oldest people in the tribe, as well as those who stand out for their courage and bravery, gain some limited influence by providing advice during disputes, but there is no actual chief as such. If decisions need to be made concerning the common interests of the tribe, then the men consult. The women are excluded from participation in these deliberations; they generally live in a miserable condition of profound degradation and are kept by the men in a state of oppressive slavery. While on the move, they have to carry the load, the weight of which is often increased by small children, while the men carry only their weapons. In doing so they do not even provide for the women, but rather when they reach their destination leave it to them to build their hut and to gather supplies. And as these poor people neither throw spears nor are able to climb trees to catch possums, they are often dependent on the most meagre nourishment and have to make do with roots and leaves if the man does not deign to cast a piece of meat their way. The skill of some of them is evident by the baskets and mats woven from a kind of grass and by the blankets sewn together often artfully from possum skins. For the threads they make use of the muscle fibres of the kangaroo, taken from the tail of the freshly killed animal; a sharpened bone is their needle. The manner in which the men for their part seek to attract the women already determines their enslavement. If a young man has reached the age of maturity, that is, when the beard regrows after the first tufts of hair are torn out, then in the company of two or three companions he lies in wait in the vicinity of an enemy tribe's camp and expertly takes the opportunity to steal one of the women who pleases him. This wife-stealing every now and again causes wars between the individual tribes, especially when the return of the woman is refused by the man. Some men have three to four wives, and it is suggested they must be very jealous of them. They do not appear to love their children very much, because generally only one of the girls is allowed to remain alive, and once a small boy was offered to us for purchase for a shilling.

The weapons of the natives are very simple and consist of 12-foot-long, very thin and light spears and short clubs (waddies). With the former they hit their target from a considerable distance (from 30 paces they can hit a hand-sized piece of paper), but if the target is further than their arm strength allows, they employ a two-foot-long instrument onto which is secured at one end a kangaroo tooth, which they nestle into the bottom end of the lance so as to catapult it greater distances. They use the clubs for close combat or presumably throw them at their enemy. One other weapon distinctive of the New Hollanders, which however does not appear among those living in South Australia, is the *waumra*, which is said to be constructed in such a remarkable way, that it flies back to the thrower after it has struck the object toward which it has been hurled. It follows from the very simplicity of these weapons that their wars cannot be very lethal. The preparations for battle consist of warlike dances which each party conducts for itself, and in which through words and gesticulations they incite each other to courage, at which point the actual fighting begins. Both parties confront each other along a line of battle. If spears are used – agreement will have been reached in advance as to which weapons are to be used in the battle – then the encounter begins when a warrior, after he has issued a form of challenge with mocking words, hurls his spear at the opposing party, and lasts until some warriors are wounded or the spears are destroyed. Often screaming women dart among them, probably to throw the enemy off his target or to protect their men with their bodies. If after the spear battle there is a desire for a fight with clubs, then one warrior steps forward from each party, and after they have well and truly cursed each other, and probably spat on each other, one of them leans his head forward as if he is tempting and testing the courage of the other to see whether he would dare to strike him. The blow takes place, delivered with such strong conviction that the victim falls to the ground. It does not take long before he picks himself up again, and now it is his turn to administer a blow, for which the opponent without hesitation offers his head. As soon as it has been struck, everyone breaks into a frightful howling and, seething with rage, attacks each other at close quarters.

Apart from the warlike dances mentioned above, at their big gatherings, attended from time to time by more than 300 people, or on other festive occasions, the Aborigines have national dances (corroborees). They take place at the time of the full moon, and to stage them at night a number of preparations are made. One tribe takes on the staging of the event and makes sure there is a roaring fire as well as a number of campsites made of branches and dry leaves. That tribe receives the guests, among whom the women and children form a large circle, while the men march with a certain military order to the central point and set themselves down there. They are all at their finest. Their whole body, especially their hair, is smeared with fat and red ochre and is then strewn with flame-like patterns made from powdered calcium chalk. As soon as all have settled, one of them starts a melodious wail, after which, one by one, the others join in, and once the chorus has reached its loudest crescendo, they suddenly all jump up to begin the dance. The women remain seated in a circle, and with their hands beat an animal skin, either rolled up or stretched over their knees, providing the rhythm for the melody. The dance consists mostly of a mix of unusual body poses with a simultaneous movement of arms and legs. Soon the dancers stand on their toes and clap their thighs together, then stretch out one or both arms, or swing a club or green branch around their head at great speed, during which time the chant accompanies the dance, and from time to time increases to a piercing cry. They like to have European onlookers at such festive occasions and feel flattered by their presence. Probably similar festivities are connected with religious concepts. The latter are very minimal and are limited primarily to the fear of an evil spirit, to whose influence they attribute every adversity in life, disease and death. Of life after death they have an unclear understanding, taking the view that after death they will be turned into white humans. Should one of them die, they make loud noises and jump around to prevent the evil spirit Tong Kinjargall taking possession of the dead. The funeral procession that precedes the burial of the body appears to have the same purpose. The body is wrapped tightly in clothes and covered in furs and fastened to a stretcher carried by four strong men on their shoulders, while women and children accompany them, howling a lament. The procession moves slowly at first but gains in pace, until finally the bearers run as fast as they can. Suddenly they stop, fall to their knees and, as if possessed by the evil spirit, they tear at their hair and thrash about wildly. At this point the body is returned, and the mourners depart, but only after they have collectively emitted one last, piercing scream. The women of the tribe as well as the deceased's next of kin make an open display of their mourning by covering their bodies with a mixture made of charcoal and grease.

The number of Aborigines has diminished considerably since the Europeans have settled among them, in part due to the diseases which the newcomers brought with them, and partly due to the increasing difficulty of supporting themselves. If they do not succeed in adapting to the growing trend toward farming or industry, then within a few decades the coloured race will completely disappear from the areas where European culture has blazed new trails. Unfortunately, any such attempts to date have had little success, but perhaps because they were inappropriate for that purpose. So far one has been more concerned to educate children in schools, to teach them to read and write and to familiarise them with Christianity's doctrine of salvation, rather than to occupy them with easier mechanical work or agricultural pursuits and such handicrafts suitable for their natural needs. If this were done, if one gave the up-and-coming ones a piece of land to work and made sure that by practising their acquired skills and talents they could earn a living, then it would be possible to exert an influence on their spiritual and moral improvement, and at least introduce the next generation to the benefits of the culture which one offers in vain to the current generation. It must be said to the credit of the English government that it is not indifferent to the lot of the natives, but rather that it commits not inconsiderable sums to bring about an improvement. It pays public servants, protectors, to uphold the rights of the natives within the borders of the colony and, moreover, to take care that no injustice is done to them on the part of the settlers. It distributes food and clothing to its black subjects, establishes schools and employs teachers. Therefore, it is all the more regrettable that to date better results have not been achieved. Earlier the children of the natives received their schooling only in the mission schools, and then they were released back to their people by giving them food to take with them, which was to be prepared for them at home. However, generally the food was consumed by the adults, and furthermore life with their family members readily swept aside the impressions that the children had acquired at school. For that reason, there was later a move away from that system and the children were given lodgings and food in the schoolhouse, without however entirely removing the earlier flaws, because when the parents moved close to the school, they had almost daily opportunity to exert a negative influence on their children, especially as the children, in particular the boys, gladly participated in the games and activities of their tribe. In addition, the parents do not at all like to see their children taken away from them, because for them that produces no advantage but certainly a disadvantage insofar as they have to make do without their help in getting things done, and they also recognise that in the eyes of their children their standing is diminished by the influence of the school, and the children become alienated from the customs of their people. If one could make the parents inclined to allow their children voluntarily to attend school by conceding certain benefits to them in exchange, and if the children could be kept away even from the community of the members of their tribe, then the success of efforts to bring culture to them would be greater. One more thing, however, and that is that one has to not limit oneself, as has been the case to date, of keeping the children to their 14th year (girls often leave school as soon as in their 12th year), rather, one would have to continue looking after them, placing the boys perhaps with a farmer, a master craftsman or as a servant, while similarly the girls would be placed in a position which would not force them to return to their tribe, where naturally everything good that they had learned at school would be lost. The children in the schools learn to speak English very easily, and there is a lot of evidence that the natives do not lack the ability to receive instructions and to make use of them.

The language of the original inhabitants of Australia is reportedly divided into dialects which vary starkly from each other; it also appears to be rather poor. Thus it contains just two words for numbers: *mätä* one and *dankull* two. Some other words are *bedaio* father, *jnakaio* mother, *lubra* wife, *jnankö* son, *maika* daughter, *babukko* head, *kulbko* hand, *tünja* foot, *dako* mouth, *korlo* eye, *knappo* I, *ullnu* you.

Emil Jung,
'The Murray Estuary and
Its Inhabitants'

Karl Emil Jung was born in Gross Machnow in Brandenburg in 1833. He emigrated to Australia in about 1858 and travelled extensively through the continent, pursuing a particular interest in his fellow Germans. He settled for a time in Tanunda in the Barossa Valley and taught modern and classical languages at St Peter's College in Adelaide. From 1872 to 1877 he was Inspector of Schools in South Australia and for a time served as Professor of Classical Languages at the University of Adelaide. Eventually he returned to Germany and settled in Leipzig, where he pursued a number of literary activities. Among them was his four-volume work Der Weltteil Australien *(1882–1883), which cemented his reputation as one of the great experts in his time on this part of the world.*

Back in Germany, Jung also served for a time as General Secretary of an organisation called the Kolonialverein *(Colonial Association), which advocated for German participation in the European quest for colonial empires. After Germany established formal colonies in the mid-1880s, Jung and other colonial enthusiasts maintained a keen interest in German settlements in other parts of the world, including British colonies such as those in Australia. In his last major work,* Das Deutschtum in Australien und Ozeanien. Der Kampf um das Deutschtum *– published in 1902, the year of his death – Jung promoted the importance of maintaining connections between overseas Germans and their homeland.**

---

* *Further reading:* Gaston Mayer, 'Jung, Karl Emil', in: *Neue Deutsche Biographie* 10 (1974), 676 [Online-Version]; URL: https://www.deutsche-biographie.de/pnd117659711.html#ndbcontent

Source:
Extracts from Karl Emil Jung, 'Die Mündungsgegend des Murray und ihre Bewohner', *Mittheilungen des Vereins für Erdkunde zu Halle* 1, 1877, 24–47.
Translation: Harald and Aileen Ohlendorf.

It is a remark often made that the character of the natives of a country is essentially conditioned by its geographical situation as well as by its productivity. If, therefore, on the great waterless and treeless Eyre Peninsula to the west of the Spencer Gulf, we find that the Australian natives there are of stunted growth and that the arid plains of Western Australia are inhabited by miserable wretches, we may expect that on a river such as the Murray whose banks abound in wild game and whose waters abound in fish, the natives will contrast favourably with less fortunate tribes.

The mighty Murray, whose length is more than 500 German miles, springs in the Australian Alps and drains the waters of an area measuring more than 30,000 square miles (a complex of countries roughly equal in size to France, the German Empire and Austria-Hungary combined) into the Southern Ocean. A shallow stream at the end of summer, with sandbanks across its bed that hinder navigation, it swells mightily in spring, fed by the melting snows of the Australian Alps as well as by the rapidly filling large and small tributaries, carries its turbid waters through the many branching arms, forming large islands, spreads out over wide lagoons and fills the lakes that lie along its banks. It carries immense quantities of sand and clay suspended in its floods, washed down from the mountain sides or torn from its banks, and finally deposits them where its waters are met by the mighty impact of the Southern Ocean in Encounter Bay, in numerous large and small islands and tongues of land, after spreading over a wide area in Lakes Alexandrina and Albert.

Close to the barely recognisable Murray mouth a long narrow arm of water stretches far to the south-east. This is known as the Coorong, where numerous fish are found in the mostly salty waters, and which is the habitat of flocks of pelicans, swans and ducks. A narrow spit of high sandy dunes separates this arm from the roaring sea, whose thunder-like roar can be heard from afar. [...]

The estuary of the Murray with the former seats of the Narrinjeri, by Dr E. Jung

In this wide area, on the coast as far as Cape Jervis to the west, southeast along the Coorong to Lacepede Bay, around those two great lakes surrounding the Murray mouth, and north almost to the great bend of the river, a large black population once lived. The number of tribes was given as 18, and, if we estimate each tribe at about 150–200, this would mean something over 3000 souls, an assumption which agrees with those of the missionaries. Now about 600 natives eke out a miserable existence in this vast area. Although farmers have penetrated only here and there with their ploughs, herds of sheep and cattle have replaced kangaroos and emus. Native wildlife has all but disappeared, while some species, like the strange platypus, are extinct altogether. In the protective reed meadows of the lakes and the inaccessible polygonum thickets of the lagoons, the pelican and black swan still find safe refuge, and the immense flocks of smaller species of wild fowl still manage to protect themselves from the long-range weapons of the white man with extra vigilance. The natives of the country hardly hunt them any longer. The older men, who still hold firmly to the traditions of their forefathers, lack strength and skill; the younger members of the tribes, who have acquired nothing but vices from the culture of the Europeans, do not make any effort; and the small number of those to whom the zeal of the missionaries on their stations has imparted the skills of civilised peoples, prefer to replace the occupation of the hunter with the more peaceful one of cultivating the land.

These tribes of the lower Murray, eighteen in number, together bear the name Narrinjeri from Narran (man) and injeri (belonging), i.e.: belonging to men; they say: the neighbouring tribes are savages, but we are men. They are very proud of this name.

Among themselves, the Narrinjeri tribes were almost constantly squabbling, but in their favour it must be said that they always showed a united front against the neighbouring hostile blacks. Their greatest grudge was against the Merkani in the east, who had a reputation for cannibalism; and if a Narrinjeri possessed a particularly well-built woman, he never left her without protection, for fear that she might be dragged off and eaten by the predatory cannibals.

The Narrinjeri have little to say about their past, but their traditions seem to indicate that they moved down the Darling and Murray Rivers to their present homes.

The colour of the natives is uniformly black, their hair curly, their nose flat, their mouth large, their chest broad and arched, but their arms and legs less advantageously developed, their whole body, especially the back, is often covered with a thick growth of hair, even in very young children, and older women sometimes have a rather impressive beard. But the dexterity with which they use their

An Indigenous South

Tarkeorn. – Taganarin tribe. Old man, famous healer.

Naraminjeri. – Karatinjeri tribe. Unmarried young girl,
16 years old (?), baptised and educated.

James Unaipon – Lathinjeri tribe. Church warden of the mission congregation at Point McLeay.

hands and feet is astonishing. With their nimble fingers they knit nets without the aid of needles with a precision that the most skilful knitters of other peoples could not achieve; the way they use their feet is reminiscent of the hands of apes. Often seated, they seize objects within their reach with the toes of their feet, without using their hands, and climb the highest trees with ape-like skill, using as their only foothold a projecting bump in the bark or an indentation made with their sharp stick, their whole weight resting on their big toe. Forrest and MacKinlay, like other travellers and myself, have often had occasion to admire the cat-like agility with which even elderly men and women, who could not escape as quickly as their younger tribesmen, climbed up smooth trunks to the tops to save themselves from the terrifying apparitions of horse and rider.

The religious beliefs of the Narrinjeri are confusing. Their myths tell of heroes who performed great deeds on earth, who later raised themselves to heaven and still exert their influence, helping or harming, on the inhabitants of the earth; but even before their appearance the earth existed, there were humans and animals, and those heroes themselves were humans, like others, only of greater stature and gifted with miraculous powers. These myths are often very absurd, even more often obscene.

[Here Jung recounts two Ngarrindjeri origin stories.]

Each tribe has its protective deity – *ngaitje* – in the form of birds, fish, insects or crawling worms, and members of the tribe are strictly forbidden to harm these animals. Sometimes, of course, necessity does not even recognise this commandment, but then one must destroy every remnant of the animal eaten, in case an enemy seizes it or the animal grows in the entrails. It can sometimes be dangerous if a white man is staying with the natives and kills animals they have chosen as their patron gods.

It has often been said that the Australians do not recognise chiefs among themselves, and yet nothing could be more untrue. In all the tribes that have not yet lost their particular institutions through prolonged intercourse with the whites, there are men to whom a certain authority has been delegated by their fellow tribesmen. The *rupulle*, that is the name given to the head of a tribe among the Narrinjeri, is the mediator and spokesman in all negotiations with other tribes; his advice is sought in all disputes and his authority is supported by the heads of the families. In war, he fills the leadership role, and he is carefully protected by all his fellow fighters. In the past he also had the right to distribute the booty taken in the hunt, but this custom is seldom observed nowadays. The role of the chief is not hereditary; the brother or a younger son of the deceased chief has as much right to be elected as the eldest son. As a rule, the chief's prestige is based on the right of the strongest, but even more important, especially among younger men and women, is the fear of the magic powers he claims to possess.

Another erroneous assertion is that the Australians practised sexual intercourse without marriage. In any case this has not been proven and it certainly does not apply to the natives of the Murray. On the contrary, the blacks there follow certain rules, and a violation of these is considered to be tantamount to a crime. The principle by which marriages are contracted is that of purchase or exchange.

Although the father has a right to give away the daughter as a wife, this right is usually in the hands of the brother, who in this way helps himself to a wife by exchanging his own sister for that of another. This right can also be transferred to somebody else, and it happens that a candidate for marriage, who does not himself have a marriageable person at his disposal, acquires such a right by purchase, in order to be able to marry. It is generally considered by women to be a great disgrace not to be given away by exchange in the usual way. The ceremony is a very simple one. The bride is led by her relatives to the groom as soon as the sun has set and then usually dancing and singing begin, which lasts until morning. Very often a double wedding takes place, namely when the bride's brother also gets married. If the bride is still young and not fully grown, the groom tries to promote her growth by rubbing fat into her skin, and she is also allowed to stay away from her husband for a longer period of time and live with relatives. The girls marry very early, from the age of 10 to 12 years, but they also mature very early in life, as is generally the case among dark-coloured peoples.

Not many children are born in these marriages. It is impossible to determine how many children are actually born; the number raised is very small. For most certainly a large number are killed immediately after birth. As a rule, this happens when the preceding child is not yet capable of following the parents on their wanderings. A black woman will not carry two children, and it would never occur to the man to take this burden upon himself. Considering the almost devious cruelty with which some mothers kill their new-born children, one can hardly understand the tenderness that is shown everywhere to those left alive and can only be mystified by the deep pain with which they mourn their loved ones snatched away by death. According to the best testimonies, undoubtedly more than half of the children were killed before the arrival of the whites. If the parents decide to bring up the child, it is treated with total love and devotion, and the father's rage when it is injured knows no bounds and all those who come within his reach, whether they are guilty or innocent of causing the accident, will bear the brunt of his wrath. At birth the children are of a very pale colour, while only a dark, dirty-looking spot on their forehead indicates their parentage; but in a few days the dark colour has spread over the whole body.

Up to the age of 10, both boys and girls live in the wurleys, i.e., huts, of their parents. When they have reached this stage of life, the girls are usually married off, but the boys enter the period of initiation, from which they transition into manhood. The young ones may then neither comb nor cut their hair and are not allowed to eat thirteen different kinds of game. Failure to comply with these rules results in disease and premature old age. I once persuaded a native boy with a gift of sugar and tobacco to clean and comb his very dirty shaggy hair, which was contrary to custom. The parents reproached me bitterly for this, and indeed the boy fell ill the same night, of course, as a result of the imagination and fear of punishment stirred up by his relatives. The rules against eating certain animals were probably made by the older people for good reasons. These animals are easy to kill. If the whole tribe were allowed to eat them, the animals would perhaps soon be wiped out. Moreover, when the younger people hunt, there is always something left over for the older ones, since the younger ones never fail to kill the forbidden animals if they can, but always hand them over to the elders to eat.

> [Here Jung provides a description of an initiation ceremony, followed by a description of reactions to death and forms of taking revenge, and finally a practice to establish intermediaries among different groups.]

The customs and rules I have talked about are mostly a thing of the past. Even if the few surviving old people cling firmly to their traditions, the younger part of the population is increasingly turning away from them and towards European customs. In a few more years there will be no trace of them either, and the blacks of the Murray estuary will have disappeared, just like the emu, kangaroo and platypus in this region.

Some observations about the language of the Narrinjeri.

As early as 1846, a small book was published by the missionary Meyer, in which, in addition to the customs and traditions of the natives at Encounter Bay, some attention was also paid to linguistic peculiarities. The remarks referred mainly to the Raminjeri (cf. the map above), one of the eighteen tribes into which the then still relatively numerous Narrinjeri people were divided. These very limited notes were expanded by the pastor of the mission station established on the shores of Lake Alexandrina some thirteen years later. With rare enthusiasm the Rev. G. Taplin studied the people with whom his arduous ministry brought him into closest contact. His notes and oral communications – my official position prompted frequent visits to the Point McLeay branch – have been of the greatest importance to me, although my own observations have often led me to conclusions different from those to which the missionary believed himself entitled.

Language has, I think unjustifiably, been given a very high status. It cannot be denied that, judging by the present spiritual condition of those who speak it, it is surprisingly sophisticated, but I believe that in judging its structure, there was a tendency to be guided by principles taken from the languages of civilised peoples and which do not apply to the dialects of these natural people. The sounds of speech can be represented approximately by the written characters that civilised peoples use; approximately only, of course, because in the case of some double consonants, such as ng, nj and dl, it is almost impossible to give a representation in our alphabet. Ng at the beginning of words is very common, but it is also very often omitted; it is precisely this sound that is most easily dropped in abbreviations. It is difficult to render it correctly; it is also found, as is well known, among many tribes in the interior of Africa.

[Here follows a discussion, with detailed examples, of the method used by Jung to examine the language of the Ngarrindjeri.]

While it is difficult to represent the words of the Narrinjeri by letters known to us, it is almost impossible to do full justice to such sounds that cannot be regarded as signs of certain ideas, but only as outbursts of feeling.

Interjections used to express physical or inner emotions are extremely numerous. They often consist only of a shorter or longer grunt or other inarticulate sounds, which one may not dare to represent by letters. A very common exclamation of astonishment is: *Kai, hai!* The exclamation *Kooh*, pronounced in a very extended manner, is a sound of desire, a call to either attract the attention of another or to invite him to come. Incidentally, this sound, which is common among several other tribes, has already become so common among the European settlers that *kohi* is as familiar to a white inhabitant of Australia as it is to a black, and is also used just as exclusively by the settler in the interior. The same word *Koh*, pronounced with a short vowel, is an introduction to a question or would correspond to the German: Hm? In this case, the terminal h is strongly aspirated. The exclamation *Jackai!*, usually two to three times in succession, is widely spread all over Australia and just as versatile in its meaning as our German Oh! The intonation and the way it is uttered gives it all its value, all its meaning.

Old women often use a certain greeting when meeting friends, and the more intimate the relationship and the more heartfelt the welcome, the more often it is repeated. The one-syllable word *kao*, uttered several times in succession, is a constant greeting of welcome amongst the female sex. This *kao, kao, kao* sounds, as has been remarked quite rightly, remarkably like the cawing of ravens or crows.

I will add some more interjections to these, because they have the same value as the otherwise meaningless actual interjections. Both old and young Narrinjeri often exclaim in response to painful sensations, whether physical or emotional: *Nanghai, nanghai, nanghai!* or *Nainkaua, nainkaua, nainkaua!* The former means: My father! the latter: My mother! The male population, from boy to old man, uses the former, the female population the latter exclamation. 'It is,' says the Rev. G. Taplin, 'often ridiculous to the highest degree to hear an old grey-headed man, whose parents died years ago, call out like a child for his father when he has hurt himself.'

A similar exclamation to express astonishment is: *Porluna!* Oh children! also very commonly and also without the meaning the words might indicate. It is only an expression of feeling.

Closed statements, expressions of thoughts, entire longer compositions are perhaps more instructive than knowledge of the word forms of a people. I will therefore briefly add a few sentences here, in the translation of which I will maintain the exact word order as used by the Australian. I have chosen a few expressions which may also shed some light on the Australians' mental states in other respects.

A common farewell formula is: *Kaljan ungune luin*, i.e. here you are sitting, to which the person who stays behind replies as a farewell greeting: *Nginte ngoppin*, i.e. you walking, to which the traveller usually replies: *Ei aur au*, i.e. Walk must now, i.e. I must go now; the final verb is omitted, since according to the circumstances it is self-evident for the native and is thus omitted as superfluous. This omission of verbs whose meaning can be understood from the context is indeed very common, in fact the rule. *Boru el ap* or ape, literally means: I will go up; meaning: I will go. Mare el ap or *ape*, literally: Down will, i.e. I will come. Likewise *Loru el ap mantangk* – Up I will to the hut, i.e. go. The same is true for questions: *Jaral inde aur Murundald* – When do you have to go to the Murray? Murundi is the name of the river above the lakes.

Expressions such as *Kung itje ellir* – Enough he has been, i.e. he has died, are significant. Additional phrases to indicate the construction of the language more precisely:

Nakkin ile itjan, i.e. Seeing through him it – He sees it. *Nginte nak aur itjan* – You see must it – You must see it.

Nakemb ile itjan or *Kile jan nakemb*, he has seen it; but the first form has the meaning of the recent event, the second of something long past. *Kil itjan nakkir*, he saw it recently. *Nginte jan nakkin* – you seeing it – you see it.

Nak aur itjan – See must it – Look at it. *Nak al jan* – See with him – Let him see it! *Nak al um itjan* – See with you it – May you see it!

Finally, a chant as they are wont to sing at their festivities, called corroborees by the whites, *ringbalin* by the Narrinjeri. I owe it to my friend Rev. G. Taplin, through whom I also had the opportunity to listen to this peculiar song. The fact that the stanzas end evenly, as in the following, is coincidental; the Narrinjeri have no idea of rhyme.

> *Puntin Narrinjerar, Puntin Narrinjerar, o, o, o! Puntin Narrinjerar,*
> *o, o, o! Jun terpulani ar, Tuppin an uangamar,*
> *Tjiuewar ngoppin ar, o, o, o, o! Puntin Narrinjerar and so on.*

> Coming the Narrinjeri, coming the Narrinjeri, o, o, o! Coming the Narrinjeri, o, o, o, o!
> Soon they will appear, Carrying (them) kangaroos, Walking fast (they), o, o, o!
> Coming the Narrinjeri and so on.

Such a verse is repeated *ad libitum* and usually *in infinitum*.

The Narrinjeri hardly ever produce longer compositions of more than one verse. The songs usually contain descriptions of hunting incidents, travelling or their battles. Others are not even known to the missionaries who stayed among them for many years. On the other hand, they learn the *ringbalin* of another tribe with great pleasure, even if they do not understand the words, and often sing it both at their festivities and when they are sitting in the *dolce far niente*, full of sweet food, in their leaf huts or in the shade of a tree. Such foreign poetry must appeal to their ears especially in its rhythm, in its timbre, for them to immediately prefer it to their own. These songs are sometimes brought back by envoys who are sent from one tribe to another to settle disputes, trade, etc. They are especially popular at festivities.

Missionaries

Christian Gottlob Teichelmann, 'Letters, Diaries and Reports'

Christian Gottlob Teichelmann was born on 15 December 1807 in Dahme, Saxony. Leaving school at fourteen, he became a carpenter before transferring to study in preparation for missionary work at Jänicke's Mission Institute in Berlin in 1831 and then at the seminary of the Dresden Mission Society (DMS) from 1836. Initially Dresden had been home to a Mission Aid Society supporting the work of the Basel Missionary Society in Switzerland. From 1836, however, Dresden broke its links with Basel and undertook its own missionary training and commissioning.

Teichelmann and Clamor Wilhelm Schürmann were the first graduates in 1838. Very soon after they were ordained, the two men were sent to Adelaide aboard the Pestonjee Bomanjee; *a fellow passenger was the incoming governor, George Gawler. They arrived on 12 October 1838 and immediately – as the passages below indicate – wrote to the DMS to inform them of progress.*

With their work based on Lutheran principles, Teichelmann and Schürmann saw their first task as learning the local language so as to be able to offer religious instruction in it. With this in mind, the two undertook intensive investigations into the Kaurna language, eventually publishing their foundational Outlines of a Grammar: Vocabulary and Phraseology of the Aboriginal Language of South Australia, Spoken by the Natives in and for Some Distance Around Adelaide *in 1840. Alongside his primary role as pastor and teacher at his school, 'Piltawodli', on the banks of the River Torrens, Teichelmann also went on to compose a book on Kaurna customs and beliefs, as well as to compile a second Kaurna dictionary. He worked as the government's Kaurna language translator and collected hundreds of specimens of birds and insects to send back to Germany. Contrary to the views of many of his contemporaries, he was of the view that Indigenous people had the capacity for complex conceptual thought and were just as capable as Europeans of being educated.*

In 1843 Teichelmann married Margaret Nicholson, with whom he had fourteen children. 'Piltawodli' was closed in 1845, and from the beginning of the following year the Dresden missionaries decided to relinquish the work they had undertaken at Ebenezer and Port Lincoln to focus on Adelaide and Encounter Bay. After his period as a missionary, Teichelmann worked as a farmer, postmaster and part-time pastor in various locations in South Australia. He died at Stansbury on the Yorke Peninsula in 1888.*

Source:
Lutheran Archives. Adelaide Missionaries [Dresden] Collection, Box 3 TA Teichelmann *Diary.*
Translation: Marcus Krieg (diary) and Geoff Noller (letters).

Letter to the Dresden Mission Society[†]

4 July 1839 [...]

We could often have had the whole house full of Aborigines and it would still be full if we – I at least – had not blocked that. The reason is that they do not yet value great friendship and possessions but, on the contrary, misuse them. It is also just if we have so many that we

---

* *Further reading:* Heidi Kneebone, 'Teichelmann, Christian Gottlieb (1807–1888)', *Australian Dictionary of Biography* Supplemental Volume, 2005, https://adb.anu.edu.au/biography/teichelmann-christian-gottlieb-13213; Christine Lockwood, 'Teichelmann, Christian Gottlob (1807–1888)' German Missionaries in Australia, http://missionaries.griffith.edu.au/biography/teichelmann-christian-gottlob-1807–1888; Rob Amery and Mary-Anne Gale, 'They Came, They Heard, They Documented: The Dresden Missionaries as Lexicographers' in Ghil'ad Zuckermann, Julia Miller, Jasmin Morley (eds.), *Endangered Words, Signs of Revival* (Adelaide, Australex, 2014) 1–19 https://www.adelaide.edu.au/australex/conferences/2013/amery_and_gale.pdf. Additional information courtesy Christine and Greg Lockwood.

† This is the first report by the missionaries on their activities in South Australia, a previous letter having been devoted to financial matters. Teichelmann includes in his communication extracts from his diary.

can learn the least since they are averse in front of each other to saying anything and are demonstrably impertinent and troublesome and want only to have what they can see. They might meet us on the street, or wherever, and then they call me by the name that they have given me: 'Cartanmeru! Maii wa? Wa birkiti? And similar. Cartanmeru! Where is food? Where biscuits!' And they visit us just with this in mind. They know nothing more than eating, drinking, sleeping, playing, sleeping. That is how it goes, year in, year out. From this, dear Brothers, you see that if we wanted nothing, we would just not need to go to the Aborigines, but they would come to us into the house. However, this is only a sign of the still great inaccessibility to their hearts. Indeed, if the missionary always wanted to be with them, where they travel to, he would have to have at least two pairs of legs and be content with what he may find to live on the way. The biggest supply of provisions that he could possibly take along with himself would be consumed in a couple of days by his black companions, and even before then.

The Aborigines are formed here into clans, without a chief. Each clan has its land, and in this land every family has a specific place in which to search for their sustenance. After they have camped at a particular place, they go on further. In the meantime, the whole group is divided into individual families and scatter, but after some time they come together again. In winter they live in one place, because they build more secure huts and vermin do not force them out as is the case in summer. Their food consists of possums, kangaroo, birds, large butterflies, witchetty grubs, chrysalis of other insects, lizards, green plants and other small vegetables, for instance the gum from small gumtrees, which exudes in large quantities. It tastes quite pleasant, either raw or roasted. The latter, namely the gum, is also a good preventative against climatic dysentery. They clothe themselves mainly with the skins of possums and kangaroos, which they sew together into a four-cornered covering after they have made it pliable with a stone or a stick. The needle is pointed bone. The thread is the sinews of these animals or also a top knot. Most of the time they are clothed in black, i.e. naked, because they appear to have no concept of shame. However, this is more the men than the women. They usually carry the smallest child on their backs with a covering around it, and sometimes they also have a child sitting on their shoulders along with other packages and utensils of the men hanging on them. The woman is the beast of burden for the man. For that reason, each man has at least two assistants for this. They must first let the man also have the best of any nourishment found, and the remainder is shared with the children. The man, by contrast, if he has caught some meat, takes what his preference is and then throws the remainder to his family. Therefore, it is quite frequent for a man to strike the woman on the skull, or to want to punish her till she is half dead and covered in blood. Break up of marriage, adultery, self-pollution, paedophilia and especially what the holy apostle Paul says about the heathen in Romans 1 and 2 is found very frequently with them. Therefore, the mistrust they have towards us single missionaries must be stated. They are not idolaters in the usual sense of the word. However, they want superstition which is endless, and, as I believe, is more damaging than the first. I will deal with this in more detail in the report which we are to send to the Governor. They are a race of people of the usual size i.e. compared with those in Europe, both large and small. However, the majority, above all the women, have weak extremities, even though this belongs less to their race than to their lifestyle. Many of them have now already moved towards eating English and German foods shown mainly by the young and suckling children, where the circumstances are for beautiful children. Indeed, all of them have a high chest but also thick stomachs which the gum and, from time to time, their gorging distends. Mostly they have long curly hair with only a few having straight hair. The colour is black. The men have a proud, noble gait, their net bags hanging around them and carrying their weapons. The colour of all is a dark black-brown, and newborn children are a yellowy brown colour. However, all fat if they can get it is later smeared on their bodies and mixed at times with a coarse red pigment (this is mixed with the fat and is the usual hair dressing). In part insects are kept away in this manner, and partly their stings (which burn severely and swell up) are rendered harmless. Generally they have a rather wide mouth and a somewhat flat nose, but still a little curved. On the whole, whoever sees this race of men must say that they, like us, have descended from one ancestor, and it belongs to the confusion of the spirit to say that they resemble Orangutangs.

Report to the Governor*

On 14th October 1838 we set foot for the first time on the land which we longed for and which was the goal of our journey. After a brief stopover on the shore of the sea we undertook the two-hour distant walk to the town of Adelaide. At once we had the joy of meeting together with the people to whom our brothers had sent us. They asked us: what name? We told them ours and then asked for theirs. We left them behind and met others who repeated the same thing. On the following day we went to their camp site and, using the same questions, investigated the names for parts of the human body and other visible objects. In this way as early as on this day we acquired a fairly large number of words from their language. When later on we repeatedly examined these at the camp sites, a picture, though incomplete, was building up at the same time in us of their talents and ability. We could compare what was presented by them with what we had acquired through reading of reports about them out of Europe. However, no matter how acceptable these were, we found ourselves exceedingly deceived. There they were portrayed as a race of people who were totally akin to the great apes. Here we saw that the people were formed like all people. In those reports we read that they had the least capability of being taught of all people on earth and were on the lowest rungs for the education of their intellect. Here, however, their natural liveliness and their motivation were revealed, and it was evident that they must be endowed with the same talents and ability as any other nation on earth. Later experiences have not only confirmed

---

* This document was written initially as a report by Teichelmann and fellow missionary Schürmann for the Governor. It was later appended to a copy of Teichelmann's diary and included in a communication to the Dresden Committee on 4 July 1839.

this but have widened the first impression that in every regard they are a capable nation for education.

They demonstrated the usual ability for any kind of handicraft as soon as they received the necessary method and had just as much patience with them as with a European pupil. On the one occasion I put a plane in the hand of an Aborigine after I had shown him how to use it, he planed a board of 7 inches wide by 4 feet long with amazing skill. (I am convinced when I took a plane in my hand for the first time, I was not so skilled in going about it, as he was.) One must see them weaving, for which they use either their own hair or the local flax or sinews from the possum, kangaroo or other long-legged animals. For instance, out of these things they prepare thread for net bags, nets and the like. They braid bags from rushes into a very pleasing form. They prepare skins either with sharpened stick or a stone after they have spread them out and then dried them in the sun or over a fire. Then they sew these together with a pointed bone and sinews into a large, neat covering (with double stitching). When a strong Aborigine wears one of these, he looks very like an old Roman in his toga (they use it also as a bag). Two sorts of wild dances or play acting, of which they have many, are led by the men. These are accompanied by the women with wild singing in a monotone and beating on a ball made of skins of different kinds wrapped together, but only the men beat their small weapons together. It is done rhythmically, which incontrovertibly shows that they have a general skill for music and a feel for precise movement. One can make a similar comment when they fight (in earnest), when every movement happens according to the rules of duelling.

Frequently they demonstrate an understanding and ingenuity which is astonishing and can be observed only by those who are always around them and among them. On one occasion we had an Aborigine with us for the purpose of learning something of the language. Since they have no written language and no actual pretence of a grammar or dictionary such as we have, it must not be viewed as a trifling thing if this Aborigine makes us aware of something happening outside, without our asking, that we should add it to our collection. They make an appropriate distinction between persons and situations, and women whom we meet do the same kind of thing. This plainly shows that they understand our plans with their language and getting to know the language itself (at least better than thousands of Europeans understand theirs).

With regard to the preaching duties that we have been directed to perform among them, we have considered it to be our priority first to learn their language. Without being able to find even the slightest preparatory work done by others in the colony, and without being able to acquire (except through questioning) what should have been known of their language, we had to undertake the difficult task and continue to so with God's blessing. The one collection of words was done by Wyatt etc. Currently we are in possession of pronouns. We believe that we should devote our entire time and energy to attaining this object, because not only is the name of God to be praised in all languages and tongues, but also because it is far easier for us to learn their language than for them to learn another language. Therefore, it would be necessary to grasp the revealed truth not only in another language, but also in other concepts which are totally foreign to them.

Jointly we have taken the trouble to discover their religious and spiritual concepts. However, there is no more difficult business than this, and nothing we do is able to get their cooperation. In this regard, they are very reticent, and even more so than with their language. Apparently it has something to do with an initiation. As such Schürmann has concentrated on the tattooing. He says: 'The tattooing is in no way to be considered just as some kind of decoration but is much more an initiation through which the young men are made familiar with the secrets such as incantations and the like, something which is not permitted for women and children to know.' This latter circumstance appears to be the main reason for this reticence of the Aborigines. They are only telling us the things we already know, which we are led to see as an indication that they are giving us their confidence which is certainly no achievement of success. What is more, an Aborigine said to me the other day that he expects that we will speak in the same way as the Episcopal preacher does, and then they will sing like Englishmen. To this we must add circumcision which is practised among many tribes and is usually done in youths in early puberty. A host of ceremonies accompany this before and after which remain incomprehensible as long as we are not allowed access to the issue.

From what I have heard from them, it appears that they touch also the feet of the circumcised with the foreskin, which would be worth noting. I am keen to be able to attend the entire action so that a greater light can be thrown on the matter. The circumcised person bears a special name and also a covering for his shame while he is sick and, in addition, still other marks of distinction. The men from the Murray and Encounter Bay areas are not circumcised and are considered to be evil by those here, because they live uncircumcised in the state of marriage. Also the special nature of the initiation is a characteristic of the different tribes.

The first of the religious concepts that we have come across among them has to do with the duration of the soul after death which ascends towards the west and lives among the stars. The body, however, is confined to the earth and in fact lies on its side (their position for sleeping), the head in the direction to which the soul goes. Their attention and amazement seemed to be stirred up when we spoke to them about the resurrection of the body and its reunion with the soul (I believe quite rightly, because this is unquestionably only a revealed truth, which is confirmed in Christ, the Risen one). Another tradition (among many tribes) appears to be that there is an evil being, resigned to his fate, small of stature, very overreaching in evil, who fears fire (and therefore especially light). In the nights he comes to their huts, and if they have no fire, he creeps in among them and into any part of the body, the hollow of his stomach, or between the breast and the shoulder blades and causes sickness, vomiting and death. He comes in and leaves with the cry Ngar! (pulled inside through the nose of the person). If they are far from their huts at night, and hear the cry, they are terrified and run back to their hut. This appears to be a cause of natural death. Superstition also appears to be the reason why they will not leave the camp site at night, without carrying a fire brand with them (or it simply serves as a lantern).

Schürmann says of cases of death among them: 'As with all uncivilised people of nature, so also it is with the South Australian Aborigines in cases of death of greater significance; to these they attach extraordinary and interesting concepts, practices and customs. The cause of death in their opinion consists in many cases in an evil black man slipping into the place where people are sleeping in the night. After he has lifted the covering, he shoves his bore-worm dagger (it is actually made of bones) from below and upwards into the body (various parts of the body). Then he pinches the wound tightly shut so that no blood comes. He replaces the covering and leaves without the wounded person waking or being aware of anything. Just because that stroke of the dagger has damaged the lungs (especially the bowels), that person must, in due course, die. This superstitious opinion is the basis of explanation for just about every death by an unknown murderer. The corpse is (now) wrapped up in old clothes and grass and laid on a bier so that he can be carried around his last camp site and is asked at brief intervals if someone had stabbed him. The brother, or alternatively the closest relative of the dead man, delivers the oracle under the name [redacted]. Not only does he say 'yes' to every question but also, if now the following mention of more suspects' names of the murderers is listed, begins to totter and then quickly leaves. As a general rule, the oracle finds the murderer among the hostile East men. Should the unfortunate person, however, by chance be present, at once each person presents arms himself, in order at once to take up the examination which the preceding verdict either confirms or cancels. This consists in the following. The relative of the deceased throws a number of large spears at him and then a number of small ones. If the murderer is fortunate to be skilled and daring enough to parry all of those spears, and if finally he also survives a blow on the head from a stick, he is considered innocent and a good man. This is strikingly reminiscent of the medieval concept of 'divine justice', the forerunner of the duel. The burial customs of the Aborigines have already been written about elsewhere. Schürmann had submitted an article on the subject for printing in the *South Australian Gazette*, even though it was the first burial that he had seen. However, I considered it a bit premature to publish something on the basis of a single experience without sufficient knowledge of either the language or the event. But he writes and thinks about everything here. What can be mentioned, however, is the loud wailing for the dead, in which each one continuously repeats the name which the deceased bore as his relative, who cried out: 'My mother!' And another: 'My father!' Or whatever the case may be. But it does not always involve the entire wailing. I have seen it happen that two or more men and likewise the women form one group, throw their hands around the necks of those opposite them, sit down and then just weep.[...]

To date we have not found a word for spirit. Or the language for being a spectator, for revelation and similar, because this seems to be the concept. A kind of revelation or rapture.

Two to three men put their arms around each other and walk like that for a period around the campsite, making no sound whatever. Thereupon they let go of each other and run raving in different directions, with hostile movements and grimaces. If the fires have not carefully been put out previously, these men fall on these and stamp them out with their feet. The effort for this procedure must be quite severe, because in doing that they groan miserably. Next day quite frequently they have a headache and similar and say nothing and are besides unwilling to do so if someone should address them. If one should ask the Aborigines about the purpose of this *Maljo* (*Mailjo warra*), they say that their heads go up where they see many deceased people. In addition, it should be noted that women too often join in this practice. At this point I should comment that whoever knows how closely these things are joined to the lust of the flesh with other people, and it is just these sins which are must customary among the heathen, will divine the purpose of this *Mailjo warra* very well. They will see it as a work of darkness whose real moving force they are smart enough to cover up.

> [*Here follows a telling of a creation story and a discussion of religious concepts.*]

There is another which is really a humorous characteristic prevalent with them, and which indeed leads them to share their provisions with one another. Should this brotherly love be demanded but refused, a quarrel follows and finally ends up in a battle, which quite frequently ends in the loss of life for one or more Aborigines. However, this love appears partly to remain with their own tribe, and partly stretches to neighbouring friendly tribes. Otherwise, the desire for nourishment rules among them just as among Europeans. This envy, apart from many other reasons, therefore causes many bloody battles. One example can serve as proof. When Oldham, the school teacher for the Aborigines, took over the distribution of biscuits and the like to the Aborigines, the Adelaide tribe camped for quite some time partly in and partly around the old location. The others, however, did not come there and also did not receive their rations. I went there and took the rations to them. And they were overjoyed when they got something. In the meantime, the others were unwilling and dissatisfied with what they received. On the same evening of the day when they were having a public midday meal and had received woollen blankets and shirts, the local Aborigines said to the other Aborigines that they should now go back to their land. The moon was full and there were many stars in the sky, and it was good time to catch fish. They took away their food and clothing. They are the ones who also kill Europeans. A few evenings later, the two tribes quarrelled. It seems that an old man quarrelled with another man, saying to him: You get your houses built and we have to live in wurlies. That is why you kill no Europeans and still more and more are coming. Still, the same Aborigine with whom he quarrelled said to the first: we kill no Europeans, because if we are hungry we can go to them. The reason for this envy could well lie in each tribe having its own land, and each family having its own area from which they must seek their sustenance. Apart from all this, and this has a direct influence on our task, our main inspiration has been up till this moment to get them working, because idleness is the beginning of all vice and work guards against many sins and vice. We have worked together for that, and with many of them, and found a few workers who stuck with it. A few of them are very anxious to earn money so that they have no need to go around begging like the others. Certainly this requires masters who are concerned for their physical and eternal wellbeing. We can hope with great confidence that in time many of them, if properly treated, can become useful fellow members at least of the civic society, namely that part of it which requires the necessary participation as such. There is therefore a great need if they could find suitable employment on site to earn money as part of their physical support. Among other things this has the benefit which they receive from those whose calling it is to work for the wellbeing of the Aborigines full time. They could then in every possible manner be instructed willingly. And this would at the same time have a much better outcome of raising the ability among them more quickly so as to reach sooner the level of independence required to make them members of Christian and civil society. The chief concern is that the more intelligent among them will be held back by the corrupting familiar acquaintance and influence of their brothers from pursuing an appropriate manner of living.

Letter to the Dresden Mission Society*

13 November 1839

22 August 1839

I visited an Aborigine in prison, which I frequently do, and we had a discussion over the immortality of the soul. Among other things, he said that the soul prior to birth or conception of a person finds itself in PINDINGA, comes from there, enters the body of the mother and there

---

* In this letter to Dresden from 13 November 1839, Teichelmann copies in 'those of my notes, or diary, that I wish to communicate impart to you', hence the separate dates in the letter.

is united with the body of the person she is carrying, and then the human being is born. After death the soul goes back again whence it came. PINDE = pit, grave; INGA or NGA in which 'e' is transposed into 'i' is the ending for designating the place *where*. However, they also called the Europeans *Pinde meja*, much like they are western people or foreign people. It prevails in these days as a great tension between both the tribes existing here. The tribe looking for strife partly belong here as their home and made their camp in the middle of the town and no doubt with particular reasons. Thus two Aborigines accompanied a herd of cattle from Sydney as guides, and certainly like the Europeans were paid for that out of the property. Now that they have money in hand and have nothing to do, they are living with Aborigines here, and in particular in a family of 4 women and 1 man. They bring all kinds of titbits to the man, and he rents his wives to them with the promise that if they should come here again, they should bring their wives along and make them over to him for his use. We indeed found out this abomination only later on, and from it we determined the cause of some of their indifference towards us.

1 September 1839

Sunday 1st September, Schürmann came to me and said that the Aborigines were just then discussing a fight and a battle with one another. We went to them and spoke with the ringleader of the party looking for a fight. He alleged that one man from the other tribe had stabbed his brother during the night. We countered with the unreasonableness of this procedure and said to him that this was long since past tribal hatred, which is what he wanted to carry out now. Even though they did not concede this, they appeared to be disarmed by our bold attempt at mediation, and the fight did not take place on that day. In the evening we went to the other tribe, who received us in a friendly manner, and we had to relate to them what we had done with the others. One of them led us from one hut to the other so that we could report to all of them. At this point we took the opportunity of demonstrating to them that they consider such action only with those among them who had died a violent death, and where they had found unequivocal evidence of a murder. All others, however, had died as a result of a sickness or some such thing. For this time they appeared to accept this all the more willingly as the murderer was supposed to be among them, and still not one of them bore any knowledge of guilt. The fight was supposed to take place on the Monday. However, since two kangaroos were seen in the vicinity, the ones itching for a fight went on a hunt, and the fight is still in limbo.

Diary*

24 November 1839

Today we had a discussion with the natives about the usual religious themes. Two women and a man with whom I usually work on the language showed that they had retained and understood everything which I had told them earlier and again today. How well I understood the hypocrisy of the two women, who are their tribe's chief magicians and sorcerers. Indeed, they now presented themselves as highly delighted with what we told them and urged us to go to the rest of the natives and tell them what we had told these, because they had not yet known it. Now this was a straight-out lie, because we had in their presence frequently told the others the same things. This was, of course, purely a pretext to rid them of our troublesome presence. However, we must leave the outcome of such discussions to the Lord of the vineyard who alone can satisfy them, since we in addition to all this are able to make only slow progress in the language, first because it is difficult to learn much from such an uneducated people, and second because they always deliberately withhold it from us.

28 November

When on the 28th I was on my way to the natives, three of them met

---

* From this point on, as the correspondence with Dresden had become more regular; rather than including diary extracts within letters or reports, Teichelmann simply forwarded the copied diary in instalments. This extract is part of the first such instalment. The period covered is from 24 Nov 1839 to 12 December 1841; translation is by Marcus Krieg.

me and said that a European had forbidden them to cut wood in the parklands, which really upset them. For the native here can as little do without fire as we can without clothing or house. So I took this opportunity to draw their attention to what we had already told them earlier, namely that they should set themselves up on the already begun settlement and occupy the houses which had been built for them, because there was wood and equipment for cutting it. They now had to learn for themselves what we had already told them, namely that if they did not settle like the Europeans they would be driven out. Even now that is more progress than they can achieve in their present circumstances, unless God's spirit inspires them. But it is much more likely for an educated European to employ such a native than for a native here a European, because this life-style is much easier and more comfortable for the body but totally destructive for the spirit. So I scolded them for their laziness and indolence, urged them again to lay aside their nomadic life-style and settle like the Europeans and not live like wild animals. It had, as I learned later, and even as we spoke, made only a fleeting impression on them. I left them finally and went home.

29 November
On the 29th I saw six men sitting alone at some distance from their huts. On the way back I went up to them and noticed one spattered all over with blood, three blots of blood lying on the ground and another native with a bandaged vein on his left arm; in addition there were four or five new wooden daggers lying on the ground, streaked with blood on the handles. I asked for the reason and was told that the one who was spattered with blood had been initiated as a warrior and hunter, and likewise the daggers were for killing. Of the ceremony itself I had observed nothing. Next, they made fires over three flecks of blood and left. In each such an initiation to a higher stage of manhood I believe that one finds a corresponding deeper initiation into their superstitious secrets.

30 November
On the 30th they returned to the Location, and we again had them

present in the neighbourhood for several weeks, without being able, however, to do anything much with them. But the unpleasant feature associated with this was that every evening we had to listen to their awful row until late into the night, and for almost a fortnight every day there were fights among them which all had the women as their cause, and which we frequently had to interfere in, not infrequently preventing the worst of consequences. Polygamy, of course, causes a shortage of females, add to which, quite often, when the number of girls exceeds four, the female children are killed. Hence fornication and adultery are a daily occurrence among them; indeed, often a female of 14–15 years old must oblige 2 or 3 at once. The result is a fight. It is also customary that the men lend their women as a favour, and so it is not allowed to cause problems if Europeans use their services and satisfy their lusts for a trifling amount – men who are considerably enticed to such an act by the almost totally naked bodies of the female sex. The women are given to understand even indirect or direct demands; indeed, one man asked me how much money I would give him if he brought me a native girl – this is what determines the field of our labours.

22 October 1840*
Went to Encounter Bay with the Protector, Mr. Moorhouse.

Between Adelaide and Willunga spent the night at a colonist's; we went to Willunga, spent the night in the Governor's house, occupied by the constructor of roads, Colda, where Stow caught up with us on the following morning, and so all four of us rode to Encounter Bay the next morning. Arrived there Friday evening; I stayed with Br. Meyer, Moorhouse with his sister, Stow with a former preacher, Newland, the man in the Government's house. On Saturday we called on the few natives there, who were staying near a deserted whaling station, near a hemispherical-shaped hill, which plunged into the sea. They were occupied in making and repairing nets; the material for this they

---

* *The following entries through to the end of 1840 relate to travels to Encounter Bay and then east to Ngarrandjeri territory around Lake Alexandrina.*

obtain from a reed-like spear-grass, which they split into strips, chew and then twist into two stringed binding strips with their hands on bare thigh, and then knit the mesh of the nets with their fingers. At our request they went fishing in the sea, and in one draught with two nets they caught about 3 dozen small herring-like fish. After spending some time with them we went back, ate our midday meal and then went south to the Murray and along it to the seashore. But, since we met a troop of natives on the way, who told us there were no natives in that direction, after spending a bit of time with them and after I had bathed in the sea we returned. In the evening there were some natives near Br. Meyer's house, and we visited them; and because I always addressed strange natives in our language to find out if any of them understands it, and every year some natives come from Enc. Bay to Adelaide, I did the same with these and noticed that one old man understood and recognised me, which pleased him and me greatly.

4 December 1840

Received with friendliness at the Station, we stayed until the following morning. Here we came upon our first family of Aborigines who were very friendly towards us, and who the Station inspector told us were very good-natured and trustworthy as well, so much so that when he went to the town the eldest of them would guard and protect his house. Leaving our horses behind, we set out in a boat to cross the river, which is very slow-flowing, to a survey station. Treated in an equally hospitable way, we spent the day there, during whose course natives arrived. All of them were very trusting, and so much more so when I gave them to understand that I spoke a language of the natives, even though they spoke a different one.

Towards evening we went down to the river-bank, where we saw several families of natives who all, as usual, proved friendly and trustworthy, when I spoke to them in our language to find out if any of them understood me. After spending some time with them we went back, promising to come again the following morning.

8 December 1840

Tuesday morning we set out on the way down the river to go to Lake Alexandrina, at whose end was a survey station which we wanted to visit. After travelling for about an hour, we came upon several natives bearing on their heads three bodies, which according to their custom had for preservation been wrapped in nets and matting.

They were all, as usual, very friendly, and when we inquired about the survey station, which they knew about, they wanted to give us a guide, immediately organised for us a boy of about 15 years old, who accompanied us on the 6 hour-long journey, on which we met native families, interpreted for us, picked Karkarla fruit, a kind of small cactus fig, for us and was especially extraordinarily obliging. All in all, we met about 150 souls between the station where we had crossed the river down the Murray to the lake, around the lake as far as the channel which leads into the probably only recently discovered Lake Albert. All the natives spoke the same language which has only insignificant differences from that of Encounter Bay and is basically the same, but somewhat different in its endings. When we reached the station where many Aborigines were just cooking crabs, at our asking they gave us as many as we wanted to eat and showed us how to eat them. To our greatest pleasure we found among the surveyors two boys from Enc. Bay who had attended school in Adelaide, had got so far as to be able to read and understood our language, whom we now used as interpreters.

9 December 1840

On Wednesday we researched the pronouns in the language, singular, dual and plural and several other things of that sort, making as much progress in a few hours in this language as we had previously only been able to make in 6 months among our own natives. As the station was not quite at the end of Lake Alex., with my companion I went to Lake Albert channel on whose opposite side the so-called MILMENRURE natives are. According to the reports given to us, their number should be very great, hence we were very much inclined to seek them out. But we did not have our horses with us to be able to ride through the Channel – we either had to go on foot around the whole of Lake Albert – about 2 days – or swim through it, which I could not do; in addition, we were seriously advised not to go without weapons and without horses. So this was not done, and indeed for my part that was preferable, since the purpose of my journey, namely to research how far to the east our language was understood and spoken, had been achieved. Thus, at the same time, it was established how far Br. Meyer's sphere of activity could extend; for the area in which the language is the same, extending from Encounter Bay or later perhaps from Lake Alexandrina outward, is the district in which it would be possible to provide the preaching of the gospel, which would require a fellow-worker for Br. Meyer.

10 December 1840
Thursday, the 10th, we commenced the return journey and stayed overnight on the same side of the river. When we were close to the survey station where we spent the night, several natives approached us and presented a fish to us. We went to their camp with them, where we were given a second fish. Each of the fish weighted about 7–8 pounds. Such courtesy, which we had never yet experienced from our natives, impressed us greatly and attracted me considerably to these people. It is their regular custom to share everything with one another; but then a reciprocal act is required; in other words, a custom among them which is based on self-interest, and failure to comply with it is strongly condemned.

11 December 1840
The natives along the river and around the lake live on the young and soft parts of the reed which grows in broad fields along the shore. They chew out these parts and throw away the stringy parts, and hence they have to stuff large quantities into their mouths. You see whole families standing up to their knees in water and chewing until their stomachs are full. Hence it is no wonder that the mouths of these people stretch

much wider than those of the Europeans. That is why each year they burn the old reeds so that there is space for the young reeds, and an easier approach is provided for the eaters. In addition, they live on the roots of a reed which, in my area, is called the *Rohrpumpe* and which, when roasted, is similar to a potato and very floury. After these have been thoroughly chewed, they use the residual fibres which, as a result of the chewing, have been prepared, as thread (twine). River mussels, fish, crayfish and tortoise eggs form a significant part of their diet. Wild animals seem to be less numerous than in the more wooded regions. In Lake Alexandrina a boy can catch about a water bucket full of large crayfish in half an hour. With a rush bag in his mouth he goes into the water above his hips, feels for the cray with his feet, dives under and emerges with it in his hand, sticks it into the bag, and meanwhile there is already another one under his foot, so that a spectator sees a constant diving up and down during which the bag continues to swell with crayfish. Since wood is scarce in this region, a kind of dense, low-growing shrub serves as a pot, hearth and fuel. Onto this the crayfish are thrown, the bush shoved into the fire, and the crayfish are cooked. The men eat the tails, the women and children the claws and the rest. For catching fish they have: nets made from a type of sword or rather a form of sabre-grass. Through chewing it is made into a kind of flax or hemp but is not as durable. The twine is spun, double, on the haunch, and twisted at the same time, and suddenly the mesh is hooked over the fingers. We saw a net over 20 feet long made in this way just like a European one, with a bag worked into its end.

 They spear the larger fish with a spear that is like a harpoon or, rather, that is based on one to which the two pointy bones are fastened on each side so that the whole is like a fork, and which at the same time serves as a rudder to steer the canoe made of a large piece of bark. This latter is made in the following way: after a large tree has been selected, an oval shape 9–12 feet long and about three feet wide is marked on the bark, the bark (which is about 1½ inches thick), is dug through down to the wood and then left exposed to the sun, which separates the canoe from the tree. After this the ends are bent to a curve in the fire, and any joints are smeared with a fat clay. Such a canoe usually carries a man and a boy. Instead of the usual covers of [illegible] hides that we have, these have round mats about 3 feet in diameter made of reeds or rushes, with which they cover themselves at night.

The male sex goes about naked without exception; the females wear a twine lap-lap, or at least are supposed to until their first pregnancy, after which they also go naked. So it is no wonder that fleshly lusts play a significant part in their lives, which indeed seems to be the source of all the other evil in their lives. The European would suppose that under such circumstances temptation could not be so strong nor so powerful, but even though this side is finer for civilised people than for the Aborigines, it can lead to a gentler stirring of emotions; so these are the same that are stirred in the Aborigines where they produce harsher tones. I had the opportunity of observing two labourers at the survey station who were bantering with the two wives of a native, and there was no difference between the black women in this case and how white women would have behaved. So even if the Europeans do not increase the sins of the flesh among these people, they do contribute by their participation, with the result that the natives are encouraged, because when I speak to the natives about their lack of chastity and advise them to give up this evil, they answer: You hate this sort of thing and are good, but very many whites sleep with our women, and even take them into their houses when they go into the city.

[Here follows a detailed description of ceremonial burial practices along the Murray.
At this point Teichelmann is once more visiting fellow missionary Eduard Meyer at Encounter Bay.]

14 February 1841
Feb. 14. For the past 14 days a tribe of natives from the upper Murray has been here, making themselves important to ours through the

practice of a futile faith-healing. They treat ours by either sucking out small pieces of bone with their mouths or by drawing small sticks of wood out of the affected parts; these small bones are presumably put into the body of the patient by the dead using witchcraft, thus causing the illness. Once the bones and the small sticks have been extracted, the doctor sucks the bone out of his staff with his mouth. They introduce all sorts of other gimmicks which are too boring to write about.

21 February 1841
This morning all the natives left the town in order to tattoo Ngultanna. Klose and I followed them. As I was watching this boring ceremony for the first time, I cannot make any particular comment on it other than that the whole procedure is utterly barbaric in that the back, the breast and shoulders are not just cut with glass but are rather lacerated.

> [A letter dated 10 June 1841 containing a detailed description of a burial ceremony is omitted.]

31 July 1841
Towards evening we visited the natives there who had gathered in large numbers, because it was currently whaling season. To one old man among these who understood my language I spoke a few words of life which he then translated for the others. They were apparently sincere, but what they felt in their hearts I cannot say. We took the old native with us to Meyer's house and on the way, something I had not noticed, the old man pointed to the moon saying: "Do you see the moon, how dark it is?" I looked up and a total eclipse was visible between 8 and 9 p.m. I asked, 'Who did that?' and the old man replied: 'A NOKUNNA (equivalent to an assassin, or perhaps devil) has covered the moon so that it does not shine on the earth.' I asked, 'With what?' The old man, 'with strips of plaster!' (The legend has it that a NOKUNNNURLO) has covered the moon with blood and so darkened it. The old man: 'So that the moon can eat the black men's

livers, and ... kill them.' I tried to give him a different explanation for the eclipse but, naturally, without much success. On 3 August I left Encounter Bay and arrived well in Adelaide on the 4th.

7 August 1841

KUDMOBURKA died, leaving a widow and a son of about 4. He was a model even for Europeans in his care for the child, kind-hearted and hard-working. During his illness I visited him often; but how difficult, indeed almost impossible, it is to direct a dying heathen towards Christ in a language still so inadequately understood! The burial was exactly as I described the one on 10 June.

[*A further description of a burial ceremony follows here.*]

The natives reported to me that on 2 August one of their fellows had been shot by a European. I reported this to the Colonial Secretary, who in turn reported it to the Governor. As a result, a policeman and 2 natives were sent to the place but could not discover anything. On the 13th, with two Aboriginal children who had remained, I went to the place where the murder was said to have taken place (12 German miles away) and found the bloodstains on the ground and a part of the gun with which the dead man had been shot. I made a report to this effect and the perpetrator was brought in with 2 of his companions. The murderer is now awaiting his formal investigation. Repeatedly I have had to appear before the magistrate and give my declarations. In my view the man was shot without a reason, because he was there in his hut, alone with his nine-year-old daughter when he was shot. The murderer is a criminal who has come over from Sydney. During this time I had a conversation with a native to whom I have already often in my weak efforts tried to impress the Word of God. He was not unreceptive to it, but still thanks me for it. I told him of the resurrection of the body and said that just as Christ had lain in the grave for three days, had again risen from the dead and gone to heaven and was living with his Father, our Jehovah and Father, so would we also become alive again. He, taking the Word said, 'So, if Christ had not risen, neither would we rise'. I replied that this was so. This clarity with which he had understood me gave me great pleasure. As I had already earlier taught him to pray, I asked him about it again, and directed him further in it. May the Holy Ghost open his heart and understanding so that he may see the bright light of the Gospel.

16 September 1841

September 16. In past weeks roughly an additional 50 natives have been shot on the Rufus (See the newspaper *Southern Australia* Sept. 7, 1841 about it). Even though a stern law of God has been proclaimed against these souls, after this they will experience a much sterner one; the appalling depravity exercised against the natives first incites them to such attacks, but is often glossed over here. O that the Lord's help would come!

Clamor Wilhelm Schürmann, 'Letters and Diary'

Clamor Wilhelm Schürmann arrived in South Australia with fellow missionary Christian Wilhelm Teichelmann in 1838. Like Teichelmann, Schürmann had initially been trained at Jänicke's Mission Institute in Berlin before moving to the Dresden Mission Society (DMS) in 1836. The two men were the first of the so-called 'Dresden Four' to be sent to Adelaide from Saxony, the later arrivals being Samuel Klose and Eduard Meyer.

One of the features of Schürmann's activities in South Australia was that he had prolonged stays in a number of regions and, through his work, became familiar with a number of Indigenous communities and languages. His first letter below references his travels along the Murray, while 'The Natives of South Australia' and 'Five Days in the Bush with Aborigines' are from his time in Adelaide and Kaurna Country. In 1840 it was planned that Schürmann would begin a mission at Encounter Bay, so he started learning the Ramindjeri language.

Instead, in September of that year he was sent to Port Lincoln as sub-Protector of Aborigines. When that position was abolished in 1842, he remained on the Eyre Peninsula, reporting on the frontier violence there and advocating – unsuccessfully – for land and government assistance for an Aboriginal settlement. Similarly, his requests to government for support to found a school at Port Lincoln were denied. Nonetheless, Schürmann learned the local Parnkalla/Barngarla language and, in 1844, published a grammar and vocabulary of the language.

With a decision to concentrate missionary work in Adelaide and Encounter Bay, Schürmann was asked to join Eduard Meyer at Encounter Bay. He farmed there with Meyer and with Ramindjeri people and married

Wilhelmina (Minna) Charlotte Maschmedt in 1847. There followed a second spell in Port Lincoln as a government-appointed protector and interpreter, until in 1853 he became a pastor in Victoria. He died while visiting Bethany in South Australia on 3 March 1893.*

Source:
These select letters by Clamor Schürmann to the Dresden Mission Society, the undated essay titled 'The Natives of South Australia' and an account headed 'Five days in the Bush with Aborigines', are from the box labelled 'Adelaide Missionaries (Dresden) 2. Schürmann–Meyer. Folder S', Lutheran Archives, Adelaide.
Translation: Marcus Krieg except where otherwise indicated.

[*The following letter refers initially to an expedition to the Murray River that Schürmann undertook in the company of the German geologist Johannes Menge.*]

Letter to the Dresden Mission Society

19 June 1839 [...]

The frequently encountered camping places, the well-trodden footpaths on both sides of the Murray, seem to indicate to me that there are more of them than is generally believed. Two cattle drovers on horseback who caught up with us on our return journey, and who had followed our tracks for two days, were astounded to hear that we had escaped with our lives, because they had been assured that to the east of the Murray on the part of the natives there had been considerable problems; later parties were said to have had even greater trouble and, it is said, fired all their supply of powder and lead; all

---

* *Further reading:* Heidi Kneebone, 'Schürmann, Clamor Wilhelm (1815–1893)' *Australian Dictionary of Biography Supplemental Volume 2005*, https://adb.anu.edu.au/biography/schurmann-clamor-wilhelm-13284; Ted Schurmann (ed.), *I'd Rather Dig Potatoes: Clamor Schurmann and the Aborigines of South Australia*, Adelaide, Lutheran Publishing House, 1987; Rob Amery and Mary-Anne Gale, 'They Came, They Heard, They Documented: The Dresden Missionaries as Lexicographers' in Ghil'ad Zuckermann, Julia Miller, Jasmin Morley (eds.). *Endangered Words, Signs of Revival*, Adelaide, Australex, 2013, 1–19.https://www.adelaide.edu.au/australex/conferences/2013/amery_and_gale.pdf. Further information courtesy Christine and Greg Lockwood.

agree that very fine and crafty people live to the east, and those who had formerly visited Adelaide confirm this, while the people from the north appear very poor. The hitherto good relations between the Aborigines and Europeans have unfortunately been shattered recently in a sudden and gruesome way by the murder of two shepherds. Six Aborigines were arrested as responsible, of whom three were later released as not guilty, one sentenced to one year in gaol with hard labour, and two were hanged on the 31st of May. One of the two latter named BAKAMBARTI JARRAITJA continually denied his guilt; the rest of the natives also deny his involvement, therefore it would have been better and more advisable, especially because the inadequate knowledge of the language means the hearing must be unsatisfactory, if they had not been sentenced so quickly. The other, a quite young man of about 18 or 19 years old, confessed, even before the hearing, in the gaol where we visited them a few times, to striking the whites on the shoulders with a small club, but another person had hit him on the head and killed him. The effect which the execution of these two has had on the rest of the natives is in no way favourable to the Europeans; that could already be concluded from the constant denial of their guilt and the unusually long continuation of mourning which they carried on for the two, but even plainer is their displeasure with the execution, shown by the fact that immediately following it the brother of Jarraitja went away to tell his relatives and fellow tribesmen what the strangers had done. Then, on the 18th of June, these really did come to carry out *Nurutti*, highly dreaded and frequently mentioned by the rest of the natives, as a result of which all the Europeans and they themselves would die.

(That they mean by the above statements a sort of magic is certain, because it is in the water, and because the smoke which is supposed to kill us as it rises into the air, without the use of either club or spear, but how they actually conceive this *Nurutti* process to act I do not know.)

However, Konuitja or Gudnuitja, one of the most intelligent and best of men, went to intercept them not far from the town and persuaded them not to carry out their magic; the strangers were not angry, but would give them rusks and such like. I saw them just as they were coming into the town and immediately asked them their intentions, but Gudnuitja, obviously uneasy, told me not to speak of it because he himself was not yet certain what they had in mind, and he wanted to divert their attention as far as possible away from their purpose. What great power the superstition of the *Nurutti* is supposed to exercise is evidenced by the situation where the magician and his men were at most 10 in number, while the rest of the natives amounted to at least 100 (not counting the whites at whom it was actually directed) and that they were still so afraid.

[Here follows a detailed description of how a determination was made as to whether a murder had been committed, of ceremonial burial practices and of beliefs about the afterlife.]

The above is evidence enough that the Aborigines of New Holland are not the stupid animal-like people similar to the orangutang as some travellers (who either from prejudice or ignorance were incapable of assessing them) have portrayed them, but that the busy, never-resting spirit betrayed the image of God also in them. That they led a continuous wandering life with all its cares and roughness was very natural and necessary since the nature of the land produces neither domestic animals nor grains, nor any significant kinds of vegetable.

Much as I feel obliged to speak for the natives whenever an injustice is done them, equally may I not hide from you [illegible]. Of polygamy I have written before, but there also exists a form of polyandry, namely, in that a brother uses the wife of another or lends his, or however else one can express this disgusting thing; fornication and ravishing of boys as well as other heathenish abominations are common among them. Hence they have certainly received the reward of their wrongdoing and are still receiving it; many have died from dysentery which has dominated here, but a few also from a ghastly illness from which many are still suffering, and of which few or none are cured. In this case this illness has positively been introduced by the Europeans, but they knew of it even before they had seen the Europeans, have their own name for it and understand its infectiousness. Another vice they have in common with the Spartans, namely, that they do not rear, do not pick up as they say, malformed children, but let them lie, irrespective of whether they are male or female. Among them the missionary finds enough sins and difficulties which oppose his effectiveness; but when to these are added those of another race, such as drinking, cursing and such-like, one must fear for a blessed outcome of all teaching and labour. But then I am amazed that the natives have not sunk even further because of their constant association with a class of people like the English rabble, rough and ungodly beyond all comprehension. Therefore, the plan of bringing the natives into active contact with Europeans, indeed, where possible to allow them to be scattered among them as the Governor and the former Protector of Aborigines foster, is highly destructive for the latter, at least for the first decade.

But it also must be said that the Governor, if the natives wanted to settle in a separate place, has no power to appropriate an area for them. This limitation appears to me to be so much more unjust in that the Aborigines as members of a family are the owners of specific sections of land which the father of each family has inherited from his father. If one asks them whom their land belongs to now, they say that they had given it to the whites. I have recently written these facts in a letter to Mr. Angas in the hope that he, as a member of the Society, would use them for the protections of the Aborigines.

A few friends of the natives are of the opinion that we should instruct the natives in English and have criticised us for following a different approach. But I rather hope that we will receive the approval of the Society, as the natives speak only a little and a very common English and, as the nature of the human soul as well as the information extracted from them in their own language show, one can only get close to the human heart by means of one's own familiar language. I should have thought that the abuses perpetrated before the Reformation through the use of Latin would have sufficed to dispose of all differences of opinion on this subject. Certainly it takes time, care and patience to learn the native language, but the riches and especially the fluidity of the same promises to compensate us richly in the future. The proximity of the town, although it has a beneficial influence in some ways, makes more difficult for us the learning of the language, because it attracts the natives into it and draws them away from us, and on our parts prevents us from making ourselves as close to them as we would wish. Certainly we could have groups of them in our houses, but then they only want to eat and drink or they will go somewhere else. Recently I tried to take a boy into my house, but he did not last longer than four days, even though I allowed him to spend the greater part of the day with his playmates. But, even if he had stayed I would have been obliged to let him go because of a shortage of provisions.[...]

But here I do not want to have sung an ungrateful song of complaint, much rather I thank the Lord for his faithfulness and generosity, whereby he has hitherto given me my daily bread, but I do lament the loss of time and the inactivity in my present situation. Otherwise I should long ago have made a journey to Wirramu or Encounter Bay in company with a few natives, where there is a powerful race of people whose female part is now exposed, without protection or guidance, to the animal lusts and shameful diseases of whale fishermen there. That area commends itself so much the more to visits from us or to the settlement there of one of us because it is the key to the whole of the east; however, the reason stated locks it for us for the time being. Nevertheless I envisage, as soon as it becomes possible for me, organising a visit to the natives in that area.[...]

I remain, Your devoted

C.W. SCHÜRMANN

'The Natives of South Australia'

Our knowledge of the natives can naturally be only very incomplete, because the only means whereby we can acquire it, namely their language, we still have not mastered. But we have now come so far that we can speak with them about the most common subjects that come to mind, and the advantage thus gained is already considerable since the way is now open for us to achieve our aim, and we have won their affection and trust so far that they visit us so often and in large numbers, so that they have become a pleasant but real burden.

But this is still a long way from being adequate to question them about such concepts which could be the most attractive e.g. about their origin, religion and the like. Indeed a few want to claim some sort of veneration of the moon but the expressed reasons for this are far better explained differently, and in order to rely on their own statements, one has to approach the subject indirectly because they have the habit of repeating the words of someone else, especially if they do not fully understand them. Whoever frames his questions so that it appears he expects an affirmative answer will definitely be wrong in nine cases out of ten. So much appears definite, that they are not crude idolaters.

What is most notable about their language, it is unfortunately only too true that the various tribes speak very different dialects. I use this expression with caution because in spite of our meagre knowledge we believe that a certain similarity is to be found; this we conclude more from the similar accents (and from the circumstance that the various tribes understand each other as also from individual words, otherwise we would instance that TANDANJE (in English: Adelaide) tribe calls the moon KAKIRRA and the RAMONY (English Encounter Bay) tribe MAKIRRI. We are naturally learning the dialect of the Tandanje-tribe partly because it encompasses about 200 souls, and it is not likely that a more numerous tribe is to be found in the vicinity, partly because we were directed to them and especially because many strangers, by name Ramony, are coming here who say that gradually (purro purro) many more would be coming. A few days ago a woman from the Murray was here who told us that there were many black men and women there who gradually intended to come.

Whenever these strangers come here, they immediately take on the local dialect and so we hope that this will become the main language in future.

An Indigenous South

The customs and manners of the Aborigines of South Australia are naturally rough and uncivilised, but there is occasionally something which merits a mention.

[*Here follows a description of cultural practices and customs.*]

The natives use a small number of artefacts: they make clubs and spears of hard wood, which is hardened even more by burning; additionally shields of thick bark; woomeras; tools with which the spears are sharpened, at their points a kangaroo-tooth fastened with a sinew of the same animal against which the spears are chiselled. Their skill makes these apparently insignificant weapons so murderous that people, kangaroos, emus, birds and other creatures are felled with them. In addition, they stitch themselves really good covers out of kangaroo hides which serve as clothing during the day and bedding by night; as well the women spin and knit nets and bags from the wild flax which would not be shamed in a German industrial exhibition. Remarkable is that the people build themselves no house of any kind; the reason for this is that their living places are constantly changing because of their nomadic life and the many fleas. Their camps consist of nothing other than tree branches laid on top of each other and if they are more particular, of bark placed together. Recently news came from Sydney that a tribe had been discovered in New South Wales which lived in proper houses and who were superior to all their countrymen in every respect.

It is not unknown to us that the Aborigines of New Holland have no good reputation in Europe as well with reference to their bodily physical condition as to their intellect, but we are not afraid to declare, at least of those we have seen, that that report is quite baseless, and those informants who brought it to pass must either have had so little knowledge of them as to be able to form a fair judgement, or may even have intended to say something striking and extraordinary. But, one will say, how is it that one finds almost no signs whatever of culture amongst the Aborigines: Our opinion is that it stems rather from the impoverished nature of this country which produces naturally neither fruits nor other means of subsistence which are necessary for a strong nature, nor draught nor beasts of burden with which one could farm the land. The most striking external features of the people are: a brownish-black skin colour, a long and dense growth of hair, in part strong limbed (but many, especially women the extremities, arms, legs, etc. excessively thin) a high chest and a proud gait; in height they are more or less like Europeans.

By nature the natives are peaceable, friendly, kind, open, without prejudice, and honest; but one quality they have which is not to be boasted about, namely laziness. What I have said here is naturally generalisation; but that there are many exceptions and especially that sin in all its possible forms rules over them their whole condition bears witness. It is also known of them that infanticide, especially the killing of girls, has not been uncommon, and in that case where the second youngest was still breastfeeding when the youngest was born it was considered an unavoidable necessity. But because of that one must not believe that the parents are without any human feelings, oh no, for they weep and mourn for many days over every single death, and the mothers, even though they have given their agreement, let the children be torn from them only by force, but as they say, they believe that they cannot nourish the children. However, this information rests not on my own but on a stranger's experience.

Finally, we have to get to what the government has done for the natives as compensation for what has been taken from them. First, a protector has been appointed who is to represent them to the government. The present one is called Wyatt, a friendly and pleasant man who among other things has directed us to our present dwelling. We will admit that this appointment has brought honour to the government; but if it really was so serious about the welfare of the natives, it would not have loaded the protector with two other offices. In addition an interpreter, named CRONK has been installed, and lives next to us. This man has been a seaman and has not the slightest education, so we have absolutely no use for him. But worst is that he has a very bad influence on them; the people depend greatly on him because he is always joking with them and chiefly because he dishes out their biscuits to them.

The government, because all the wildlife has been driven away in the vicinity of Adelaide, apportions some rusks to the natives, but not enough for them to live on; what more is needed they earn from the whites by carrying water or wood. Apart from that a small piece of park or government land has been fenced off for the Aborigines, and several huts of split boards built on it as well as a school-house and a store room; but the natives use their huts only in times of utmost need, when it is raining very heavily, because they cannot move for fleas inside them. These houses, it is rumoured, are to be moved to another site, but whether one foot of land will be set aside as property for the natives is extremely doubtful, since according to the law every single inch of land is to be sold, and the government here has hardly enough land for its own needs, so that least of all it is able to buy land for the Aborigines. This is one of the bragged about fruits of a self-supporting colony.

I cannot refrain from relating the description of an incident that happened here only today. The following incident that took place as recently as today is evidence of the tender love of the parents for their children. A small child of the Kartammeru died, whereupon all who were present mourned so deeply and so loud that it was moving to see and to hear. The father held his child wrapped in a kangaroo skin, on his lap, his head covered with a blanket and poured out streams of tears which were constantly renewed when the others, one after the other threw themselves down beside him, lowered their faces over the child and brought him a rich offering of tears. The burial is still to take place today, but they will go a long way away with the body, so we will not be there to see it and the natives apparently do not want us to be there either. Oh how strongly this reminds one of the apostle's statement that the heathen are so sad over death because they have no hope. True, we still do not know whether the Aborigines have any concept of soul and immortality, but judging by their excessive grieving, if they do have one, they do not believe death to lead to an improvement in the state of the person. How death rules over the whole world and over all people. It is very disheartening for us that our meagre knowledge of the language does not permit us to use this present moment to talk to the natives about death, the immortality of the soul and eternal life. But we have the hope that before the passage of half a year we will, God willing, be in a position to do so.

All that we have said here about the Aborigines of South Australia applies to the Tandanja tribe and to the few who now and then come here from Ramong. Of the rest of the tribes we have not the least knowledge; if one can rely on what the people here say namely about the multitude of tribal names, there must be many more in the inland. If we had the means to buy a horse or other beast of burden for the carrying of our provisions, we would make a journey at least as far as the Murray to provide information on the numbers of the people living there to pass on to you. We consider such an expedition necessary, not because there is not enough to do here, but because we assume that the results of such a journey would help you with the choice of a destination for the rest of the brethren to provide vital services. This much already appears certain to us, that the Society has to consider not only the numbers but even more the widely distributed tribes of the natives in the appointment of missionaries.

And, with this, let this account conclude until time and God's guidance set us in a position to provide you, beloved brethren in the Lord Jesus, with more comprehensive and accurate reports. But, may the God of grace and love, who has begun the bringing home of this forlorn people, continue and complete His work though you and us.

'Five days with the Aborigines in the Bush'*

9 September. Yesterday a group of about 30–40 Aborigines set out for the bush, accompanied by their European dogs, in order to hunt kangaroos. For a long time I had been wanting to spend a few days observing the life and activities of the Aborigines in their natural

---

* This is an excerpt from Schürmann's diary from the period when he was in Adelaide in September 1839. Translation by Greg Lockwood.

surroundings. I was convinced that not only would this serve to give me a closer insight into their whole way of life but would also be the best way of practising their language. So the opportunity to fulfil my wish, offered to me today by two young Aborigines, Tuitpurro and Kadna Ipiti, who were following the others, was very welcome. It was also most pleasing that Brother Teichelmann decided to go along.

My entire equipment for this excursion consisted of a woollen blanket, some tea, ship's biscuit and salt. The hunt was to supply us with the remainder. And in this we were not disappointed, for about three German miles from the town we found some of the group that had set out yesterday already occupied in preparing a kangaroo which they had just hunted down. The method used by the Aborigines in making a kangaroo edible is worth commenting on and may therefore find a place here:

As soon as the prey is killed, they look for a suitable place in the vicinity for baking. It must be dry and have enough wood and stones. Then they carry the animal there, and the most skilful person prepares himself to skin it as far as the head and the largest point of the tail which is then cut off and hung in the fire. Meanwhile another man digs a hole about 1½ feet deep in the earth, a third fetches small stones, and a fourth fetches wood and, when the hole is ready, a fire is kindled in it in which the stones are heated until they glow. By the time the fire has burnt itself out, the butcher has already gutted the animal, cut off the legs and shanks, and slit open the thick flesh of the thigh three times. During the latter process another person has been cleaning the large intestines and making a sausage from the blood that accumulated in the chest cavity. After this is done, the stones are pulled out of the heat, and the smaller ones are placed partly in the breast and stomach cavity and partly in the split-open shanks, mixed with the foliage of the small gum tree for flavouring. Branches from the same tree are now also laid on the coals both directly underneath as well as on the kangaroo. Then the legs, the tail, the sausage, together with the choice parts of the entrails are placed into the branches lying on top, and the whole lot is covered with glowing stones. During this process one of them has detached a piece of bark from one of the trees nearby, big enough to cover the kangaroo from head to tail, and placed it on the roast. The gaps between the bark and the edge of the hole are now filled with earth, so that no air can pass through.

Now everyone rests contentedly for half an hour. Then the grave is opened, and the cleanest and most delicious roast is pulled out. Now it is the butcher's task to play the part of carver, a role he plays a little less cleanly, making more use of the club (*wodna*) pointed at one end than the knife. With the club he tears the ligaments of the joints in a very skilful way, dividing the whole kangaroo into about 8–10 large pieces. When each of them has to some extent satisfied his appetite, they pack up the remainder in order to consume more of it the following evening and morning with the hangers-on, consisting of women, children and some men who take no part in the hunt but merely move from one campsite to another looking for roots and similar edible plants.

Today's roasting spot was so far distant from the campsite, and we set out so late that we only reached the site when it was already quite dark. Therefore, as it was too dark to erect our own shelter, we had to make up our minds to sleep in the shelter and by the fire of an Aborigine. There was at first great amazement and joy over the fact that Brother Teichelmann and I wanted to accompany them. No less did the supply of meat bring good cheer among the group, so that they sang in their manner deep into the night. I took this opportunity to gather some of the verses that the Aborigines are accustomed to use in their songs. These are remarkable because they contain the impressions that the coming of the Europeans has made on the Aborigines' minds. The first one that I let them tell me reads: Waienenuma Burlokka witte, that is, Be very afraid of the bullocks. Another one: Pindi mai birkibirki, that is, Peas are a strange food, and so forth.

10 September. The next morning the Aborigines advised us to go back, ostensibly because they would be going very far, but in fact because they were afraid we would eat too much of their meat. Brother

Teichelmann allowed himself to be persuaded to go back. It seemed to me that he did so because of excessive sensitivity as well as the inconveniences of the previous night. I however persisted in my plan, all the more so as not to allow the Aborigines to break their word, as they had promised to give us kangaroo meat. It seemed to me that in Brother Teichelmann's conduct there lay a weakness that fostered selfishness and the breaking of one's word and must therefore have a detrimental effect. How completely the Aborigines understood the injustice of their demand became evident not only in that the two young people who had taken us with them from Adelaide sought to avoid us when we reminded them of their word, but also because all of them wanted to have Brother Teichelmann back when they saw I was determined to stay with them. As he did not come back, they sent a man after him, so that the Ngukunna, the Assassin, might not kill him. They tried again on this occasion to persuade me to turn back. I might perhaps have gone if we had not already been a distance from our campsite when we heard about Brother Teichelmann's escort.

Here the large group divided into two smaller ones. The one that I joined consisted of about 20 young people, except for two men and a strong woman with her child. She participated in everything at the side of her man. As we travelled today through a region devoid of game, it was fast going and [we] covered a wide area. So I was very happy when a halt was called.

This took place on a mountain ridge from which you could overlook the plain that bordered on it. Down on the plain our main hunt was to take place.

This evening I made myself a hut and a good fire so as not to be exposed to the same frost as in the previous night. But so many young people camped around me that I had little [reward] for my trouble. At first, I did not prevent them because I spoke with them about the creation, heaven (God's house above) and hell (the fire-hole below), the future judgment of the world, etc., and succeeded to the extent that they did not laugh (as they usually do) but listened attentively to my broken sentences. As a result, I could not get rid of them later.

11 September. The hunt did not go [down] onto the plain, as I had believed it would, but sideways onto the last spurs of the hills. At 11 o'clock we already had one kangaroo which the dogs had driven into the water or which, more likely, had jumped into the water in fear. Then it was clubbed to death by the Aborigines hurrying after the barking dogs. While it was being prepared, two young men hunted down a second kangaroo in the vicinity, which was carried there and roasted in the same hole. There were only a few of us, as the larger half of the already smaller group left us this morning. As a result, everyone had so much to carry that he could only drag it along. When we came to our campsite, we found the whole group gathered in full once again. Some of them had just brought a third kangaroo which our dogs, running ahead, had hunted and which was captured by them. Although it was already dark, this one was nonetheless immediately slaughtered and roasted.

I had already asked about a tail when the first kangaroo was captured. I wanted to present it to my Bertha as a sign of how close she had been to me even in the bush. But they always put me off till the next time. Now, from this third kangaroo I thought I would surely get the tail, and most of them claimed it for me. But an old skinflint was unwilling. Now I acted very offended and reproached them for not keeping their word, and when they again referred me to 'tomorrow,' I said: 'Tomorrow and the day after tomorrow they would still be saying "tomorrow," and so tomorrow would never come.' That made them laugh. Meanwhile my brother Tuitpurro, who always spoke up for me, said that if I did not get a tail tomorrow he would get angry.

12 September. Satiated and still amply supplied with food, most of the Aborigines just lay around their fires today in contented indolence. Only I, Tuitpurro, Kadnaipiti and one other went hunting. Meanwhile our best dog had been so badly wounded by the last kangaroo that he could not run, so we had to come back soon, empty-handed. With the three other good dogs, Tuitpurro had strayed from us. When he returned home in the evening, he brought the news that here and there he had killed a kangaroo in the water, but because he could not swim, he had to leave it there. For me time was now hanging heavy on my hands, and I wanted to return home tomorrow, all the more so as it began to rain this evening, and it looked as if the rain would set in. So the Aborigines set about building shelters from tree bark for protection against the rain, but I [simply] turned my leafy shelter that I had already slept in yesterday with only my brother Tuitpurro. I turned it against the wind which had changed direction and improved it with even more branches. I had chosen the place purposely so that there was room only for two. This was [already] done by the time my brother returned from the hunt, and again we both slept quite comfortably together.

Now my ship's biscuit was almost completely finished. Yesterday I had very few left, as others had assiduously helped me eat them. But Tuitpurro did not let me go lacking but shared as much meat as I wanted to eat and, into the bargain, insisted that if I was hungry, I should ask for more. When the others kept begging for biscuit he forbade them, because I no longer had any myself. Many of the older Aborigines were very sorry for me, because I had no more food and was homesick, being so far from home (it could well be 25 English miles). Tidlaitpinna, the most respected among them and to some extent the leader, shared with me some of the small amount of rice that he still had. I let them know that I would be returning tomorrow, and my brother Tuitpurro would accompany me. They all agreed to this, and moreover they encouraged me, as they said, on account of my homesickness.

13 September. Although it had been arranged yesterday evening that my brother Tuitpurro would escort me back, this morning the Aborigines made objections to this. I do not know on what grounds. Allegedly, it was because, without him, they could not find the kangaroo they had mentioned. Instead, they proposed other companions. But as that proposal seemed groundless to me, I insisted all the more on our agreement yesterday. Tuitpurro himself would rather go with me than stay, and the others who had been suggested were lazy people with whom I could hardly have reached the town in a day. After a long debate about this I finally, out of impatience and with the intention of showing the Aborigines my unalterable decision, set out on the way alone, convinced that thereby the deliberations would be brought to an end more quickly than by all my arguments. As soon as they saw me go, all hindrances were removed, and Tuitpurro soon came after me, well loaded up with meat for us and for some relatives of the others who had stayed behind in Adelaide. Through unprofitable waiting and talking we had indeed lost a good part of the day, and I was almost afraid we would not complete the strenuous day's journey. However, my companion marched so well that we were in Adelaide by 7 pm, albeit tired and limping.

I cannot conclude these five days in the bush without [making] some observations that are worth remembering. What I promised myself from this trip in terms of a closer acquaintance with the way of life and [the] language of the Aborigines, I found more than confirmed.

Making progress in the language lies not so much in the number of new words but rather in a greater appropriation and more fluent use of the words you already know. So, for example, there was also the discovery of a *modus conjunctivus*, which is formed by appending the little syllable 'ma' onto the stem of the verb and is used very regularly in the situations where we use the subjunctive for the recent and the distant past tense.

Furthermore, I was very surprised and delighted with the propriety and good manners among the entirely free and equal Aborigines and, especially, with the willingness of the young to follow the older men.

Still, I hope that I was not the only one to profit from this living in the bush, but that it was also of some use to a few of the Aborigines. Before the all-seeing eye of the Lord, I freely confess with shame and humility that I have not always practised and maintained the proper foresight and earnest decorum which, admittedly, was no easy task given the fluctuating circumstances and the forwardness of the Aborigines. Nonetheless, I am convinced that with one or two a basis has been laid for wakening the sleeping conscience, as this became evident from the seriousness and the questions with which they accompanied my clumsy, feeble descriptions of eternal life and eternal reward. So they asked, for example, where their relatives were now, in God's dwelling above or in the fire hole below. I replied that if they had been good, they would be in the former, [but] if bad then it was in the latter abode. A short discussion among themselves, which of course I did not understand, often followed my words. However, from their expressions and their tone I could draw conclusions about their interest and their approval. May the Lord in his mercy bless the delicate individual seeds that are now beginning to be sown in this virgin soil and check the endemic and foreign weeds.

Letter to the Dresden Mission Society
Port Lincoln, 27th December,
1840 Beloved and respected Brothers,
[…]
On my arrival here, favourably recommended by the Governor, I was very received with great friendliness by the settlers, but the attitude towards the Aborigines I found very unfavourable, with the exception of a few. I hoped that this dislike would diminish with time and with closer acquaintance with the natives, but the sad happening which occurred soon afterwards shattered my hope and justified, at least so it seemed, the longstanding distrust of the colonists. Namely on the 6th October of this year, Frank Hawson, a boy of 11 who had been left alone on his father's station about 2 hours distant from the town, was speared by two natives. Both spears were thrust into the breast and had pierced the lung, so that he would soon have died if his attempt to pull them out had succeeded. But this was impossible even for the doctor, because the spears had been fitted with a barb or barbed hook. Twelve long, lonely hours the boy had to endure before anyone knew of his lot, and five agonising days before he gave up the ghost. He bore his suffering with great steadfastness but found it difficult to suppress the natural desire for revenge and to forgive his murderers, although

he admitted that he should. The natives were immediately followed the following day by the magistrate and the police, and these succeeded first in discovering their tracks and, two days later, their camp site, but the stony and bushy nature of the country gave them the opportunity to escape. On the 8th of October, while the pursuing police were still out, a group of nine native men came to the settlement without weapons, unsuspecting and for our part unsuspected, because in no way did they fit the description which the unfortunate boy had given of his murderers. Nevertheless, the intention was on the following morning to lead them to the boy, who was still alive, to see whether he also would declare them innocent. So during the night they were watched from a distance, and on the following morning, as they made to leave, perhaps because they aroused suspicion, the police threw them into prison with considerable force and with injury to several of them. No sooner had they been captured than Dr. Harvey, who had been chosen to lead them to Hawson's house, arrived and, moved by the unexpectedness of the situation and the complaints and distressed wailing of the natives, without authorisation released them again. This only made the bad situation worse, even though his intention was good, because the poor Aborigines could, of course, not understand why they were treated so roughly, and it was thus only right to expect that fear and anger would arouse in them a strong desire for revenge, which we were denied the opportunity to placate. I had to regret this incident, so much the more because these were the first Aborigines with whom I had come face to face, and this seemed to me a very ominous beginning.

Several investigations were set up into the behaviour of the police and Dr. Harvey, but nothing came of them except that the Governor issued a proclamation saying that anyone who laid hands on a native, except in cases of unavoidable self-defence and protection of his property, would be punished with the full force of the law. Almost a whole month passed after the above scene before I was able to get to see even a trace of the Aborigines, even though I occasionally visited the stations inland, and otherwise tried to make contact with them.

On the 7th of November of this year a fire was noticed at the head of Boston Bay, and accompanied by my brave Gottfried, I set off there on foot, commending us to God's protection, because I must admit that the commonly held fear of the natives had not left me untouched. The place is about 12 miles from here, and, as it was very hot, we had a difficult journey. When we were still about nine miles away from them, they became aware of us, called out to each other and returned our waving. At the same time two of them came running towards us, and because we could not see for the scrub if they were armed, we were not a little concerned. But their intention was only to indicate to us that we should not come any nearer, and as we stayed still only indicating that they should approach us, in a short time we were surrounded by 10–12 men and boys, to whom we distributed our rusks, and of whom five accompanied us back to the town. They stayed with me for two days, then went back, and two days later one of them brought 8 guests to the town. With these Dr. Harvey and I went to Boston Island in a boat, where we spent two days, so that I had enough time to convince myself of the suspected relationship between their language and that of the Adelaide people. It gives me great pleasure to be able to report to you that the basic components of the language spoken here are the same as in Adelaide. I have, of course, gathered only some 400–500 words; only many names of common objects are different, but the pronouns and verbs are, at least as a rule, the same except for very few exceptions. Now and then the natives continue to come to Port Lincoln for a day or two, and recently they also gave the names of young Hawson's murderers and accompanied the police to Coffin Bay, evidence that they want to live in friendship with us. But they never bring their wives and children and will never allow one to visit their huts if one meets them in the bush, but always come to meet one and ask one to leave or to go another way. This seems to be evidence that they put no great trust in the purity of the mission. And when one considers that even among themselves the abduction of women is very common, as well as that the crab-catchers on Kangaroo Island at the founding of the Colony, who were found to possess many abducted native women, have probably visited this part of the island: one cannot wonder at their distrust.

In so far as I have had opportunity to observe the local Aborigines, in character and outwardly, they appear to differ very little from those in Adelaide; circumcision, tattooing, polygamy, the dance [redacted] and other customs are identical. Only two differences have struck me here, namely the spears fitted with barbs and a mutilation of their bodies which, out of consideration for your sensitivity I would not describe if I did not believe that you would wish to know of it because of its unheard of rarity. It is a slit in the male penis from its tip to half its length so that the urine canal lies open, or in other words, the cylinder is cleft to the middle, and that on the underside. Dr. Harvey is of the opinion that this operation so alters the performance of that member that it limits the natural increase of the natives, but I believe that the reality contradicts this. This custom appears to be exercised only in the fullness of youth, but its basis and purpose I have not been able to ascertain and can just as little surmise. I hope that you will find nothing indelicate in this description, but should that be the case, I ask that you take no offence at one whose feelings are made tolerant by seeing this every day and in frequent conversations.

What kind of future the Aborigines of this area and I in my relationship with them as missionary will have is impossible to predict, but this much is certain, that the situation will take a form different from that in Adelaide. There they gather in a city whose population is increasing daily, where in return for small services, or out of pity, people give them their daily bread; here the number of inhabitants diminishes daily, and the few who remain have scarcely a crust left over, so they will not, at least for the present, gather in Port Lincoln. Here perhaps the best and only way to proceed would be to try a plan which I have always considered the best, namely to undertake land and cattle farming for them. I am not unaware that this undertaking would require much money and people and that it also has its problems, but one should always first and foremost be prepared for the worst. One favourable circumstance I still do want to mention, which is not of minor importance, is namely that two or three station owners inland are favourably inclined towards the natives, who will try whether from principle or from a sense of duty to maintain a friendly relationship with them. These men are Quakers, a society which, it is well known, has always distinguished itself for its friendliness with the Aborigines in the colonies. [...]

C.W. Schürmann

Letter to the Dresden Mission Society

Port Lincoln, May 18th 1842

Sir,

I regret that my absence from town at the time when the *Governor Gawler* sailed for Port Adelaide prevented me from writing to you last month.

The particulars of the cruel murder of Mr. Biddle and of two of his people by the natives, I presume are already so well known, that it would be superfluous to say anything more about it. I shall therefore at once proceed to make a few general remarks on the Aborigines at Port Lincoln, in order that the occurrences which I find it to be my painful duty to report to you may be the better and more easily understood.

The natives of Port Lincoln are divided into two principal tribes, called in their own language the one Nauro and the other Parnkalla. The former of these frequent the coast to the South and West of the settlement and live chiefly upon fish; they are generally speaking a strong race of people and often met in comparatively large bodies, not unlike the natives of Encounter Bay. They differ considerably in dialect and customs from the other tribe, and the males have the distinguishing mark of a small ring or circle engraved on each shoulder.

The Parnkalla tribe are spread over a far greater extent of Country from Port Lincoln to the Northward beyond Franklin Harbour and over the greater part of the interior country.

They divided themselves again into two smaller tribes, viz. Wambirri yurarri, i.e. Coast people and Battara yurarri, i.e. Gumtree people, so called from their living in the interior of the country, where the gum is plentiful. It is to be understood, however, that these tribes are not so entirely separated as not to mix occasionally; on the contrary, they often visit each other in small numbers, whereby it becomes explicable that stolen property is often found with other tribes than were implicated in the robberies or murders. The natives of both the Western and Eastern Coast have always and unanimously maintained that the murders at Mr. Brown's and Mr. Biddle's station have been committed by the Battara yurarri or inland tribe. It may perhaps not be amiss to mention the names of those that are designated as murderers; they are the following: Milli, Mita, Multa, Mulya, Munga, Ngaltya, Nganki, Ngarbi, Ngurpa, Tyinga, Wonda, Yailga. Only one half of this number are said to have been present at the murder of Mr. Brown and his hutkeeper.

On the 2nd of April, four days after Mr. Biddle's death, a mounted party under Mr. Driver started in pursuit of the murderers accompanied by myself and six natives as guides. I went with the party at the request of Mr. Driver, partly as interpreter between him and our guides, partly to communicate, if possible, with those natives we were in search of. Towards evening we came upon them to the Westward and within four miles of Biddle's station, in a narrow valley surrounded by scrubby hills. They all fled the moment they saw us, with the exception of one who endeavoured to screen himself behind a tree but was shot down by one of our party. Three or four others who had stopped halfway up the hill were also pursued and fired at, but none of them fell. Taking a short route over the hills we returned to the camp of the natives, where our guides had remained, with whom four strange Natives were again observed. Three of these ran off, but Ngulga, one of the two natives that first gave information of the particulars of Mr. Brown's murder, remained, declaring that he was no murderer and supported by our guides, wherefore he was spared. The party followed those other three, but they were immediately lost in the scrub, and when we came back, not a vestige of a native was to be seen, even the man that was shot had disappeared. We now encamped in Malli, the name of this place, where we collected a great number of spears, wallets, cloaks, etc. etc. all which were burnt, and a considerable quantity of stolen property, among which was also a chair and a wheelbarrow. Towards morning we proceeded to Biddle's station, in the hope of finding our guides there, for they had been told that we would go there before we fell in with the murderers. They were however not there, and we had to return home, persuaded that without guides we should not find the murderers again. A day or two after we had come home, our guides also returned, bringing half a dozen valuable forks and spoons with them from Malli, which we had overlooked. It appeared from what they said that they were frightened by misunderstanding one of our party, who urged them on to show us the fugitives, and they encamped not far from us among the hills the night that we passed in Malli. They had learned from some of the fugitive natives that two men had been shot by Tubbs, Mr. Biddle's shepherd, that one was in a dying state, and that the other, who is the same man that was shot by one of our party, was wounded in his leg, wherefore he was unable to run way with the rest. Besides these two, another native had been wounded by our party while running up the hill.

I think it right to say that I was induced to accompany the party because I was given to understand that the murderers should be made prisoners if possible and not be shot if it could be helped. If I had known the mode of proceeding which was adopted beforehand, I should have felt it my duty not to be present.

April 19th. The soldiers and a mounted party went out this day in pursuit of the murderers. Messrs. Driver and Hugonin wished me to accompany them to point out those tribes of natives that had not participated in the late murders. The latter gentleman said that his instructions were to take the whole of the Port Lincoln natives either dead or alive without discrimination, but since he understood that these were distinct tribes and that the murders had been committed by one tribe only, he thought I ought to go with them to save unnecessary bloodshed. Under these circumstances I thought it better to transgress my former determination than to have to reproach myself afterwards that through my not going, innocent blood had been shed, and I accordingly accompanied the party with two Port Lincoln guides.

April 22nd. Headquarters were removed from Biddle's station to Palanna, a place about 15 miles to the West from town. When approaching this place our guides observed fresh tracks and told us that there were natives probably encamped at Palanna. The party was therefore divided to surround them, but they must have heard us coming, for they were gone when we came to their fires. It having in the meanwhile become quite dark, pursuit was impossible.

The following morning the mounted party struck into a scrubby plain in the direction of Coffin Bay, where a fire had been observed. We soon fell in with numerous tracks and natives which we followed to within four miles of Coffin Bay. But it had by this time become so late, and the country so stony, that it was determined to return to the camp and to resume the pursuit the next day on foot.

April 25th. We set out on foot to Coffin Bay, where the natives that we had been tracking the day before yesterday, were supposed to be fishing. The party consisted of Mr. Hugonin and the military detachment under his command, Capt. Hawson, myself, Tunba a native of Port Lincoln and one Adelaide native. When we approached the beach we could hear natives' voices about one mile from us; we therefore went some distance from the beach through trees and bushes to prevent the natives seeing us. Tunba now said they might be Yumbalta and his friends or other natives of the Kauo tribe and wished me to tell the rest so. I communicated this to Mr. Hugonin, adding: If he would not ascertain who the natives were and what they were before he allowed firing upon them, if it should come to that. His answer was: 'We shall soon see what they are made of when we come to the beach'. As soon as we had proceeded so far that the natives were between us and the sea, we ran towards them spreading in such a manner as completely to surround them. Tunba, who saw them first, now exclaimed: 'Let them alone it is only Yumbalta', but he was told to be quiet, because it was feared that he might wish to afford them an opportunity to escape, as the natives often did on former occasions. The moment the natives saw us, they jumped up, spread out their arms and declared that they were not the murderers. Mr Hugonin directly ordered not to fire, saying: 'That's enough no! no!' and I myself called out as loud as I could not to shoot, but notwithstanding all this one of the soldiers snapped a pistol at Yumbalta, which, however, was fortunately not loaded. There were three men, two women and a few children employed with roasting fish, but presently a fourth native came up, looking rather wild and presenting the most appalling sight; a musket ball had passed right through his abdomen so that his entrails came pressing out of both wounds. He said to me: 'I am Kappler, very good, I am no murderer, you saw me in Wadnelli, I am an acquaintance', and in a similar manner did the other natives remonstrate with me. All this was very true, [I had seen] them the very day Mr. Biddle was murdered in Wadnelli, a place only two miles from town, and Namma the wounded man had been so familiar at my house that he adopted the name of my servant boy Kappler. The soldier who had shot him maintained that the native had a spear and attempted to spear him. True, he had a spear, but the other natives said for the purpose of spearing fish, which appeared to be very obvious, for the native was in the water when he was shot, several fish were lying by the fire, quite fresh, and numbers of others were playing about in the sea. The soldier also contradicted himself, for I heard him say that the native was running back into the water, when he saw the gun pointed at him. A few things were found in the natives' wallets which seemed to have been taken from Mr. Biddle's station, however Yumbalta, who had been one of our guides to Malli, accounted for them by saying that he had picked them up in that place. Mr Hugonin first intended to take the wounded man to the Doctor and the rest prisoners, but on my statement that I had seen them on the day when Mr. Biddle was murdered, he desisted from this plan, and Numman prayed so hard to be left where he was, that it seemed cruel to remove him, moreover he was evidently dying. When we left, he stretched out his hand for my pocket handkerchief, with which he covered his face, saying again: 'I Kappler very good'. Before we left, 12 or so other natives of the same tribe came up to us, probably attracted by the report of the musket. Tunba went to meet them, and they approached unarmed but shy. I knew them all with the exception of three or four whose names however did not correspond with those of the murderers. They seemed friendly, taking little notice of the wounded man, but desiring us to go away. No sooner, however, were we gone, than they commenced a loud and pitiful lamentation over their then probably departed friend. After the crying had ceased, one voice was heard, uttering very violent and abrupt sounds. I asked Tunba what it meant, when he answered that they were scolding him for having brought us to them, and that by and by they would spear him.

Seeing now that the object of my accompanying the expedition had been frustrated, and that it was not likely to be attained for the future, I left the party next morning and came back to town. I felt it to be inconsistent with my missionary character und injurious to my good faith with the natives to witness transactions as that described above. The party returned in about a week after me without having seen any more natives.

May 7th. In consequence of a report brought to town by some fisherman, that there was a numerous party of natives assembled on the southern coast of Port Lincoln proper, the soldiers and a few volunteers went in a small craft after them. From the fact that the place where this body of natives was collected is in the Nauo country, and from the description given me by one of those that had seen and hunted kangaroo with them, namely that they had been all painted white, which is the sign of mourning with Port Lincoln natives, I felt persuaded that they could be no other than the Nauo tribe. On the following day the party returned, bringing Palubba, an old white headed man already in his dotage, and two women with their little children with them as prisoners. I heard that two men had been shot dead and that some more must have been wounded. Wornawas, one of the female prisoners, stated that five had fallen – Munta and Iubus, two of our former guides, Tyilye and Jalerilla, two boys of about 10–12 years of age and Ngulga, who was found among the murderers in the camp of Malli. Some stolen property had been found with the natives, part of which was admitted by the prisoners to have been given to them by the murderer Ngarbi, and the other part, a dog and a piece of canvass which had been stolen from Driver's station subsequently to the murders, had been given to them by Tyukalta one of the Eastern Coast tribes. They were set at liberty by the Magistrate the same day and went back to their tribe on the following morning.

Since this time no natives have come to the settlement and, I apprehend are not likely to come for some time, at least not in a friendly way.

I have the honour to remain, Sir,

Your most obedient servant.

C.W. Schürmann

Samuel Gottlieb Klose, 'Letter to Dresden'

Samuel Gottlieb Klose was born in Löwenberg in Silesia (today's Lwówek Śląski) on 27 December 1802. Little is known of his life before entering the Dresden Mission Society. Along with Christian Gottlob Teichelmann, Clamor Wilhelm Schürmann (both of whom arrived in Adelaide in October 1838) and Heinrich August Eduard Meyer, Klose was one of the so-called 'Dresden Four' missionaries sent to South Australia by the DMS. Klose arrived in Adelaide with Meyer on 9 August 1840, both men having been directed by the DMS to work with Teichelmann and Schürmann as equals.

Much of Klose's early time in Adelaide was spent at the Native Location (Piltawodli) near the Torrens Weir, where he moved into the house previously occupied by Schürmann and dedicated himself to the education of Indigenous children. The government, however, ultimately decided to close both that school and another at Walkerville, transferring all the children to a school on Kintore Avenue. It is not clear to what extent Klose and his wife Elizabeth Duncan were involved in the new school. From 1846 Klose was pastor to a Lutheran congregation in Adelaide. A petition he and the other missionaries made to Dresden to discontinue their work among Indigenous people was granted by Dresden in late 1847. For reasons unknown, Klose was dismissed by his congregation and followed the flow of hopefuls to the goldfields of Victoria. He did, however, serve out the final years of his life in South Australia, for a time at the Happy Valley Congregational Church. He died in 1889.*

---

* *Further reading*: Christine J. Lockwood, 'The Two Kingdoms: Lutheran Missionaries and the British Civilizing Mission in early South Australia,' PhD thesis, University of Adelaide, 2014. https://digital.library.adelaide.edu.au/dspace/handle/2440/84754; Christine Lockwood, 'Klose, Rev. Samuel Gottlieb (1802–1889)', http://missionaries.griffith.edu.au/biography/Klose-Rev-Samuel-Gottlieb-1802–1889.

Source:
Joyce Graetz (ed.), *Missionary to the Kaurna: The Klose Letters*, trans. Erich Meier and Marcus Krieg, 'Adelaide Friends of the Lutheran Archives, 2002.'
Translation: Erich Meier and Marcus Krieg.

Letter to the Dresden Mission Society

Adelaide, 4 January 1843

To the Committee of the Evangel. Lutheran Mission Society in Dresden Respected Brothers in the Lord,

Since my last letter to you six months have already flown by. A long time indeed. But no ship has arrived here, either from Europe or any other place, which was sailing back to Europe. At the end of last month the first ship for this year arrived here, and in a few days it will go to Mauritius and from there back to London. The harbour has never been so free of ships for such a long period since the coming of the Europeans. The Brothers Schürmann and Meyer have both come here and are living with me, which is the reason I have been somewhat hindered from writing more fully to you, nevertheless I will report on the most important things as far as time permits.

Concerning the work of the mission in general, progress is very slow, because each one of us is busy learning the language; especially when compared with the report of our dear brother Cordes in Tranquebar (1842 No. 11) where congregations are formed one after the other, where a third and fourth preacher can be provided for, where their children come to school in their hundreds, there are such pleasing reports. Thank the Lord that this is so. But when I contemplate the natives here and see their blunted moral sense, it appears to me almost impossible that we will ever see even one converted Christian among these people. However, I know that it does not depend on us, and that with God nothing is impossible, so I will continue to punish and to encourage wherever I find an opportunity. From the following tale you will see how hard the attitude of the natives is. On the 19th of last month, very early in the morning a native woman was delivered of a healthy and strong daughter. Both mother and daughter were healthy even though the night had been cold and wet, and she was lying under a tree here on the Location with only one woollen blanket. At about 9 o'clock in the morning the Protector, Mr Moorhouse, came and visited her. While he was there another Aboriginal woman came up, exceedingly angry, picked up the child by the legs and wanted to kill it. Mr Moorhouse immediately asked what she intended doing; was she about to kill it? The answer was, 'Can't you see that she already has one child (of 1 year and 4 months) to carry – she cannot carry two'. It will be known to you that the natives suckle their children for up to three years and carry them about on their backs wrapped in a blanket. Mr Moorhouse replied that if she killed the child, he would have her thrown into prison. You will also be aware that the punishment of death, of which they are terrified, follows. Thereupon she threw the child to the mother, who appeared to be totally unconcerned, and stormed off weeping and swearing. The child is still alive, and I believe it has escaped from this form of death, because usually they are said to kill their children straight away after they are born. If one proclaims the Word of God to them and draws attention to their sins, while referring to such truths as the fact that Jehovah will punish them in eternity, they burst out in loud laughter. Unbelief has the upper hand here.

Their ancestors believed (according to the statement of an Aborigine last Sunday) that the soul lived on after death, but they had abandoned that belief and now believed that death was the end of everything. Only after the arrival of the Europeans, of whom they had never previously seen or heard anything, did they again take up this concept, so that many now believe that the whites are their ancestors, and that when they die their souls go to *Pinde*, which is supposed to lie to the west, or to England, where they receive a white body and become Europeans. But many also see that the Europeans are born and die, just as they do. When I told the children in school of this callous mother and said that no creature on earth sacrificed its young to be murdered, they told me of another mother who, because she did not want to carry and nourish her child, had thrown it alive into the fire and burnt it. And another one strangled hers for the same reason.

But since I have been here this sort of thing has never happened.

Since the section of land has been bought, Br Teichelmann has settled there completely. It lies about 12 English or 3 German miles south of Adelaide. Whenever he does not come to town, I gather the adults and children on Sundays. On the 2nd Sunday after Trinity, I told them the story of the great banquet: Luke 14:16, explained to them what God wanted to be understood by it and made as an application that we too had come to invite them to this great feast. Br Schürmann sat among the adults and gathered from them that they had understood me clearly. Even though my language was still broken, I was delighted, and was encouraged to continue. The children would have understood me better, because they are better acquainted with the story of the Old Testament. The Bible pictures you sent me are very helpful and for these I again thank you sincerely. Before receiving those pictures, I had the opportunity to borrow an English illustrated Bible. If the German illustrated Bible has more pictures, I ask you to send me one at my expense, as well as a German-Hebrew dictionary, since Br Teichelmann took his with him.

Two of the older schoolboys, about 12 or 14 years old, send you some of their writing as a token of their gratitude for the playthings they received. They contain their own thoughts. I told them that I was again sending letters to my friends in Europe, and asked if they would also like to write something: whereupon these boys decided to write. Up to now we still have found no word to express thanks. Usually they express it through the use of names for relationships. Namely: *ngaityerli* (you are my father); *ngaityaii* (my mother); *ngaityo yunga* (my elder brother); *ngaityou panyappi* (my youngest brother); to friends they say *ngaityo taru* (my friend – actually my in-law). Similarly with addressing children they use the suffix *anna* which means the directing to an object. Certainly Kartanya would also have written if she were still attending school. But she left last year, lived with her husband and already over the past four months has been suffering from venereal disease which is prevalent among the Aborigines.

Heinrich August Eduard Meyer, 'Manners and Customs of the Aborigines of the Encounter Bay Tribe, South Australia'

Heinrich August Eduard Meyer was born on 5 May 1813 in Berlin. Beginning his professional life as a plumber, he then studied with the Dresden Mission Society. He was ordained in February 1838 and expressed a desire to join his friend Clamor Wilhelm Schürmann in South Australia. His request was granted, and prior to leaving he married Friederike Wilhelmine Sternicke in March of the same year so that she could join him in South Australia. While in South Australia they had six children.

Meyer arrived in Adelaide on 9 August 1840, but rather than join Schürmann and the latter's colleague Teichelmann, Meyer and his wife were sent to work with the Ngarrindjeri people at Encounter Bay. While his efforts to create a functioning Indigenous school largely failed, his attempt to record the Ramindjeri language resulted in two books, published in 1843 and 1846. Initially he had thought that teaching would offer him the opportunity to learn the language, but he increasingly found that his language acquisition was best done in the evenings around the campfire.

In the end, Meyer's mission school at Encounter Bay struggled to attract Indigenous students and sufficient funds; in 1848 it closed. Meyer then moved to the Barossa Valley, where he became a minister for the German Lutheran population in the region. He died on 19 December 1862.*

---

* *Further reading*: Christine Lockwood 'Meyer, Heinrich August Eduard, Rev. (1813–1862)' in German Missionaries in Australia http://missionaries.griffith.edu.au/biography/meyer-heinrich-august-eduard-rev-1813–1862; Rob Amery and Mary-Anne Gale, 'They Came, They Heard, They Documented: The Dresden Missionaries as Lexicographers', in Ghil'ad Zuckermann, Julia Miller, Jasmin Morley (eds.) *Endangered Words, Signs of Revival*, Adelaide, Australex, 2014, 1–19, https://www.adelaide.edu.au/australex/conferences/2013/amery_and_gale.pdf

Source:
Extract from Heinrich August Eduard Meyer, *Manners and Customs of the Aborigines of the Encounter Bay Tribe, South Australia* (Adelaide: George Dehane, 1846), 1–15.

The Aborigines of different parts of the province are distinguished by differences of language, customs, manners, and traditions. Thus there appears to be no similarity between the Adelaide and Encounter Bay language, and the same may be said of their manners, habits, and traditions. In what follows, therefore, I am only to be understood as speaking of the manners, customs, traditions, &c., of the natives of Encounter Bay and the lower banks of the Murray. These people, who speak one language with slight variation of dialect, are divided into different tribes, as Raminjerar, Lampinjerar, Karkarinjerar, Pankinjerar, &c., and these tribes consider themselves as large families, and are more or less connected with each other by marriage. Each tribe derives its name from the district to which it belongs, and which they claim as their own property, as Ramong, the district belonging to the Raminjerar, the affix *injeri* (plural *injerar*) having the same signification as "er" in English, as Londoner, &c., &c. Although these tribes are, as just observed, related, they are nevertheless extremely jealous and suspicious of each other, and almost constantly at war.

In giving an account of these people, we shall endeavour to trace the life of one from his birth upwards.

When a woman is near her confinement she removes from the encampment with some of the women to assist her. As soon as the child is born, the information is conveyed to the father, who immediately goes to see the child and to attend upon the mother, by carrying firewood, water, &c. If there are unmarried men and boys in the camp, as there generally are, the woman and her friends are obliged to remain at a distance in their own encampment. This appears to be part of the same superstition which obliges a woman to separate herself from the camp at the time of her monthly illness, when, if a young man or boy should approach, she calls out, and he immediately makes a circuit to avoid her. If she is neglectful upon this point, she exposes herself to scolding, and sometimes to severe beating by her husband or nearest relation, because the boys are told from their infancy, that if they see the blood they will early become grey-headed, and their strength will fail prematurely.

If the child is permitted to live (I say permitted, because they are frequently put to death) it is brought up with great care, more than generally falls to the lot of children of the poorer class of Europeans. Should it cry, it is passed from one person to another and caressed and soothed, and the father will frequently nurse it for several hours together.

Children that are weak or deformed, or illegitimate, and the child of any woman who has already two children alive, are put to death. No mother will venture to bring up more than two children, because she considers that the attention which she would have to devote to them would interfere with what she regards as the duty to her husband, in searching for roots, &c. If the father dies before a child is born, the child is put to death by the mother, for the Father who provides for us all is unknown to them. This crime of infanticide is increased by the whites, for nearly all the children of European fathers used to be put to death. It is remarkable that when the children are first born they are nearly as white as Europeans, so that the natives some-times find it difficult to say whether they are of pure blood or not. In such doubtful cases the form of the nose decides. When the child commences to walk, the father gives it a name, which is frequently derived from some circumstances which occurred at the time of the child's birth; or, as each tribe has a kind of patron or protector in the objects of nature, as Thunder, the protector of the Raminjerar, a kind of ant, the protector of the Kargarinjerar, the pelican, a kind of snake, &c., &c., of other tribes, the father often confers the name of this protector (as the pouch of the pelican), or a part of it, upon the child. Grown-up persons frequently exchange names, probably as a mark of friendship.

Children are suckled by their mothers for a considerable time, sometimes to the age of five or six years; and it is no uncommon thing to see a boy playing with his companions, suddenly leave off and run to his mother to refresh himself with a draught of milk. When weaned, he accompanies his father upon short excursions, unless he should be delicate and unable to bear the fatigue, upon which occasion the father takes every opportunity to instruct his son. For instance, if they arrive at a place concerning which they have any tradition, it is told to the child if old enough to understand it. Or he shows him how to procure this or that animal, or other article of food, in the easiest way. Until his fourteenth or fifteenth year he is mostly engaged in catching fish and birds, because already, for some years, he has been obliged to seek for food on his own account. Thus he early becomes, in a great measure, independent; and there is nobody who can control him, the authority of his parents depending only upon the superstitions which they have instilled into him from infancy; and the prohibitions respecting certain kinds of food— for different kinds of food are allotted to persons of different ages—are enforced by their superstitions. The roes of fishes are appropriated to the old men, and it is believed that if women or young men or children eat of them they will become prematurely old. Other kind of meat they consider diminishes the strength of the muscles, &c., &c. At certain seasons of the year, when a particular kind of fish is abundant, the men frequently declare it to be *rambe* (holy); after which, all that are caught must be brought to the men, by whom they are cooked, and the women and children are not allowed even to approach the fires until the cooking is over and the fish are cold, when they may approach and eat of what the men choose to give them, after having previously regaled themselves.

The boys, besides being taught to obtain their own food, are also exercised in the use of the spear and other weapons; and when arrived at the age of fourteen or fifteen years, they take part in the wars between the tribes. A few years afterwards, when sixteen or eighteen years of age, according to the growth of the beard, he is admitted into the rank of the men, and becomes *rambe*, or sacred in this way.

[*Here follows a description of cultural practices.*]

A rude kind of tattooing is practised amongst them, consisting merely in making scars without applying any colour, and for this there seems to be no particular time allotted, as sometimes boys of ten or twelve years of age may be seen with several large cuts upon the breast and shoulders, and others, several years older, without. They consider it not only as ornamental, but also as a means of alleviating pain, and giving freedom of motion to the arms, and enabling them to use the spear and shield with dexterity.

The education of the females is simple. As soon as weaned they receive the fringe, for covering the pubes, which is the only article of dress considered absolutely necessary; for the skins or mats which they sometimes wear, are worn only at pleasure, and both men and women generally go uncovered, or wear some article of clothing given to them by the Europeans, only, as just observed, the female is obliged to wear the fringe until near the birth of her first child; and, should she prove barren, it is taken, away by her husband while she is asleep, and burned. They are given in marriage at a very early age (ten or twelve years). The ceremony is very simple, and with great propriety may he considered an exchange, for no man can obtain a wife unless he can promise to give his sister or other relative in exchange. The marriages are always between persons of different tribes, and never in the same tribe.

Should the father be living he may give his daughter away, but generally she is the gift of the brother. The person who wishes to obtain a wife never applies directly, but to some friend of the one who has the disposal of her, and should the latter also wish for a wife, the bargain is soon made. Thus the girls have no choice in the matter, and frequently the parties have never seen each other before.

At the time appointed for the marriage, the relations on both sides come and encamp about a quarter of a mile from each other. In the night the men of one tribe arise, and each takes a fire-stick in hand. The bride is taken by the hand and conducted in the midst and appears generally to go very unwillingly; the brother or relation who gives her away walks silently and with downcast looks by himself. As soon as they approach the camp of the other tribe, the women and children of the latter must quit the hut, which upon this occasion is built larger than their huts usually are. When they arrive at the hut, one of the men invites them to take their places; but before they sit down the bride and bridegroom are placed next each other, and also the brother and his intended wife, if it is a double marriage. The friends and relations then take their places on each side of the principal parties. They sit in this manner, silent, for a considerable time, until most of them fall asleep. At daybreak the brides leave the hut and go to their nearest relations, and remain with them until the evening, when they are conducted to their husbands by their female friends, and the tribes then separate and go to their own districts. When married very young, the girl is frequently away from her husband, upon a visit to her relations, for several months at a time, but should she remain, the man is under obligation to provide her with animal food (providing vegetable food is always the duty of the females), and if she pleases him, he shows his affection by frequently rubbing her with grease to improve her personal appearance, and with the idea that it will make her grow rapidly and become fat.

If a man has several girls at his disposal, he speedily obtains several wives, who, however, very seldom agree well with each other, but are continually quarrelling, each endeavouring to be the favourite. The man, regarding them more as slaves than in any other light, employs them in every possible way to his own advantage. They are obliged to get him shell-fish, roots, and edible plants. If one from another tribe should arrive having anything which he desires to purchase, he perhaps makes a bargain to pay by letting him have one of his wives for a longer or shorter period. The Europeans and others are aware of this, and therefore if any woman whose company they desire refuses to go with them, they commonly go to the husband with some bread or tobacco, or article of clothing, who then compels her to grant what the white man desires. Miserable and degraded beings! When will they throw off these diabolical practices and become obedient to the laws of our God.

Their mode of life is a wandering one; but the whole tribe does not always move in a body from one place to another, unless there should be abundance of food to be obtained at some particular spot; but generally they are scattered in search of food. Sometimes of a morning two or three of the men will leave the camp to go fishing. If they are fortunate, after having satisfied their hunger they will lie down and sleep for several hours; they then perhaps get up and search for another meal, and if they have obtained more than they can consume, they return at sunset to the camp with the remainder, which they distribute amongst their wives and children if married, or if unmarried, amongst their friends and relations. Sometimes the men go out with their wives and children, when the men employ themselves, according to the season, either in fishing or hunting emus, opossums, kangaroos, &c., while the women and children search for roots and plants. If food is not found in the neighbourhood, they remain out sometimes a month or longer, wandering about from place to place. Upon these occasions the aged and sick, who remain at what may be considered their head-quarters (the place from which the tribe derives its name), often suffer severely from want of food. Having to search for food is not the only cause of their wandering about from place to place, but also their frequent wars, and the meetings of the different tribes for purposes of amusement, and the wish of the women to visit their relations in the tribes to which they originally belonged.

These circumstances taken together make their residence at one place very uncertain. This wandering life must be considered as the cause of their having no permanent habitations, but merely huts of the rudest construction. Arrived at a place where they intend to remain for the night, the women and children proceed to obtain some branches, which are placed in a semicircle open to the side opposite to that from which the wind is blowing at the time, placed a little closer and with more care in bad weather, so as to afford some shelter from the wind and rain, and constitute the hut. Near the sea, if they are likely to remain for some time, they cover the hut with sea-weed, and the branches composing the framework being arranged something in the form of a quarter of a sphere, or the half of a bee-hive cut perpendicularly, it makes a pretty good defence against the weather. Yet the children and sick persons, no doubt, suffer considerably in bad weather, and the former, left to themselves as soon as weaned, lie huddled together to keep themselves warm.

Before the arrival of the Europeans they had two modes of catching fish—with the net and the spear—to which must now be added the hook and the line, which they have learned of the whites. They use the spear at the Murray in catching the large fish, *mallowe*. Going into the river as far as he can to use the spear with effect, the native stands like a statue, holding the spear obliquely in both hands ready to strike his prey as it passes. Standing motionless, he is soon surrounded by fish, and the first that passes his feet is pierced by a certain and powerful thrust. Sometimes they make use of a canoe made of bark, from which they spear the fish, and have a fire in the middle, upon which they are immediately roasted. The nets are precisely similar in texture to European nets, though made without mesh and needle, and they display considerable patience and ingenuity in the manufacture. The string of which they are made is composed of the fibres of a kind of flag. It is prepared by roasting the leaves, and afterwards chewing them; the leaf is then divided longitudinally into four, two of these are twisted by being rolled upon the thigh, and are then twisted together by being rolled the contrary way; other lengths are added until as much line is made as is required. In the operation of netting the twine is wound round a short stick which answers the purpose of a needle, and the meshes are formed and the knot tied by passing the string over and between the fingers. Thus are made long pieces or ribbons of netting twenty or thirty feet long, and about a foot broad, which are afterwards put together to make a fishing-net. The net is kept extended by pieces of sticks, placed across at the distance of about four feet from each other.

Some nets are furnished with a bag or pouch of netting, with smaller meshes placed at one end of the net, into which the smaller fish are driven as the net is hauled in. When the fish approach the shore the natives enter the water with the net, and swim about until they get the fish between themselves and the shore, they then spread out the net, those on shore directing them, so that they may enclose the fish, and as soon as this is accomplished they are drawn to the shore.

Swans, geese, ducks, and other birds, which are plentiful at the Lake, are caught with a noose at the end of a long stick, with which the native steals upon them amongst the reeds which border the margin. Shell and crayfish they get by diving, the last generally by the women; in obtaining which, one woman last year lost her life, having by some means or other become jammed between the rocks at the bottom of the sea.

In hunting the kangaroo they sometimes go a number together, and sometimes singly. When going singly, the native takes care to have his spear in good order; he places it over the fire to straighten it, sharpens the point with a shell, and barbs it with pieces of quartz or glass, fixed on with the resin of the grass-tree. Having prepared his spear he takes his *koye* (basket) upon his shoulder, which contains his throwing stick and other weapons of defence, and goes in search of his prey. When arrived at the place where he expects to find some kangaroo, he seems quite a different man. He is now silent; rolling his eyes from side to side, and looking in every direction, he moves forward with long strides, his body erect and arm motionless, the spear grasped in both hands, and held obliquely in front. As soon as he perceives a kangaroo he stops suddenly, and watches an opportunity to steal upon it while holding down its head to graze; when near enough he fixes the spear in the throwing stick, and taking his aim he sends it flying at his prey, which seldom escapes him. When a number go in company they endeavour to surround the kangaroo, and gradually close in upon him, and at length despatch him with their spears and sticks.

The emu is hunted in the same manner. Other tribes are said to use large nets in taking the kangaroo and emu; but it is quite foreign to the practice of the tribes of whom we are now speaking. The opossum is hunted only by some tribes.

In this district the Raminjerar are the only opossum hunters, and they manifest considerable dexterity in getting them from the hollow branches of trees which they inhabit. Before ascending a tree they examine the bark to see if an opossum has recently gone up, by the marks which their claws leave upon the bark. Having determined that there is an opossum in the tree, one commences to climb, and in a few seconds ascends thirty or forty feet without any branches to assist, and this accomplished only by means of a stick about two feet long, pointed at one end. With this stick he first makes a small hole in the bark, into which he inserts the great toe of the left foot, and then driving the point of the stick held by the right hand into the bark as high as he can, and embracing the tree with his left arm, he lifts himself up, and now supports himself upon the toe of the left foot, and by the left arm embracing the tree; and taking out the stick he makes another hole at a convenient distance above the first, then again driving the stick into the tree he holds on by it while raising the left foot to the second hole, and lifts himself up as before, and so on until he arrives at the branches. Here arrived, he ascertains by tapping against the branch in which the opossum is, where the hollow terminates. If the hollow is of small depth, he puts in his hand, seizes it by the tail, and striking its head two or three times against the tree throws it down to his companions. If the hollow is deeper there is more difficulty. He makes a hole where he considers the hollow to terminate, and endeavours to seize the opossum; but if it has ascended, he applies fire, the smoke of which speedily drives the animal out of the top of the branch, where the native is ready to seize it.

The preparation of their food is extremely simple. Fish, cray-fish, opossums, and small birds, are roasted upon the fire; roots and shell fish are roasted in the ashes; some plants, the flesh of the kangaroo, emu, &c., are prepared in the following manner: — A hole is dug and a fire kindled therein, stones are added, and when sufficiently heated, the fire is removed and grass placed upon the hot stones; the article to be cooked is placed upon the grass, covered with more grass, and the whole covered up with earth; if they think there will not be sufficient steam, holes are made and water poured in.

In proportion as these people are removed from the true knowledge of God so they are deeply sunk in superstition, as witnessed by their notions of diseases, the means adopted to cure them, and the observations in disposing of their dead. There are but few diseases which they regard as the consequences of natural causes; in general they consider them the effects of enchantment, and produced by sorcerers. They fancy that they can charm or enchant by means of two instruments, one called *plongge*, the other *mokani*. The *plongge* is a stick about two feet long, with a large knob at the end. They believe that if a person is tapped gently upon the breast with this instrument he will become ill and die, or if he should shortly afterwards receive a wound that it will be mortal. The charming is generally performed upon a person asleep; therefore, when several tribes are encamped near each other there is always one keeping watch that they may not be charmed by any of the other tribe. Should a man have an enemy whom he wishes to enchant, and he can steal upon him while sleeping without being discovered, he thinks to throw him into a sounder sleep by striking in the air before his face as though in the act of sprinkling with a tuft of emu feathers which have been previously moistened in the liquor from a putrid corpse, and having performed the same operation upon any others who are sleeping near, to prevent their awaking, he taps gently with the *plongge* upon the breast of his victim. The *mokani* is a black stone, shaped something like the head of an axe, fixed between two sticks bound together, which serve for a handle. The sharp side of the stone is used to enchant males, the other side females. It is used in the same manner as the *plongge*. The *ngatunge* is another instrument to cause illness and death. Enemies watch each other, and search diligently for places where they have eaten ducks, parrots, cockatoos, a kind of fish called *ponde*, &c. If any one has eaten of either of these animals, and neglected to burn all the bones, his enemy picks them up. But if the other has been too careful to enable him to do this, he takes one of these animals and cooks it, and offers it in a friendly manner to his intended victim—having previously taken from it a piece of bone. This he keeps carefully, and fixes with grass-tree resin upon the end of a small needle-shaped piece of kangaroo bone about three inches long. This is the *ngadungnge*, which he places near the fire, in order to produce illness and death. While in possession of this instrument, he fancies he has the other in his power. Should a man become sick, if he is satisfied that his illness is not owing to the *plongge* or *mokani*, he attributes it to the *ngadungnge*, which he supposes an enemy of his has placed near the fire. If he has, or can obtain from one of his friends, a *ngadungnge* giving him power over the person whom he suspects, he immediately places it near the fire. If he is only certain of the tribe to which his enemy belongs, without knowing whom to suspect, he gets as many *ngadungnges* as he can, giving power over individuals of that tribe, and places them near the fire; should he become better, his recovery is attributed to his enemy having removed from the fire the *ngadungnge* which made him ill; and as soon as the others are attacked with illness, in consequence of the *ngadungnges* which he has placed, he removes them also. Should he become worse and die, the *ngadungnges* are left until the resin is melted and the pieces of bone come apart; which they think will cause the death of their enemies. If a person is convinced that the death of a friend or relation has been caused by enchantment, and he can obtain a *ngadungnge* having power over the person whom he suspects, he places it in the thigh of the corpse, believing that this will cause the suspected person to die a lingering death. If any person should die, and his friends are ignorant of the cause, his death is attributed to sorcerers, called *melapar*. They apply this name to the Adelaide and more northern tribes, and believe that they have the power of transforming themselves into birds, trees, &c. Both young and old are very much afraid of these *melapar*, and, in consequence, do not like to be away from their huts after sunset. Nearly every tribe has its own doctor, who has but one remedy for every disease; but every doctor has a different one, and this is the object, animal or vegetable, which he regards as his friend or protector—thus one has a snake, another an ant, another sea-weed, &c. &c. The sick man may either go to the doctor, or send for him. If the doctor is prepared, he knocks against the hut with his fingers, and upon the shoulder of the patient; then squeezes the part affected between his hands, and sucks it with his mouth; having done this for a minute or two, he spits out (if this is his protector) seaweed upon the hand of the patient, which he is to keep carefully until it is dry. In the evening, the doctor and friends of the patient assemble round him, and sing as loud as they can to drive away the disease.

The doctor sits in front of the patient with two sticks, one in each hand, beating the air; and the women beat upon kangaroo skins, rolled up, held between their knees. He pretends to have sucked out the seaweed from the patient; and if anyone should hint his having previously put it into his mouth he becomes indignant, and threatens to send it with the disease into his body.

Some weeks ago I accompanied a man, whose eye was inflamed, to the doctor. The old man was sitting before his hut in company with some of his friends, with a large portion of cooked plants before him, which he appeared to enjoy very much. Having learned the purpose of our coming, and knowing that I would watch his movements, he sat for some time as if in silent contemplation, and then said in a low tone, 'I am not able to suck to-day; I have eaten too much of this (pointing to the plants), and there is much wind upon my stomach—I will come to-morrow.' The next morning the doctor came, and after sucking the eye it became much better, which, doubtless, it would have been without his assistance. There is another man in the same tribe who cures a kind of large boil, which the natives are very subject to, by sucking out the matter and swallowing it, saying that it is his *ngaitye* (friend or protector).

[Here follows a discussion of practices to dispose of the bodies of the dead and conduct funerals, then a retelling of a number of creation stories.]

Carl Strehlow, 'The Aborigines of Central Australia'

Carl Strehlow was born into a devoutly Lutheran family at Fredersdorf in Brandenburg in 1871. He entered the seminary founded by Wilhelm Löhe in Neuendettelsau in Franconia in 1888, graduating in 1892. At this time missionaries were being recruited from Neuendettelsau for work in Australia; Strehlow was asked by the Immanuel Synod to fill the position of teacher at the Killalpaninna (or Bethesda) mission on Cooper Creek, which he reached in the middle of the year, having been ordained at Light Pass.

A brilliant student at Neuendettelsau, Strehlow showed a particular proficiency in learning languages and soon turned his hand to learning the local Dieri language. He collaborated with missionary J.G. Reuther in translating the New Testament into Dieri. After a long courtship with Frieda Keysser, Carl and Frieda married at Point Pass in September 1895. By that time Carl had already been appointed to take over the abandoned Hermannsburg mission station (later Ntaria) in Central Australia, which would be the home for the couple and their children for much of the next three decades.

The population at the station, both Aranda and Loritja people, became the focus of Strehlow's missionary endeavours. As at Killalpaninna, his strategy entailed the learning of the languages of the local people so as to be able to enter their mental world and facilitate their conversion to

Carl Strehlow

Christianity. To this end, Strehlow translated key religious texts into local languages, just as he had at Killalpaninna. In his linguistic work Strehlow worked together closely with fellow missionary Otto Siebert, at least until the latter's return to Germany in 1902.

Strehlow's ethnographic interests were at best tolerated by the mission authorities, whose primary interest lay in Strehlow's proselytising and his management of an enterprise which relied on state and Church support to survive. As an ethnographer, Strehlow devoted himself primarily to languages, cultures and belief systems. This, together with his plainly sympathetic attitude toward the subjects of his studies, his affirmation that they had a religion of their own, and that they were not doomed to extinction, set him at loggerheads in particular with the British biologist-cum-anthropologist Baldwin Spencer, who mocked the missionaries' endeavours.

Like many of German birth or background in Australia, Strehlow and his family fell under suspicion during the First World War. Despite Spencer's best efforts, Hermannsburg was still functioning when the war ended, but restrictions on German immigration made it difficult to find a successor to take over from the ailing Carl Strehlow. More hopefully, there were signs in post-war Australia that attitudes to Indigenous people were changing, and some were visible in Adelaide. The future of Indigenous people was becoming a subject of public debate, into which Carl Strehlow was to be drawn from distant Hermannsburg. It appears likely that it was John Blacket who persuaded Strehlow to put his own views to the Adelaide public.

Serious illness the following year persuaded him to attempt to make his way to Adelaide to seek medical help, but he died at Horseshoe Bend on 22 October 1922 and was buried there.*

---

* *Further reading:* John Strehlow, *The Tale of Frieda Keysser: Frieda Keysser & Carl Strehlow: An Historical Biography*, 2 vols, London' Wild Cat Press, 2011, 2019; T.G.H. Strehlow, *Journey to Horseshoe Bend*, Adelaide, Rigby, 1978; Walter F. Veit, 'Strehlow, Carl Friedrich (1871–1922)', *Australian Dictionary of Biography*, National Centre of Biography, Australian National University, https://adb.anu.edu.au/biography/strehlow-carl-friedrich-8698/text15221, published first in hardcopy 1990, accessed online 30 October 2022.

An Indigenous South

Source:
Carl Strehlow, 'Aborigines of Central Australia: Interesting Questions', *Register* 7 December 1921, 11.

The lecture by Dr. Basedow on the Aborigines question has aroused a great interest in wide circles. It is to be hoped that the impulse which it has provoked will not vanish fruitless, but that it will deepen, and lead to practical results, which will ameliorate the conditions of the Aborigines of Central Australia, and will save them from the fate of their brother-tribes on other parts of this continent. As I have lived among the Australian Aborigines for nearly 30 years, and have for many years made investigations into the religious ideas and social organisations of the Aranda (or Arunta), and the neighbouring Loritja (or Luricha) tribes, I presume it will not be regarded as arrogance, if I give my views of the religious traditions and the mental capacities of the Aborigines, and if I show by what means, according to my opinion, the remnant of this people could be saved. As I cannot deal fully with this great problem in a short article, I shall apply myself to the utmost brevity, and touch the following questions:— 1. Are the Australian Aborigines the missing link? 2. Have the Aborigines a religion? 3. Are they cannibals? 4. What would be the best solution of the half-caste problem? and 5. Is the mission among them a failure?

— Are the Aborigines the missing link? —
The Australian Aborigines are a strange people, which have not made the least progress in the last centuries. They do not seem to fit into our time, but to be at least 4,000 years back, living still in the stone age. This circumstance has induced some scientific men to find in the Aborigine the missing link, or the primordial anthropoid. How strange! The Aborigines descended from the apes, and that in Australia, where there are no apes! But, perhaps these demi-apes immigrated into Australia in the Alcheringa time, which Spencer and Gillen, in their great work ('Northern Tribes of Central Australia', p. 745) translate as 'dream time,' in which the ancestors of the

present Aborigines were endowed with supernatural powers. When I investigated the religious beliefs of the Aranda, I asked the blacks if they knew of any 'dream time' in the past, but they did not understand me. They had never heard of a dream time before, and I could not give them any information of this mythical time. 'Dream time' sounds so scientific, but nobody can say what it implies. According to evolution, we may imagine the 'dream time' in the following manner: — In the pre-historic time there lived in Central Australia a great horde of primordial anthropoids, or demi-apes. They went in search of the different fruits, climbed up high trees for birds' eggs, and lived very happily for a long period. But unexpectedly a severe drought swept over their country. The waterholes in the creeks dried up, the fruit on the trees died off, and a very bad time set in. One day the old chief of the demi-apes had climbed a big gumtree in sheer desperation. Unfortunately, he had fallen from a branch of the tree, and broken his spine. The female members of the horde were soon squatting around their dying chief, and uttered loud lamentations, while the male members were sitting aside gesticulating and grunting. Suddenly a clever member of the demi-apes rose and called out in indistinct sounds — 'If we want to survive, we must accommodate ourselves to the changed circumstances.' Great astonishment among the demi-apes! Nobody knew what 'accommodation' meant, but — *fortes fortuna adjuvat!* Under loud lamentations and discussions the night drew near. Soon all the members or the horde fell in a deep sleep, which lasted for centuries. They dreamt the loveliest dreams. They had visions of merry hunting parties, grand feastings, and beautifully conducted corroborees. And, O, wonder! when they at last awakened, their visions were verified. They arose from the ground, and brushed their hair off their bodies, their tails dropped off themselves, and— greater wonder!— they could express all their thoughts quite easily. They possessed a well-structured language. If you see in the present type of the Aborigine the missing link, you require 11 more links from the present type of the Aborigine to the common ancestor of man and ape, because the greatest difference between an ape and an Aborigine is not the bodily structure, but the wonderfully structured language of the Aborigines, and their religious beliefs. The well-constructed language of the Arandas reminds one of the old Greek language; in fact, it has more moods than the last-mentioned. It possesses an indicative, conditional, optative, minative, and imperative, it has not only the usual *tempora*, present, imperfect, perfect, and future, but also three aorist forms, *aoristus remotus*, *aoristus remotior*, and a *remotissimus*; besides, it has a dual for all three persons. In the declension of the noun there are not only a double nominative (transitive and intransitive) and a genitive, dative, and accusative, as in other old languages, but also a vocative, ablative, a double locative, an instrumentative, a causative, &c. The derivations and compounds are often quite marvellous. Then the great number of words! It is difficult to count them on account of the many derivations and dialectical forms; but, the latter included, I estimate, that the Aranda language possesses not less than 6,000 words. This wonderful construction of their language leads one to the thought that the Aborigines must have descended from a higher state of intellect to a lower grade, because among the present members of the Aranda tribe there is none that would be able to construct such a wonderful language. My own view is that the Aborigines inhabiting now Central Australia, have centuries ago emigrated into the interior from the north, perhaps by traversing New Guinea, and possessed a higher intelligence than at present, which inferior state is due to the long isolation and the barrenness of their surroundings.

— Have the Aborigines a Religion? —
Religion is the attitude of a human being towards a higher being. All the Aborigines of Central Australia believe in such a supernatural being. The Aranda call this Supreme being Altjira, who (according to the traditions of their forefathers) is everlasting, and not created by any one. He is described as a strong man of red colour (which latter the natives like best of all colours). His abode is the sky; the stars are his camp fires. He is the good God of the Aranda, and is known by the women and children also. As he does not do them any harm, there is

Carl Strehlow

no reason why they should fear him, or propitiate him. The Loritja, inhabiting the country west of the Aranda, also believe in a Supreme Being called Tukura, who resides in his heavenly abode. While Tukura enjoys himself in his hunting ground, his wife and son are collecting yams and grass-seeds, which are growing abundantly there. During the night Tukura performs sacred ceremonies to which he invited the living men in his vicinity. Also the Dieri Tribe, living between Lake Eyre and Lake Hope, believe in this Supreme Being, called by them Mura. But, as in the Greek mythology, the Supreme God Zeus receded in the background, and the greatest interest was bestowed on the semi-gods, just the same thing happened in the religious traditions of the Australian Aborigines. They neglected the Supreme Being, and turned their main interests to the demigods, half-animals and half-men, and endowed them with supernatural powers. The Aranda call these demi-gods *Altjira-ngamitjma* (the eternal uncreated); the Loritja, *Tukutita*; and the Dieri, *Muramura* (the duplication of a word, like *mura-mura*, signifies in the language of the Aborigines a *dimunitis qualitatis*).

These semi-gods wandered from place to place, instructed their novices and performed ceremonies, by which their Totem animals or plants were produced. These Totem-gods regard the Aborigines as their ancestors and benefactors; yes, rightly understood, the Aborigines regard themselves as reincarnations of these respected ancestors. Such a demi-god or Totem-god of the wildcat people was Malbanka (or Malbonga, which Mr. Krichauff mentions, con. the article of Rev. J. Blacket, 'Our Aborigines'). He started his wanderings from Atalana, a far-distant place in the south-west, put all his novices in a pouch made of kangaroo skins, where they were transformed into wooden *tjurungas* (or *churingas*), and carried his two wives in the form of two stone *tjurungas* in another pouch under his right arm, and arrived at last at a place called Tunapapa, west of Barow [Barrow] Creek. Very tired, he went with his old father and mother and his novices in a big cave, where they were all transformed into *tjurungas*, which scene is celebrated by the old sacred song:— '*Letoppetoppa indapindama*' (in rows they are lying on the ground), '*Tloarala indapindama*' (with their white headbands they are lying on the ground). This cave is now regarded as a great wild-cat Totem-centre. When the Aborigines are performing their sacred ceremonies they cantillate such sacred songs, of which they possess several hundreds, which I have translated. These refer to the wanderings of their Totem-ancestors, and also to the peculiarities of their Totem animals and plants; and contain in their totality quite an interesting popular natural history. As a proof that some of the Aborigines possess a poetical vein, I may mention that one of the Aborigines who visit the preparatory cursus of baptism brought me a hymn of 21 verses, which showed clearly that he had closely followed the religious instructions he had received. And these people, with such mental capacities, should form the 'missing link'? Never. The Aborigines also believe that their souls after their departure from their bodies wander to the north, the land of the departed spirits, which is situated near to the ocean (*laia*). They return sometimes to their relations and friends, but are finally destroyed by a thunderbolt.

— Are the Aborigines Cannibals? —

In a recent article in *The Australasian* I saw a statement of Mrs. Bates that the blacks around Ooldea, were fearful cannibals. She told such gruesome stories of cannibalism that one involuntarily asked, 'Can it really be true?' I wonder how many cases of cannibalism Mrs. Bates has witnessed herself. I have lived nearly 30 years among the Aborigines, but I have never seen the Aborigines eating human flesh, nor have I heard of a single case of cannibalism in our vicinity. I presume that a lot of wrong information is obtained from the blacks by putting negative questions to them. Every Australian Aborigine will answer a negative question contrary to our custom positively. If I ask an Aborigine, 'Do you not eat human flesh?' he will answer, 'Yes', meaning 'We do not eat human flesh', because his 'Yes' refers to the whole sentence, including the word 'not'. The only cannibalistic notion I found among the customs of the Aranda was at the investigation of their avenging practices. When the avenging party finds it necessary to slay all the inhabitants of an enemy camp, the participants of this party open the bodies of the slain and eat a little of the kidney fat of their enemies, to appropriate the strength of them. There might have occurred in the past some cases such as that a little child has been eaten by the women in times of great distress; but has not this happened, according to the Holy Scriptures, in Samaria, too (II. Kings, v. 29).

Certainly we do not call the Jews cannibals on account of an extraordinary case.

— The Half-caste Problem —

It would be best if there existed no half-castes at all. But as this wish will always be a *pium desideratum*, the question arises— 'How can the half-caste question best be solved?' I regard the half-castes as blacks, especially when they are brought up by their black mothers, and in the saying — 'The half-castes possess the vices of both races, and the virtues of none', there is some truth. Certainly the half-castes are more skilful than the Aborigines, but they hate the work just as much as the latter, and are more sensitive as a rule. We have only a few half-castes at our station. As they behave just as the Aborigines, we breed them back; that means, we let them intermarry with the blacks. This is one solution. Another would be to take the little half-caste children away from their mothers when they are only a few years old, and transport them for ever to another part of the State. If they come back, they mostly go directly to the blacks' camp. But is not this cruel? It seems so at first; but one must take into account that it is done in the best interests of the half-castes themselves, and that the black mothers have not quite the same feelings as white mothers. There might be, perhaps, one white mother among thousands that would be able to murder her own child to cover her shame. But among the Aborigines each woman would be capable of murdering her first-born twin-child, and neglecting the other till it finds an early grave. But do not the black mothers lament fearfully at the death of their babies? Certainly; but that is to a great extent due to their customs, and there is a great lot of show in their wailings. Strange people indeed! They can murder in cold blood a new-born child, but cannot kill a puppy!

An Indigenous South

— Is Mission Among the Aborigines a Failure! —

Some months ago the Government set aside for the benefit of the Aborigines a great reserve in the west of our block. This step should have been taken years ago, to preserve the remnant of the Aborigines. But will this reserve fulfil its purpose? If there is done nothing more in the direction, its advantage to the Aborigines will be very slight. The present-day blacks are not content with their former way of life; they now want tea, sugar, tobacco, and beef. If they are confined to this reserve, they will be a menace to the neighbouring stations. In bad seasons they will enter the cattle-breeding runs, and, having done a lot of damage, will recede unpunished into their reserve. Something more must be done for them. To establish depots of rations and blankets would spoil them thoroughly. To establish working stations among them would mean to drive them away, because most of the blacks hate work just as much as chastisement. To civilize them is an impossible task. Before they are properly civilized they will be swept away from the earth. The only means to preserve the remnant of the Aborigines would be to establish real mission stations among them, and teach them according to the principle — *Ora et labora!* Bring them the best you possess — the Gospel of Christ, which has served the ancient world from destruction, and which will regenerate this degenerated people. At our station the number of the blacks is steadily increasing. When I arrived here about 27 years ago the number of the inhabitants of our station was about 60, today we count 180; the birth-rate exceeds the death-rate. But is not mission among the Aborigines a failure? Not long ago Conrad Sayce published a book 'Golden Buckles', which deals with affairs in the Northern Territory. The author writes an interesting story, and as far as the life of the white inhabitants is concerned, his conclusions are pretty correct. But, as he was not long enough in the bush he fails utterly in characterizing the Aborigines. He tells his readers that almost all the cattle killing in Central Australia is done by blacks who were educated at the mission station. I emphatically deny this charge. He pictures in his book a 'Mission Jack', who, having been whipped by a white man, revenges himself by breaking the white man's leg with a boomerang. Not content with this act of vengeance, he causes the death of the 'boss' of his fictional Marnoola Station, and commits other foul acts. His Jack is not a type of a mission boy, but of an incarnated devil. The law of the Aborigines is the *jus talionis*. A blackfellow will remember for years a wrong done to him, but when he has avenged himself once, especially if he has seen a little blood of his offender, he is satisfied. Our station blacks do not kill cattle, on the contrary they have aided us in capturing the culprits. Most whites call all blacks coming from the north-west division of the Aranda and Loritja tribes 'mission blacks', even if they have never been in the service of the mission; and all evil doing is attributed to them. But how can one know which is a real mission boy? There is a simple discrimination. If there come some Toms and Jacks and Jims from the north-west, they are not members of our congregation; but if there arrives an Aborigine bearing the name of a prophet or apostle — our blacks mostly choose biblical names at their baptismal — you may classify him as a mission boy, and if he does any wrong, we will investigate his crime. If the blacks really accept Christianity, the horrid diseases mentioned in Dr. H. Basedow's lectures will vanish too. By church discipline and homeopathic remedies (mercury) we have wiped out the venereal diseases among our station blacks. But you want great patience. The Aborigines are just like naughty children. They require a kind but firm treatment. If you really desire to do something for the remnant of the Aborigines, do not bring them rations and clothes only, do not teach them playing cards, and two-up, or to use foul language; but bring to those who have come into contact with their white brothers already, the medical aid which they require.

Geographers and Naturalists

Hans Hermann Behr, 'On the Aborigines of Adelaide Based on His Own Observations during His Stay There'

Hans Hermann Behr (1818–1904), born in Köthen in the Duchy of Anhalt-Cöthen, was a medically-trained botanist and entomologist. He spent two periods in South Australia. His first visit, reportedly made with the encouragement of mentors Karl Ritter and Alexander von Humboldt, was from September 1844 to October 1845, when he returned to Germany. He was back in Adelaide at the end of 1848 for a period of under a year, after which time he left for the Philippines and, later, San Francisco. By coincidence he made there the acquaintance of the German writer and traveller Friedrich Gerstäcker, who would soon voyage in the opposite direction across the Pacific to spend time in Australia. The two men were united in their love of travel and, it seems, in their politics. Both were 'Forty-eighters', that is, supporters of the liberal revolutions which brought the establishment of a short-lived liberal parliament in Frankfurt in the period 1848–1849.

On both his visits to South Australia, Behr's activities were centred on the Barossa Valley, but he travelled to other parts of the colony as well. His passion for botany is preserved in the native plant Behr's Pink Velvet Bush (Lasiopetalum behrii). His contribution to entomology was recognised by the Germanophile George French Angas, whom he would almost certainly have met on his first visit to South Australia. Angas named the Mistletoe Moth for Behr (Comocrus behri), and in his South Australia Illustrated *(1847) Angas noted the contribution of Behr to the recording of many new species.*

An Indigenous South

*While in Germany in 1847 between his visits to Australia, Behr gave two presentations to the Geographical Society of Berlin on the observations he had made of Indigenous South Australians during his collecting expeditions.**

Source:
'Über die Urbewohner von Adelaide in Süd-Australien nach eigenen Anschauungen während seines dortigen Aufenthalts, *Monatsberichte über die Verhandlungen der Gesellschaft für Erdkunde zu Berlin*, (9) 1848, 89–93. 'Über die äußern Verhältnisse, welche auf die Entwickelung der Australier eingewirkt haben', *Monatsberichte über die Verhandlungen der Gesellschaft für Erdkunde zu Berlin*, (9) 1848, 145–149
Translation: Harald and Aileen Ohlendorf.

Mr Hermann Behr spoke about the Aborigines of Adelaide in South Australia based on his own views during his stay there.

[*Hermann Behr from Köthen was present as guest.*]

If we compare the reports about all the peoples grouped together under the name savages, it turns out that, along with the Bushmen and some South American tribes, Australia's autochthonous people are at the lowest level of human development. It is striking that all these peoples inhabit the southern hemisphere, and our north has so far provided no example of analogous barbarism. To what extent the overall position in the world, the uniformity of the soil, the lack of structure in the southern continents and the associated impediments for these peoples in the exchange of ideas have held these tribes back in their development is beyond the scope of this lecture and is left to the broader intellect and the wider knowledge of others for discussion. I will confine myself to rescuing the much maligned Australian from the accusation of a complete incapacity for education, with a brutality that is comparable to that of animals, which has made the already

---

* *Further reading*: Allan Bretag, 'Hans Hermann Behr (1818–1904): botanist, anthropologist, humorist and dangerous?' *Papers and Proceedings of the Royal Society of Tasmania*, 150 (1), 2016, 24–27.

beginning decline of the Aborigines appear desirable and necessary in the eyes of many.

The tribes I observed during my stay in South Australia roam the area between Spencer Gulf and the lower Murray. Although strictly separated by dialect and tribal hatred, and although they differ in their customs and traditions, they all present the same, only slightly nuanced picture of aimless wandering, combined with ignorance of the first structures of incipient civilisation. The lawless group does not gather around any leader, no priest guides them through the customs sanctified by their ancestors. Just as one finds the same body forms and the same facial features everywhere, so their minds never rise above the level of tribal development. It is every man for himself. Common danger or a dark concept of religious duties immediately lead to united action; but no tribal name distinguishes tribes of the same dialect from neighbouring arch enemies. No hut, no tent marks the campsite of these tribes; a fence half the height of a man is the scanty protection against winter storms, dry branches and smouldering campfires are the only trace – soon obliterated – left by the savage wanderers.

As fleeting as the appearance of the tribes in the forest, so temporary is the memory of the individual in the tribe. The lamentation of the dead, the corroboree has faded away, and no song mourns the friend or lover, no legend recounts the heroic deeds of those who fell in combat. New Holland has no history, and if the country could speak instead of the natives, it would only reveal to us a chaos of hunger, misery, futile fighting and the commentary to *Schiller's* words:

> 'Woe to the stranger whom the waves
> have thrown on the beach of disaster!'

The Australian knows no yesterday, hopes for no tomorrow; what has been is in the past; what will be, not yet present. No hope, no aspiration attaches the present to the future; neither longing nor remorse links him to the past. No ghost with a gaping mortal wound frightens the murderer out of his deliberately summoned sleep. There is no right and wrong, and apart from the instinctive drive of the moment, there is no driving force for action.

An Indigenous South

I met a savage at the Cambunga Lagoon who betrayed his companion, who had been prosecuted for murder, to the policeman stationed in Murondee for the sake of a horse blanket, and who knew full well that in doing so he was handing his friend over to the gallows. The traitor was neither ashamed nor proud of his act; the other members of the tribe did not show in their behaviour that they found anything unnatural in this action.

All the endeavours of the Australian are apparently aimed only at satisfying basic needs, and it is only by concentrated listening that the related string sounds in the native's mind; only the most unbiased research can detect the dormant seeds of human development.

It has been said of the Australian that he is devoid of any religious concept. Only a mind which is completely ossified in its innate understanding of religion could misjudge the forms in which the native has cloaked the notion of transcendence. The Australian believes in a higher being and immortality. The fact that his ideas are vague, unclear and often unworthy is not unexpected in the imagination of such people, which is rooted in the material world. The tribes of the Murray Estuary believe that the rainbow is a direct creation of the supreme being, but they have a very obscene idea of the way it is produced, which they cannot have received from the Europeans, since their language provides the most irrefutable proof that this idea originated from a primitive viewpoint.

On clear nights at the time of the full moon, the colonist often hears strange, wild discords, chords which change according to a certain rhythm and sometimes swell to wild howling, sometimes descend to deep moans. Even from a distance he perceives a demonic throng of black figures silhouetted against the blazing campfire. The newcomer would be frightened by the natives' war paint, the apparent excitement amongst the tribe; the colonist calmly says: 'That's the corroboree;' and someone who is reasonably familiar with the natives' customs sees with heightened interest the wild groups which, as he knows, unite and separate for religious purposes. Separated from the men, the women crouch by the fire and accompany the men's dance with fervent shouting, the rhythm of which is given by the beating of two sticks. Armed with shield and spear, disfigured by bizarre body paint, the men begin the dance after each break in quiet, picturesque positions. But as the frenzied harmonies swell, the spears are swung more wildly, their poses become more lively and grotesque in rapid succession, until finally all the men of the tribe, with rigid upper bodies but with their knees moving violently, almost vibrating, form a weird row of barely human figures.

Throughout this strange ceremony, modified according to the purpose of each event, the seeds of religious feeling fight their way to consciousness. In some cases, the corroboree has merely the meaning of a funeral ceremony. Its regular return with the phases of the moon, however, points to something more general. The answer, albeit obscure, of a native, whom I asked about the purpose of the dance, proves, if I have interpreted it correctly, the belief in a higher being, a world creator and sustainer. In broken English, often distorted by Australian words, the native explained, to some extent with lively gestures, that the corroboree is celebrated for the branches of the trees, the water of the creeks, the game of the forest, for the sun, the moon and everything around. From this answer it is evident that the corroboree is a ceremony of thanksgiving and dependency, thus a religious service.

The belief in immortality manifests itself in the native's strange idea that he will become a white man after his death. I do not wish to decide whether a dark foreboding, a premonition that the black tribe will one day be displaced by the white tribe, has been propagated through generations and is expressed in this vague form, or whether the original belief in immortality has been modified by the sight of the more highly gifted, yet human-shaped strangers; but I am convinced for several reasons that this belief has not been instilled in the natives either through attempts at conversion or through the exchange of ideas. The word *Grinkari* in the dialect of Encounter Bay means a deceased person and a European, and the transfer of the word from the original concept to the new invading race proves that an original idea of survival in human form existed. It is also certain that the Autochthone initially saw in the Europeans the souls of his ancestors and that only their often very human behaviour destroyed this advantageous delusion. I could also mention here the evil spirits that in the imagination of the natives populate the local forests, how they crouch on the trees at night and throw invisible spears at passers-by, who, if not protected by fire, languish and die; the satyr-like ghost that steals young girls in the Murray scrub and other figments of the imagination that reveal little knowledge, but a well-developed imagination. A more striking proof of the seeds that lie dormant in these people is found in their languages. The idioms of these savages may often lack words for the most obvious abstracts and may in fact lack all the specific numerals; yet the rich declension, which, as far as I have been able to perceive, disdains agglutination and designates the categories of words by real inflection, provides the verb. Although the verb does not include the person in its form, it is already clearly separated from the other parts of speech and designates the finest nuances of voice by a large number of expressive inflections; all this proves how alive and tactful the power of language formation, this purely human faculty, functions in the savage hordes.

I could quote many other things here, accurate answers, unexpected flashes of inspiration, traits of deep and true feeling, which break like stars through the clouds of deep barbarism and brutish dullness. But these observations would seem to prove sufficiently that only millennia of misery have held these tribes back in their development, and that patient and above all unprejudiced effort can kindle the weak spark of knowledge and restore the half-withered branch to the tree of mankind.

Part 2.
'On the External Circumstances That Have Influenced the Development of the Australians'

On a previous occasion I had the honour of giving a lecture here on the condition and activities of the Australian natives; I have now set myself the task of discussing the extent to which certain conditions have influenced the development of the Australians. The neglected state of the race is in fact caused by unfavourable external circumstances, not by internal ones, rooted in the Australian's own character.

If we go back in history to the beginnings of human civilisation as we know them, we find that wherever the human race has reached a new level, where the old world of ideas has been enriched and expanded, an intimate integration of different races has preceded, so that the latent sparks of the intellect have been released only by the clash of different elements. The development of the nation, as well as that of the individual, has its limits; when these limits are reached, intellectual activity wanders aimlessly on the ground already fought for; the vision is limited by a horizon which only begins to unfold when a new higher viewpoint is reached. But the development of the human race as a whole is unlimited, it is an eternal rushing forward, in which an apparent regression is simply the path to new peaks. To give you some examples: the Persian Wars, the Great Migration, the Crusades, as well as the myths of all ancient religions, according to which the state of civilisation always develops from a battle of giants against Olympus, of giants against the Aesir, in short, of the indigenous against immigrants.

Australia had never known such mentally stimulating processes until the arrival of the Europeans. The tribes of the natives are all of the same ancestry; mind and body of the most distant tribes are still so alike that from mutual interaction the same, the old state, would always emerge. Malays and Chinese, who have been attracted to the north coast of the continent for years to catch trepang, remained without influence, as their presence was only very temporary. They even carefully avoided any encounter with the uncivilised Australian, and if they did encounter him, it only caused mayhem and murder.

One could mention here the eastern neighbours of the New Hollanders, the oceanic peoples of the Malay race, as an example that even when strictly isolated from other peoples, development was possible to a certain degree. These natives, however, obviously are immigrants just as the Australian negro is indigenous. Their languages clearly reveal their relationship with the idioms of the Indian archipelago, whose original culture, not yet suppressed by Brahmins and Arabs, found asylum in those remote isles. In Batavia I was shown an undeniably Japanese idol whose expression differed from those of its Brahmin neighbours and was very close to the graven images of the New Zealanders, from which, in truth, it differed only in its material, not in its design. It was made of stone, unlike those of the New Zealanders, which are always made of wood; but whoever has seen the wonderful grotesque facial images, decorated with the ever-recurring spiral in new combinations, cannot doubt that the peoples of Oceania and the Indian archipelago were originally united. We do not even have legends about the Germanic prehistoric times; but we can clearly recognise this much: the tribes migrating to the east from the west to their present home brought the ideas of a certain cultural background, to which they probably added little, but from which they lost a great deal.

The situation is different with New Holland. I don't know a single word of an indigenous language that could be traced back to a Malay language or that only hinted at it. Even if some points of contact with certain Malay idioms can be found in the sound system, this is in any case purely coincidental or a peculiarity of underdeveloped articulation, which is by no means limited to these two language families and for which there are analogies in Chinese and in some American languages. The structure of the languages is completely different. It would go too far to go into the details of the two grammatical systems here. Let me just remind you that the Malay idioms, perhaps the most inflexible in the world apart from the monosyllabic languages of East Asia, indicate the categories of words by position, addition of infixes or carefully separated particles, whereas the Australian ones agglutinate and inflect so that in some respects they are not so far removed from the Indo-European language structure. Moreover, at least the more sophisticated Malay languages, like the Semitic languages, contain almost exclusively two-syllable word stems, whereas the Australian idioms, like most other languages of the world, show a very definite preference for monosyllabic root forms.

Even if the Australian languages, as far as we know them, agree in the essential points of grammatical structure, the material, like that of the American languages, is divided into so many independent idioms that one must assume that grammatical agreement is only the result of the way of thinking which is expressed in the same way everywhere. The oceanic languages, on the other hand – and let us take those at the most distant points – always agree in the greater part of the roots and can often only be considered as dialects. But the diversity and limited distribution of the languages is certainly peculiar to the Autochthones, and the spread of a language family indicates either common descent from an ancient people or foreign influence.

We have never yet received any news of an Australian concept which would indicate descent from another country or foreign influence, and may, with the same right, see in the natives the Hindu, Malay or Mongolian people just as the English sectarians believe to recognise in them the lost tribes of Israel.

But let us suppose that some descendant of Noah had settled on the inhospitable coast. This assumption does not, in the end, change anything at all for what has to be proved, namely that the Australian was only hindered in his development by external circumstances. Such an immigrant could not possibly have brought with him a high degree of culture, because some monument would have to have given evidence of this long ago, even if only in the example of the Nordic megalithic graves and stone circles. But this is not the case.

Now the fewer resources culture provides to man, the more

dependent he is on the land he inhabits, the more he himself is a result of his country. Let us therefore draw a new parallel between the vaunted islanders and the despised continental dweller.

The oceanic archipelagos with their richly irrigated fertile valleys, overgrown with vegetation that voluntarily distributes its treasures into the lap of man, under the canopy of a mild sky, surrounded by a calm ocean: they invited agriculture and navigation of their own accord. The dense population created by the abundance, concentrated in a relatively small area due to the small size of the isles, itself determined the exchange of ideas, constitution, and religious systems, while in the barren, arid New Holland, which originally did not anywhere produce a fruit worth cultivating, an animal worthy of taming, which by virtue of its size allowed and encouraged the scattering of the inhabitants, even necessitated it because of its poverty.

According to the natural course of events, those uncivilised, nomadic tribes of hunters, split into a multitude of small groups, had to evolve, and they still roam the inhospitable wasteland, or as beggars, unwillingly tolerated and intrusive, they are pushed around among a population that is more highly developed and creates from within the means of a happy existence.

Certainly, no culture could develop among a people whose every effort must be directed to the satisfaction of the basic needs, to the most necessary conditions of a life which has its own end in itself; all energy is exhausted in the arduous and perilous struggle to wrest a meagre existence, by crude and inadequate means, from an environment hostile to mankind from the outset.

The simple conditions of Australia, not clouded by any historical storms, allow, especially in this case, a clear view and show how much man is the child of the surrounding environment. The character of the natives can be deduced from the features of the land they inhabit; that of the settler, on the other hand, is the product of a historical process whose beginnings vanish in the darkness of prehistoric times. From the far west, Indo-Germanic civilisation moved to the coast, untouched by a ploughshare and which the Hindu, the easternmost branch of the same tribe, probably never set foot on. The Celto-Teuton, having originated in the east, returns beyond his homeland and reaches out to the far south, in the midst of a race not yet touched by any historical ferment, to his fellow tribesmen who have advanced from the west.

Wilhelm von Blandowski, 'On the Aborigines of Australia'

Johann Wilhelm Theodor von Blandowski – when in Australia simply William Blandowski – was born in Gleiwitz in Prussia (today's Gliwice in Poland) in 1822. He was educated at the University of Berlin. When he travelled to Australia in 1849, his aim was to study the continent's natural history.

After his arrival in Adelaide in September 1849 he made a number of expeditions within the colony, heading as far east as the Murray River and as far south as the Coorong, Guichen Bay and on to Mt Gambier. The discovery of gold in Victoria proved a diversion, with the result that for a time he worked on the goldfields before returning to his original scientific goals.

Appointed to the post of government zoologist in Victoria, he undertook three expeditions to various parts of that colony. The last of those expeditions, to the region of the junction of the Darling and Murray Rivers, included a fellow German naturalist in Gerard Krefft, who left a valuable artistic record of some 500 drawings.

By temperament Blandowski appears to have been given to fractious and stubborn behaviour. His last two years in Melbourne were marked by a number of disputes with colleagues and the government. In 1859 Blandowski returned to Berlin and then Gleiwitz, where he took up the profession of photographer, but his attempts to publish his work on Australia were largely unsuccessful. The exception was the production in 1862, at Blandowski's own expense, of his encyclopaedic Australien in

142 photographischen Abbildungen nach zehnjährigen Erfahrungen.

Blandowski was admitted to a mental asylum in 1873 and died there in 1878. The article below is not from his self-published encyclopaedia but derives from a presentation he delivered to a natural science society in Dresden in 1861, two years after his return to Germany. While his travels to many parts of the colonies of South Australia and Victoria had exposed him to a wide variety of communities, he affirmed that in his view the Australians were of the same type – he used the English word 'race' – all over the continent, with just minor regional variations.*

Source:
Wilhelm von Blandowski, 'Ueber die Ureinwohner Australiens: Nach dem von Herrn von Blandowski in der Isis am 4. Oktober gehaltenen Vortrage', *Sitzungsberichte der naturwissenschaftlichen Gesellschaft Isis zu Dresden* (Dresden: Rudolf Kuntze, 1862), 101– 110.
Translation: Harald and Aileen Ohlendorf.

[…]

Mr *v. Blandowski* now turned to the main part of his lecture, the description of the natives.

Physically, they are a lightly built race with very curved, strong chests, strong, black, shaggy beard and hair growth, and have well-developed muscular strength. The legs are slender. They seldom attain old age, because, often suffering from emaciation, they generally ruin themselves before they reach the age of forty. Blood vengeance and other passions are the destructive elements. Civilisation has promoted the process of destruction. Tribes of 3–600 people, which *Bl.* encountered at the Darling in 1849, had dwindled to no more than 100 heads by 1857. Then Mr *Bl.* showed several illustrations with characteristic heads. Various characteristics of men and women, youth and age were depicted, even a woman with a grey beard. They are of a

---

* *Further reading:* Harry Allen (ed.), *Australia: William Blandowski's Illustrated Encyclopaedia of Aboriginal Australia*, Canberra, Aboriginal Studies Press, 2010; L.K. Paszkowski, 'Blandowski, William (1822–1878)', *Australian Dictionary of Biography*, National Centre of Biography, Australian National University, https://adb.anu.edu.au/biography/blandowski-william-3014/text4413, published first in hardcopy 1969, accessed online 4 March 2022.

chocolate-brown colour and always heavily tattooed. There is a deeper meaning to this than mere adornment. Since both men and women are painted, it serves as an identifying mark of the tribe, even if the individual's markings vary. The women never belong to the same tribe where they are found, because they are usually stolen or exchanged.

Their lives. They never provide for the following day, and therefore the lack of food often forces them to eat nothing but roots and resin for days. Only one exception has been known to *Bl.* and that is on the Darling River, where Australians harvest fruit seeds of Panicum and store them in animal skins. To do this, they skin the possum species through the mouth so as not to tear the bags made in this way. They use two methods to produce fire, both requiring a soft and a hard type of wood. In the one method, a piece of hard wood is laid on the ground, and a stick is put vertically in a hole in the wood and turned rapidly between the palms of the hands like a whisk. When one man tires, another immediately replaces him. The second method consists of inserting a piece of bast into the crack of a fallen tree trunk and moving it back and forth quickly with a stick in a sawing motion. In both ways they achieve their purpose in no more than 5 minutes.

In order to get water in the deserts, they tear out the roots of a reddish and shiny-looking eucalyptus dumosa species, peel off the bark in long strips and place the two-foot-long rootstocks upright next to each other on a gutter below. The sap drips into this and flows into a small trough at the end of the channel.

There are many methods for **fishing**. The women go into the flooded areas and, damming the narrow arms of the river except for a small opening, set up their nets. In order to ward off the influences of the evil spirit that might spoil the catch, one of the fisherwomen swings a flat piece of wood on a rope, which by its whirling motion makes a howling sound, which is further intensified by the screaming of the women. The men sail the rivers at night in the frailest bark boats and, in the light of their torches, spear the sleeping fish with their long spears, even at a considerable depth. These boats are made of the bark of various eucalyptus species, which is removed from the trees and held open only by thin sticks and are put on the water without any further work. However, they are so frail that a European could easily sink them with his heavy tread, while the more cautious, light-footed natives dare to put even eight or ten of them with all their belongings on a single vehicle to cross the rivers. The method of catching sea fish is different. At low tide they go 3–4' deep into the water and remain motionless in this position for several hours until they have killed their prey with a spear.

Their method of **catching birds** is unique. The hunter covers his head and chest with a thick wad of bushes and foliage and slowly approaches the bird with a noose on a long rod in his hand until he can pull the noose over its head. They are inventive in hunting ducks. They stretch a wet net vertically between two trees above the water and drive the ducks towards it. Once near the net, one of them throws a piece of bark among the birds, imitating the sound of an eagle. The frightened birds beat their wings frantically, rob themselves of the possibility of an easy upswing because of their wet wings, and are easily caught under the falling net and pulled to the shore.

Their daily food, however, is the opossum. Their pelts are sometimes pulled off the animals, stretched on a piece of bark, dried on the fire and thus made into blankets, while the meat, placed on glowing coals, is devoured after only 10 minutes.

Other types of rats, which build themselves substantial houses of brushwood, are caught by surrounding the nests closely with nets, then tearing open the burrow and killing the animals as they escape.

Catching wombats is, however, more difficult, but it also shows the admirable perseverance of the natives. The animal, whose meat is considered a special delicacy, digs horizontal burrows in the earth's walls. A shaft, sometimes 40' deep, is dug into the furthest corner of the burrow with the help of very crude tools. But if the animal has heard the noise and the knocking above it and digs itself deeper, the effort in digging the first shaft has been in vain. A second, even a third shaft is dug, until finally the desire of the hunters defeats the eagerness of the hunted and ever deeper burrowing animal, and the animal is caught by the rejoicing pursuers.

Kangaroo hunting is associated with special dangers. The animal can take on a pack of dogs, even humans have to watch out; it wraps itself around its enemy and tears open its abdomen with its hind feet or jumps with it to the nearest river and kills it by dragging it under. They are rarely seen in herds. When an animal has been killed, it is thrown with its skin and hair onto a pile of hot stones that have been heated for 10 to 12 hours. Other hot stones are placed on top.

After half an hour the roast is already pleasing to their palate and the cutting or better the tearing begins: So much for hunting practices.

The speaker then described the weapon dances and their weapons and warfare.

Their dances differ essentially from those of the Europeans, are performed only by men and have the purpose of displaying their muscular strength; certain moves are applauded by the women. These sit in a circle around the dancers and make music by beating the rhythm on their rolled-up blankets. When the men dance with their weapons, their stances are usually declarations of war. Their main weapon is a 3' long pointed stick for striking, while their throwing weapons include the spear and boomerang. The latter consists of a slightly curved piece of wood, which, bent in a specific way, with a cutting edge on both sides, is flung towards the enemy in a swinging motion, so that it almost touches the ground after the first third of the flight, then lifts up again, hits the enemy and, rising in flight, returns to its starting position in a high arc landing at the feet of the thrower. The weapon performs a series of arcs during its whirling flight. To increase the spear's momentum, they use a piece of wood that significantly lengthens the arm's leverage. This artificial lever, a 2–3' long flat stick on which the spear rests, has a hook on one side, which is turned backwards when throwing, and which fits into a recess at the base of the actual throwing weapon. The spear is lifted horizontally with its base over the shoulder, the end of the lever is grasped with three fingers and at the same time the spear resting on it is grasped with the index finger, and then, during the throw, as the arm swings forward from behind, the lightly grasped weapon is released, while the lever is kept in the thrower's hand. The force of the swing becomes so significant that the projectile can completely pierce the opponent's body. With the help of this compound weapon, they can even hit a duck at a distance of 80 paces with accuracy.

They have small shields of bark, which are narrow, about the length of an arm, tapering on either side.

When it comes to fighting, their weapons are first laid in glowing embers, straightened, smoothed, rubbed with fat and studded on top with pieces of glass or shards. Since the resin in which these shards are stuck softens in the wound, they remain in the body even if the spear is removed, and always make the injury fatal. Before they begin the fight, they perform athletic exercises. They rub their naked bodies with fat so that, like slippery eels, they make it difficult for the enemy to attack them and hold on firmly in the wrestling match. Then one of them steps forward and challenges the strongest man of the other party to single combat. Once a competitor has been chosen, they approach each other cautiously, finally grab each other under the arms, bend their upper bodies down horizontally against each other until they reach the ground with their hands to rub the opponent's neck with sand and dust in order to be able to grip him better.

A game, 'the emu feather', follows these exercises. A man holds up a bunch of feathers and challenges anyone to snatch it from him. The first man approaches from the enemy side, a second man from the friendly side to support the feather bearer, and the wrestling becomes more energetic. The wrestlers stream in from both sides, competing with each other, until a densely packed, lively, undulating mass of bodies forms. In this crowd, there are many who faint, who are then dragged to the side by the women who revive the men by sprinkling them with water. The quarrel sometimes becomes so violent that men in the centre of the tangle are crushed and suffocated under the enormous pressure of bodies.

After these exercises, quarrels arise between the women. The most beautiful one steps forward, dances and sings and then asks: Who on your side is as beautiful as I am; which of you can dance and sing as well as I can? Then the Venus of the other party steps forward and a lively argument ensues. The one who is better with words than the other picks up dust and throws it at the other with the words: You are not worthy of the dust that I throw at you. The other retaliates and now a mutual fight begins. The men take up arms, the partners of the two women come forward out of the ranks. The offended party remains quietly in a challenging and kneeling position, allowing the opponent to come within a step towards him, and then the duel begins, which is fought with great bitterness until one of the two sinks down wounded. This is the signal for a general fight. The wounded and the dead are received by the women with melancholy songs. Finally, peace is made: a boy is then adorned with leaves, sent forward and calls out: Let us make peace, we have always wanted it. If the other party has accepted the peace, they welcome the boy into their group for 3–4 months, while the men fix the terms of peace. Then the individual families separate from the main tribes and seek their livelihood on their lands.

They love polygamy, but it is rare, as the men can usually support only one wife. Herr v. Bl. met only a few respected people with four to five wives. Other motives for taking more than one wife can be seen in the following characteristic behaviour. A native had only one wife when he first met Herr v. Bl., later he had two wives. When the traveller asked him why he now had two wives, he replied: One cooks very well and the other one sings very beautifully.

On their wanderings they swim across the smaller rivers, placing their children and luggage on pieces of bark and pushing them in front of them.

[*Here follows a description of initiation practices.*]

Their religious concepts do not go beyond the sensory; they believe in the spirits (*uri*) of fire, water, air and earth, all of which are hostile to them.

Their priests or doctors, who declare all diseases to be influences of the water spirit, expose the patient to smoke and steam. Then they light a fire, cover the embers with water plants and also cover the head of the sick person with bushes and leaves in order to expose him to the heat and smoke while standing with his body bent forward until the frightened evil spirit withdraws.

But if the spirit persists and the sick person succumbs to his suffering, the dead person is laid on a stretcher. The doctor sits underneath and asks: What was the cause of his death? If any sound is heard which bears the slightest resemblance to the name of a person present, the prophet seizes his weapon, goes after the unfortunate person and slays him. The brother becomes the heir of the deceased, i.e. he inherits his wives who come forward. All movable property, however, especially the weapons, follow the dead man into the grave. The corpse is stretched on a wooden frame under a leaf hut erected on the spot, rubbed with ochre and fat and smoked under a constant mild fire until it becomes mummified. In some regions the body is also wrapped in bast and burnt. Or it is placed on a scaffold and exposed to the sun until the fat drips down. Then the nearest relative has to put him on his back and the whole tribe follows him. They move through the bushes until they come to an open space. Here they quickly dig 20–30 holes. They throw the corpse into one of them and cover all the holes with earth in all haste, so that the devil, who, of course, does not know in which hole it is, will not find it.

But the burial customs differ. On the Murray River, the bodies are put into boats, taken to the most beautiful areas and buried in holes without further ceremony. On the Darling, the dead body is placed on a bier and before the burial proceeds, the leader makes a speech. The body is covered with wood to keep dingoes away.

The women mourn for a long time, cutting and scratching their chests and faces, singeing off their hair and rubbing their faces and heads with charcoal, plaster or ochre, which they do not wash off until the wounds heal, or wear 10-pound turbans of gypsum, but not all day, only temporarily. In other places, as on the Loddon River, they erect shield-like monuments. The graves are examined every day until an animal track appears or until the wind blows the sand to one side. The closest heir, armed with a weapon, goes in the direction of the animal track or in which the wind has blown the sand until he meets a man, whom he kills with his spear to avenge the dead man.

When a fisherman dies, his net is stretched out over his grave. Huts of bark are also built over the graves. Or sticks are driven into the ground in a vertical circle around the grave and a hut is made of leaves; as long as the mourning widow puts a green branch into it every day, no suitor may approach her. Or conical mounds are made of earth and wood is laid on top. On the graves of outstanding warriors, their weapons are erected in the soft earth. When the first falls down, the relative goes in the direction shown by the weapon and seeks to take blood revenge on the guilty party. Other grave sites are very similar to ours. The significance of the winding passages leading between the individual graves, however, was not clear to v. Blandowsky. Indeed, even mausoleums of skulls are erected, as for example at Cape York.

But the dead are not completely forgotten. During certain festivities one can even have a conversation with them. On quiet nights, the tribesmen gather around a thick tree, among whose branches one of them is hiding. They ask him questions about the dead, but no name must be mentioned. The more accurate the answers, which reveal knowledge of the dead person from hints of special idiosyncrasies and predilections, the greater the applause of the tribesmen.

The Australians reveal the same physical characteristics, the same customs, the same weapons throughout the whole continent, and the latter only differ somewhat in form, and we are undoubtedly only dealing with a race that stands isolated and passes down ancient customs to the present, compared to which those of the four Vedas of the Hindus appear as modern products.

Charles Wilhelmi, 'Manners and Customs of the Port Lincoln Natives in Australia'

Johann Friedrich Carl Wilhelmi, known in Australia as Charles Wilhelmi, was born in Leipzig in 1827. The son of a horticulturist, he became an apprentice gardener before travelling to Adelaide aboard the vessel Godeffroy, arriving on 1 March 1849.

One of three German gardeners on the Godeffroy, the main purpose of his travels was probably to gather plants for collectors in Germany. Very early in his stay in Adelaide he encountered and made the acquaintance of a fellow German in Dr Ferdinand Müller. Müller would later become director of the Royal Botanic Gardens of Victoria and receive a knighthood due to his contribution to science in Australia, but when he met Wilhelmi he had been in South Australia just over a year, acquired property in the Bugle Ranges south-east of Adelaide, and become an avid plant collector. It appears that Müller employed the freshly-arrived Wilhelmi as a plant collector, or at least Müller purchased plants from Wilhelmi.

That activity brought Wilhelmi into contact with Indigenous people, initially during travels to the Murray and Lower Murray in 1849 and again in the summer of 1850/51.

More influential in facilitating Wilhelmi's ethnographic interest was Pastor Clamor Wilhelm Schürmann. When Schürmann was Court Interpreter for the Barngarla people and teacher for their children on Eyre Peninsula, Wilhelmi undertook a collecting expedition to the area and stayed for a time with Schürmann at his home and school in

Wallala north of Port Lincoln. Wilhelmi must have had some earlier contact with Schürmann's missionary colleague Eduard Meyer, because Meyer had written to Schürmann before Wilhelmi's visit at the beginning of 1852, explaining, 'Dr Mueller has not come here, but in his place a young Leipziger by name of Wilhelmi, gardener and botanist, who brought me your letter of introduction as an inclusion in a letter from Dr Mueller. He is a modest nice young man, and very diligent in collecting.' It appears that Wilhelmi visited Schürmann on the Eyre Peninsula at least twice in 1852 and then made a further visit in late 1854; he also trekked to Mount Gambier in the colony's south-east in the same year.

Wilhelmi followed Mueller to Melbourne in 1855 and as Assistant Government Botanist travelled extensively in Victoria. His employment in Victoria concluded at the end of 1868, at which time he and his family (he had married in 1858) returned to Germany and settled in Dresden. There Wilhelmi became a member of the 'Naturwissenschaftliche Gesellschaft ISIS', contributing his vast botanical knowledge of Australia on numerous occasions. He died in 1884.

Wilhelmi's ethnographic observations were read to the Royal Society of Victoria in October 1860 and published both in the Society's Transactions and, as a 43-page booklet, Manners and Customs of the Australian Natives. The following article, appearing in translation for the first time, was first published in 1870 in Aus allen Welttheilen: Illustrirtes Familienblatt für Länder- und Völkerkunde. In large part it closely follows the earlier English publication and has a similarly heavy emphasis on observations made on the Eyre Peninsula, supplemented by Wilhelmi's earlier observations made in Adelaide and along the Murray. In both publications it is clear that for his understanding of the people of the West Coast, Wilhelmi was deeply indebted to Schürmann, who benefitted from a sustained presence in the region and an ability to communicate with people in their own language.*

---

* *Further reading*: Phillip A Clarke, *Aboriginal Plant Collectors: Botanists and Australian Aboriginal People in the Nineteenth Century*, Dural, Rosenberg, 2008; Carl Wilhelmi, 'My Journeys in South Australia: Lecture by Carl Wilhelmi 14 September 1857. Translated and introduced by Thomas A Darragh', *Journal of Friends of Lutheran Archives*, 10 (2003), 5–24.

Charles Wilhelmi

Source:
Charles Wilhelmi, 'Sitten und Gebräuche der Port-Lincoln Eingeborenen in Australien', *Aus allen Welttheilen: Illustrirtes Familienblatt für Länder-und Völkerkunde*, 1 (1870), 113–117, 121–123, 134–136, 151–152.
Translation: Peter Monteath.

Although Australia, for a considerable time already, is known to the world in general, very little, comparatively speaking, has as yet been written and published respecting the habits and customs of its original inhabitants.

My various botanical journeys since 1849 have necessarily brought me in frequent contact with them, when it always has been most interesting to me closely to observe their manners and customs. In particular, during my two visits to Port Lincoln I have had many opportunities for making observations respecting the natives there, which were the more interesting, as these people, at that time, had as yet been so little interfered with by civilisation.

For highly interesting communications I am indebted to the Rev. Mr. Schürmann, who in September 1840 was engaged as the Protector of the Natives in Port Lincoln, went as missionary to Adelaide and Encounter Bay in 1846 and some years later returned to Port Lincoln to his former position. Entirely fluent in the language, he was able to obtain full information about the life and activities of the tribes living there.

During my stay with him in 1851, twenty-four native children attended his school, and had then made pretty considerable progress in reading, writing, etc., which was rendered the easier to them by the advantage that all information was conveyed to them in their own language by this most excellent man.

It has been remarked that the population and general condition of the natives of Australia greatly depend on the nature of the locality they occupy; where the country is sterile and unproductive, the natives are found to congregate in small numbers, and to be in a miserable condition; while, on the contrary, in fertile districts they are comparatively numerous, robust, and well made. The correctness of this observation must have been apparent to everyone who has had the opportunity of comparing the natives of Port Lincoln with those of the Adelaide and the Murray districts in particular. The former are fewer in number, of smaller size, weaker, and less expert, and not of so sociable a disposition as the latter. A Port Lincoln black but very rarely exceeds the height of a middle-sized European, and in reference to bodily strength the comparison is more unfavourable still. Among the Murray tribes, on the contrary, you will find handsome, tall, and well-made men.

Striking peculiarities in the appearance of their body are their thin arms and legs, wide mouths, hollow deep sunken eyes, and flat noses; if the latter are not normally so formed, they make them so by forcing a bone, a piece of wood, or anything else through the sides of the nose, which causes them to stretch. They generally have a well-arched front, broad shoulders, and a particularly high chest. The men possess a great deal of natural grace in the carriage of their body, their gait is easy and erect, their gestures are natural under all circumstances in their dances, their fights, and while speaking, and they certainly surpass the European in ease and rapidity of their movements.

With respect to the women we cannot speak so favourably by a great deal; their bodies are generally disfigured by thin arms and legs, large bellies, and low hanging breasts, a condition sufficiently accounted for by their early marriages, their insufficient nourishment, their carrying of heavy burdens, and the length of time they suckle their children, for it is by no means uncommon for children to take the breast for three or four years, or even longer.

Although a superficial observer will scarcely be able, on account of the apparently great similarity prevailing among them, to detect any difference in them, a closer intimacy with them will easily trace very considerable varieties, not of countenances and forms of body only, but also of colours and skins even.

While the tribes of the north, which inhabit a rather scrubby country, possess a darker and drier skin colour, that of the tribes of the south and the westward, in many instances, approaches what is termed the copper colour. Whether this is attributable to the influence of the climate or the difference of the food, it is difficult to decide. Schürmann believes that upon the whole the best fed and most robust natives are of the lighter colours. In reference to this subject, the African traveller Livingstone makes the following observation in his work, that heat alone does not produce blackness, but heat with moisture seems to bring forth the deepest hue.

The covering they generally wear consists of one or two kangaroo skins only, and seldom of rugs made of skins of the wallaby, possum, and similar animals, and which for this purpose are prepared in the following manner. The skin, directly after being flayed, is spread, the flesh side upwards, on an even piece of ground, and fastened by small wooden pegs, driven in along the ridges. When dried the small fleshy fibres adhering to the skins are scraped off with a sharp angular piece of quartz, and afterwards the skins are well rubbed over with a coarse-grained stone, for the purpose of making them soft and pliable. Thus prepared, the skins are then sewed together with the sinews of the tail of the kangaroo, a small sharp-pointed bone answering admirably for the purpose. As these skins are never tanned, the natives are required to be very careful in guarding the flesh side against the wet, as it would make them hard and stiff; on this account it is that during the rain the hairy side is turned outside.

The best rugs generally belong to the women, and more particularly so if they have young children, as they make them serve for covering both of them, while they carry them on their backs, or while resting they have them on their laps. Those children old enough to walk are decidedly the worst off as regards covering, for they have to run about quite naked, or be satisfied with the remnant of some old used-up rug. Usually the women carry their children on their backs by firmly tying the corners of the possum rug on their breast, while the net or grass braid which they have permanently hanging from them to carry all sorts of things ensures that the child does not fall out the bottom. Other tribes have only grass braids in which to carry their little ones, while still others carry them on their shoulders. If they trek across tree-less plains, they take wood with them in their baskets, and to provide the weary work of making fire by rubbing two sticks together, they take a fire-stick with them as their constant companion.

More ornament than for any imaginable comfort, the men wear a band of yarn round their heads, tying it round several times, so as to leave the crown only uncovered by it. They spin this yarn of human hair, or that of the possum, using for the purpose a kind of spindle, about two feet long, and not thicker than a goose quill, with a cross piece at one end, on which they wind up the yarn spun. They turn or roll this spindle on their legs, with their hands spread out flat.

The Murray tribes, in the neighbourhood of Swan Hill, in a similar way spin the fibres of the roots of the club rushes (*Typha Shuttleworthii*) growing in rivers and ponds to any lengths and employ it for making their nets. Those who wish to appear particularly polished add to the decoration a tuft of emu feathers which they insert into the hair above the brow. Now that they have learned to smoke from the Europeans, a small clay pipe is also woven in.

On occasions of rejoicings and of ceremonies, as, for instance, at the meeting of two different tribes, they add two small pieces of green wood, decorated from one end to the other with very thin shavings, and which have the appearance of a white plume of feathers, and these they stick behind their ears through the above-mentioned band, in such a manner that the upper ends can be joined in front, and thus, at a distance, they have the appearance of two long horns. Schürmann has seen this latter ornament only with one tribe of the north-west, and it may perhaps be confined to it. This ornament, together with their white and red painted chest and arms, is said to produce quite the impression of savageness.

Frequently they attach to the end of their pointed beards the tip of the tail of a wild dog, or a wallaby. They also wind the entire length of a wild dog's tail around their head and forehead; this is regarded primarily as a significant adornment. The natives who come in frequent contact with Europeans, instead of the latter ornament, make use of a rag of white or red cloth, or else of even a piece of paper.

The men always wear round the waist a cord, generally made of their own hair, being first spun, and then twisted into a cord of about a quarter of an inch thick, and which at times is interwoven with emu feathers. If they cannot have one of this description, they will take any kind of cord rather than do without one altogether. They always wear it tight, but tighter if hungry, as they say, in order to allay the painful sensation of hunger.

The means which the natives, both males and females, mostly use and prefer to all others for beautifying themselves, is fat; if well supplied, they rub their entire body over with it; but short of it, they confine themselves to anointing their faces only. This custom has its origin in some sound reasonable motive, as this anointing produces with them a feeling of comfort, in hot weather particularly, and when the mosquitos and flies are exceedingly troublesome.

They will ask for a little fat as pitifully as for a piece of bread. They compare this custom to that of Europeans washing themselves; they never appear in better humour than when the fat is actually dripping from the entire body, from head to foot. The colours with which they paint themselves are black, white and red. The black and red colours are the produce of a soft stone which they draw from a great distance in the north; by rubbing or scraping it they obtain a powder, which they rub into the fat which they have before put on their faces, arms, and breasts; the colours then assume quite a metallic lustre. The white colour is prepared of a soft clay or chalk. It is applied on particular occasions only, among others for dancing, and when in mourning. For indicating mourning, the women paint their whole front, a ring round each eye, and a perpendicular line about the stomach. The men on the other hand paint the breast by making drawn or punctured streaks down from the shoulders, all verging towards and joining at the navel.

The difference in the design of the painting indicates the nearer or more remote degree of the relationship with the deceased. The black colour, in some parts, is also used for mourning at the death of a relation by marriage, while white indicates the death of blood relations.

The weapons of the natives of Port Lincoln are by no means so handsome and respectable looking as those of the Adelaide and Murray tribes but are quite as efficient. The spears are made of the stems of the young *Leptospermi* or eucalyptus trees which, hardened in hot ashes, they bend and sharpen. The natives along the Murray River also possess spears which at the upper end consist of a strong reed and at the lower end wood. Because they do not sink they use them mostly for spearing fish but also in battle, because they fly further than wooden spears. The spears are 2.5 metres long and at the end of the root about the thickness of a thumb. In the upper end they bore with the tooth of the kangaroo a perpendicular hole, in which, for throwing it, they fit the hook of the wooden lever (*middla*). In order to protect the edge of the hole against breaking or splitting, they take the precaution to tie it well round with a fine sinew of the kangaroo.

Among the number of spears which every adult native carries with him, they generally have two or three of them ready provided with the barb, and for the others they always have about them sufficient to serve in case of need and can fasten them on in an instant. These barbs are simply a small piece of wood, of about five centimetres in length, and have a knee in the middle, so that in putting one side flat on the spear, the other will project from it at an acute angle. Although it is fastened on with the sinews of the kangaroo only, it is so firmly fixed as never to slip off, so that it is quite impossible to draw such a spear out of the body of a person or an animal; the entire length of it would need to be pushed through. On this account it is considered unfair and highly blameable among the natives to employ this weapon in any fight or in warfare.

Besides this kind of spear, which is always thrown with the so-called *middla*, they make use of the *winna*, about 1.5 metres long, thick and clumsy, but only for the purpose of spearing fish.

The *middla* is a kind of catapult or lever made of casuarina wood, one metre long and 5 centimetres in diameter, which gives the spear a greater force. The inward side on which the spear rests is scooped out a little, while the outward part is rounded, both sides being usually notched, in order to give a firmer hold. To the upper tapering end is attached, with sinews of the kangaroo and a little gum, a hook or a tooth of the kangaroo, which, when throwing, is placed in the opening at the flat or blunt end of the spear. In using the *middla*, it is held with three fingers, while the thumb and first finger remain disengaged, for holding the spear, and giving it the proper direction.

Throwing clubs, called *wirra* by the natives, are made from young trees and are 60–75 centimetres long, and over a centimetre thick. The thin end, which serves for the handle, is generally notched, while towards the thicker end it is a little bent, somewhat in the shape of a sword.

The *wirra* of the Adelaide and Murray tribes have generally a stout knob at the lower end, which adds considerably to their propelling power. The natives use this weapon for killing kangaroo rats and other small animals and at the commencement of their fights or battles, until they can afterwards employ their spears.

The *katta* is a cudgel or stick, roughly one-and-a-half metres long and three to five centimetres thick, the lower end of which, when hardened by fire, is sharpened something in the shape of a chisel. This tool is used for digging up roots; and as this is one of the occupations of the women chiefly, they constantly carry them along with them. The Murray tribes also employ this stick for loosening the two-centimetre thick bark off the eucalypti; it is used either for canoes and shields or as shelter against the rain. The Murray tribes generally have in their camps a piece of this bark, stretching the skins of the smaller animals, the possums and wallabies over it to dry.

The *wadna* is a piece of bent wood about one metre long, with a knee at the end. It is never used as a weapon for fighting, but only for killing large fish. On this account one sees the natives with this weapon only when they happen to be engaged in fishing.

The most extraordinary tool is the *yuta*, being a piece of bark about 30 centimetres long and 20–25 centimetres broad, in the shape of a small trough. With this instrument in the spring (September, October) they dig out ant-hills, and by using it as a kind of swinging arm, they separate out the rubbish and the numerous little red insects, so that only the big white maggots among them remain behind. The natives wrap these in a bushel of dry grass, which they chew and suck, whereby each time they fill their mouths to the maximum.

All their weapons and tools, together with various other articles, they collect in their knapsacks, which they carry by means of strings tied over their left shoulder and under the left arm. It consists either of a kangaroo skin only, drawn together with a cord, or of a coarse matting made of the fibres of a certain kind of rush. The articles contained in almost every knapsack are:– a small flat shell for drinking, a round flinty stone for bruising the bones of the game, pieces of one or more kinds of colours, a small wooden shovel, which they use for roasting roots, a few pieces of quartz, and the entire skin of some small animal, which answers the purpose of a bag, into which they put the smaller objects they require, such as sinews of kangaroo and pointed bones of various sizes, which answer the purpose of thread and needle, also some bones with sharp edges, for scraping the roots, some spearhooks, etc. To prevent anything from dropping through the large meshes of the network, they line it with dry grass. In addition to the articles mentioned, they put into their knapsacks, called *nurti*, a stock of roots and game, and then on the top they place their weapons, which are kept fast by being twisted between the strings, so that they cannot slip off. The bags of the women, called *nudla*, differ from those of the men in being of a larger size, and, if filled and heavy, are carried on the back by means of crossbelts.

An unusual tool is the *witurna*, made from a piece of wood about 46 centimetres long, 2 centimetres broad and 4 millimetres thick. Tied to a long string they swing the *witurna* around above their heads. When the string is taut as a result of the rotation, it produces a low rumbling sound at intervals, ceasing and returning with increased power. The *witurna* is carefully hidden from the women and children, as its sound indicates that the men are engaged in some of their secret ceremonies, and that they are to keep away from them.

The natives divide all their articles of food into two classes – the *paru* and *mai*, the former including all animal, and the latter all vegetable articles of food; of these are the various descriptions of roots – such as the *ngamba, ngarrureau, nilae* and others, all of about the size of a small carrot, and of its shape, of a more or less acrid taste, and which are first roasted in hot ashes, and then peeled for eating. Of the grasstree, xanthorrhoea, they eat the lower part of the stem not yet grown above the surface of the ground; it is by no means tasteless, but certainly cannot contain much nourishment; besides these they also eat various kinds of fungi.

Although to Europeans the country offers scarcely any kind of edible fruit, it yields a pretty good variety of such as affords valuable food to the natives. The most important and abundant fruit is the *karkalla*, the fruit of a *mesembryanthemum* growing widespread on sandhills near the sea, to which the English have given the somewhat vulgar name of pigfaces. From January to April they squeeze the ripening fruit between their fingers and let the sweet, sticky juice drop into their mouth. The men generally gather only as much as they want for the moment, but the women collect large quantities for eating after supper.

The Port Lincoln blacks eat only the fruit of this plant, but those living between the Grampians and the Victoria Ranges, as a substitute for salt with their meat, eat also the leaves of this saline plant. Other edible fruit grows in pods, or in the shape of berries on small bushes. Some of these they allow to ripen, as, for instance, the fruit of the santalum and that of a species of epacris, which, growing on the seashore, bears small red sweet berries called *wadnirri*. Another plant, also growing on the sea-shore, is the *Nitraria billardierii*, called *karambi* by the natives, which bears a beautiful red berry the size of an olive and is very tasty.

Other fruits they collect before they are ripe, and roast them in hot ashes, such as the berries of the *pulbullu*, and the pods of the *menka*, and the *nundo*. The last-mentioned fruits, highly valued by the natives, are of the acacias, growing abundantly on the sandy downs of Sleaford and Coffin's Bay, and by attracting thither a numerous company of blacks, they frequently give occasion for dissension and quarrels. As the actual gum tree (eucalyptus) is not abundant in Port Lincoln, there is very little of the edible resin from which the Adelaide tribes live almost exclusively during the summer months.

Any kind of game, from the kangaroo down to the smallest species of genus of the marsupials, and every description of birds, without distinction, are welcome as food to the Port Lincoln natives, nor are snakes and lizards by any means despised by them – the former of which they eat only if killed by themselves. They are also very fond of lizard eggs, which, dug fresh out of the ground, taste exactly like soft-boiled hen's eggs.

The usual method of the natives when hunting is to approach the animal as near as they can without being noticed and to spear it. On these occasions they resort to various manoeuvres. For example, one of the natives places himself at some distance in an open space of ground or behind some bushes and makes a slight noise by breaking off some branches, or in any other way, while another black stealthily approaches to within a spear's throw from the opposite side, where, of course, the animal does not suspect the least danger. This is the usual manner for killing kangaroos, emus, wild dogs, etc. If there is a number of natives together, who are aware of several kangaroos being in the neighbourhood, then they will surround the district, gradually narrowing the circle; the best spearsmen being placed at certain favourable spots, and the others driving the game regularly towards them. If such a chase happens to take place near the sea, the kangaroos will try to escape into it, but to little purpose only, as their pursuers follow them there even, and while swimming surround them. Smaller animals, such as wallabies, kangaroo rats, etc., which live in the lower scrub, they kill by throwing a club at them. At times, having set on fire entire districts of country, they place themselves before the fire to kill the scared animals which try to escape in that direction. From early childhood the natives are very expert in the use of this very simple weapon and practise it from the earliest age by rolling on the ground, instead of the animal, a dry sponge, throwing the club

Eingeborene von Südaustralien mit ihrem Kinde.
South Australian native with her child.

after it. I have frequently seen little boys seven and eight years old bringing down, in this manner, parrots off the casuarina trees, and the little girls even know well how to handle this tool.

They have a variety of signs, unaccompanied by sound, for indicating the different animals they discover. The outstretched first finger, accompanied by a certain movement, indicates a kangaroo. Three fingers stretched out, the second finger a little lower than the others, is for an emu; the thumb alone is raised for a possum. The whole hand stretched out horizontally indicates fish. The possum and wild cat they hunt when the sky is slightly clouded; saying that with a clear sky the animals can see them and will escape before they can approach them. When they discover kangaroo rats in the holes of rocks, or under heavy stones, and find that they cannot drive them out with their hands or a stick, they will light a fire at the hole in order to smoke them out.

Having no fish-hooks, they are, with respect to fishing, behind the other tribes of Australia. The larger fish they spear, but the small ones living in schools are surrounded by a body of natives, armed with branches of trees, who go into the water and drive them together and then with these branches push them onto the shore. When engaged in this occupation they allow no stranger to be near, on account of the idea they have that the fish would smell, 'pull a face', that is, push out their lower lip, and escape. Some fish species at night are attracted to light, and then easily killed; the blacks, provided with torches, made of long strips of bark, go into the water, and catch them with the hand, striking them or spearing them. There are great rejoicings with them if they have had good luck in their hunting or fishing expeditions. Quite excited, slapping their stomachs with both hands, everyone exclaims, '*Ngaitye paru, ngaitye paru*', which means 'my meat, my prize', and most liberally bestow their praise upon those whom they are indebted to for the great treat.

They roast all their meat on the fire. The large animals such as kangaroos and emus are cut up before cooking, and the former are skinned; but the smaller ones, excepting those of which they want to preserve the skins, are put on the fire with their skins on. They first singe off the hair, and having taken out the entrails, which are generally given to the women and children, they close up the opening with some small wooden pegs, and, thus prepared, place it on the fire for roasting. If connected with more cleanliness, this method of preparing the food might be strongly recommended, for the meat gains a most inviting flavour, and retains all its strength and juice; but the filthiness of these natives is so excessive, that they do not even take the pains to wash the entrails.

Eingeborener von Südaustralien.

South Australian native.

The superstitious simplicity of these natives is strikingly apparent in their manner of hunting and dividing the game. There have been transmitted to them, by their early ancestors, several short rhymes of two lines, which now are known to the adults only, and these, on pursuing an animal, or when on the point of spearing it, they constantly repeat with great rapidity. The general principle, with regard to the division of the game, is that the men eat the males, the women the females, and the children the small animals; but since there is no rule without its exception, so also in this case the men claim the right also to eat the females and small animals, while the women and children must abide by the established rules. The common kangaroo rat, however, they are all, without any distinction, allowed to eat.

[*Here follows a description of a dietary custom.*]

The natives of Port Lincoln lead a wandering life. Sometimes they are obliged to resort to the seacoast for catching fish, at other times to rove over hill and dale in pursuit of game and roots. During the unproductive months they are forced, for the smaller kinds of game, to roam through the whole country, some parts of which are covered with an almost impenetrable small scrub, and other parts complete deserts, all the time having to contend against a dreadful heat, rendered almost insupportable by the reflection of the rays of the sun, and of the surrounding burning scrub. In addition to all this, they are deprived of a sufficiency of water. In order then to allay their thirst, they resort to the strange trick of covering their stomachs with earth. The average distance which the natives travel in a day is 25 to 35 kilometres; but I can recall that on one occasion three natives, two men and a woman carrying a child, walked 50 kilometres on an exceedingly hot day. On their journey the men generally ramble about, but the women and children, under charge of one or two men, proceed in a direct course to their place of rendezvous. In the morning they are never in a hurry to make a start, and at times it requires a great deal of coaxing and persuasion, on the part of some of the older men, to get them into a regular move. On the arrival at their camp or place of rest, generally a little before sunset, the first thing they do is to kindle a fire for roasting the small game which the men have secured during the day. The larger game they roast on the spot where it has been killed, which renders it anything but desirable to fall in with emus or kangaroos when travelling in company of blacks, if anxious to reach any fixed place at a certain time. The remnants of a large roast they hang upon sticks, and thus carry it to the camp. After eating their meat, the women hand round the roots and fruits which they have gathered during the day; and after having done with these also, they chat and sing; and if assembled in large numbers, they dance until

Charles Wilhelmi

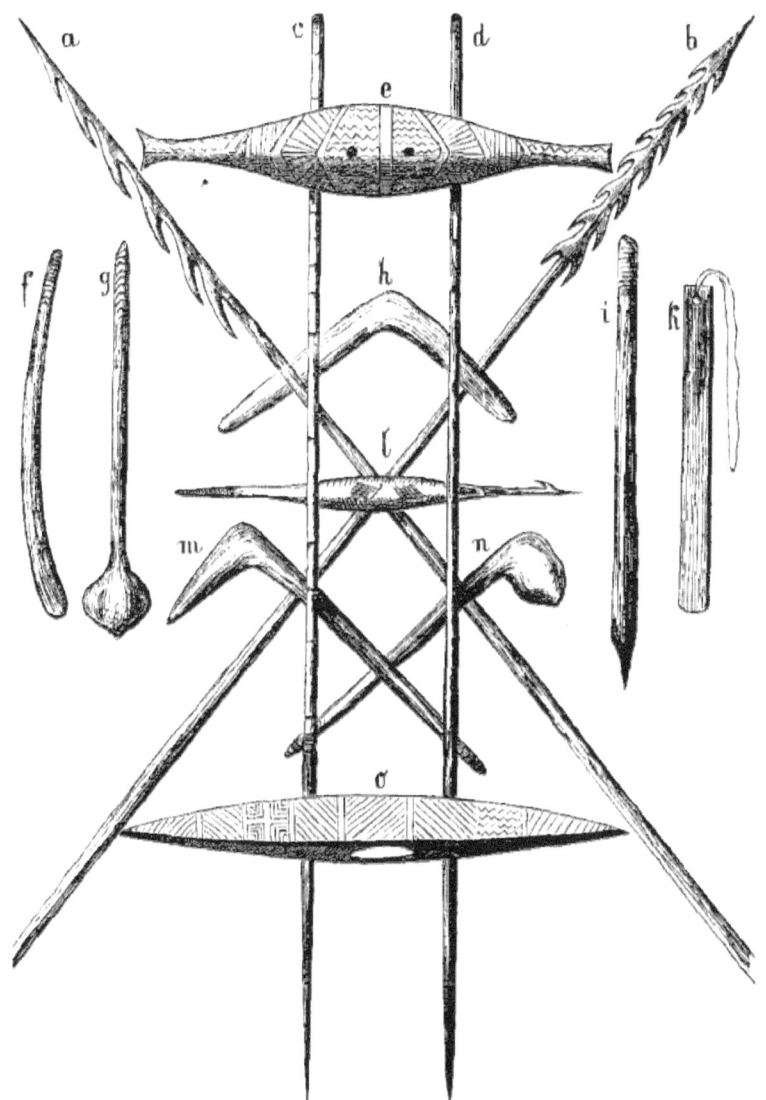

Waffen der australischen Eingeborenen.

a und b Jack-Speere. c Rohr-Speer. d Holz-Speer. e Schild von Eukalyptus-Rinde. f und g Wirri oder Wurfkeulen. h Boomerang. i Katta. k Witurna. l Middla. m Wadna. n Hölzernes Beil. o Dreieckiges Schild von Holz.

Weapons of the Australian natives: **a** and **b** Jack-spears. **c** Reed-spear. **d** Wooden spear. **e** Shield of eucalyptus bark. **f** and **g** Wirri or throwing clubs. **h** Boomerang. **i** Katta. **k** Witurna. **l** Middla. **m** Wadna. **n** Wooden axe. **o** Triangular wooden shield.

tired, then lie down for sleep. If there should happen to be a large supply of meat beyond that required for supper, they stay up the whole night to finish it; but if, after all, anything should remain over, they put it into a bag, which they make serve them as a pillow, and, on opening their eyes in the morning, their first move is towards the bag for its contents.

As patiently as these children of nature bear up against the cravings of hunger and thirst at times of want, as immoderate also are they when in abundance. The only cases in which they evince any forethought of the future is in their great care for the birds' nests, and for water, to secure and protect which against animals they cautiously cover all their springs with stones or branches of trees.

Their habitations are of a very simple construction. In the summer, and in dry fine weather, they heap up some branches of trees, in the form of a horseshoe, for protection against the winds; but in wet weather they make a kind of hut or bower with the branches of the casuarina, in the shape of deep niche, and erect them as perpendicularly as they can, thereby to facilitate the dripping off of the rain.

In those parts of the country where they have gum trees (eucalypti) they peel off the bark and fix it so well together as to make the roof quite waterproof. In front of these huts they always burn a fire during the night for warming their feet, and in the cold weather every one lies between a small heap of burning coals in front and at the back, for keeping warm the upper part of their body. As the slightest motion must bring them into contact with these burning coals, it naturally occurs that they at times seriously burn themselves.

In several parts of Port Lincoln there are isolated wells or holes in large rocks, containing a supply of water, while not anywhere else within 50 kilometres is a drop of it to be found; the natives, as long as they remain in that neighbourhood, are consequently obliged to return every night to the same camp. In places favourably situated for fishing they will extend their stay in the same camp for ten to fourteen days. The habit of constantly changing their places of rest is so deeply rooted that they cannot overcome it, even if staying where all their wants can be abundantly supplied. A certain longing to revisit this or that spot, for which they have taken particular fancy, seizes them, and neither promises nor persuasions can induce them to resist it for any time. Each family has its own particular camp, and unmarried men, of whom there are relatively many among them, also have their particular camp.

All the Aborigines are divided into two separate classes, viz., the *matterri* and the *karrarru*. This division seems to have existed among them from time immemorial, and with a view to regulate their marriages, as no one is allowed to intermarry in their own castes, but only into the other one – that is, if the man is a *matteri*, he can choose as his wife a *karraru* only, and *vice versa*. This distinction is kept up by the arrangement that the children belong to the class of the mother.

Apart from this general difference there are other limitations on marriage between relatives, simply because of the countless degrees of blood relationship, and because friendship among natives constantly takes on the forms and names of relatives, it becomes impossible to establish these differences.

Young girls are betrothed by their parents and follow the man regardless of his age or whether he is already married. The girls' inclination is not taken into consideration. To their good luck, however, it does not very seldom occur that an old, jealous matron strongly opposes herself against such a division of her husband's affections between herself and her young rival and forces him to renounce all claims upon her in favour of another man. There is no shortage of examples of abductions and of murders motivated by jealousy. Marriage generally is not viewed as holy; brothers often possess several women jointly, and the women call both their actual husband as well his brother 'husband', while the husband calls his own wives *yungaras* and those of his brothers *kartelis*.

Although the men are apt to become passionately jealous if they detect their wives transgressing without their consent, yet of their own accord they offer them and send them to other men or make an exchange for a night with some one of their friends. Of relatives, brothers in particular, it may be said that they possess their wives jointly.

The number of children raised by each family is generally limited and seldom exceeds four. If there are a lot of children, then the youngest one is done away with. From the excess of male adults alive, it may fairly be presumed that a by far greater number of girls are killed after birth. As an apology for this barbarous custom, the women plead that they cannot suckle and carry two children together, while the men plead ignorance. In the naming of the children a fixed rule is followed, according to the number of children born. The first-born is called Piri, if a boy; and Kartanye, if a girl. The second one is called Warni, or Warrunya. In addition to these names, which correlate exactly to our first names, each child also takes the name of the place of its birth. Both these names they preserve their entire lives, and only the males, on attaining the age of puberty, get a third one.

Although living in a salubrious climate and on healthy food, the natives are subject to many diseases. Among those which they suffer most from are sores, diarrhoea, colds, and headache. For removing these, or partially curing them for the time, they apply outward remedies, some of which appear to be effective. The chief ones are – rubbing, pressing, and treading even upon the afflicted parts of the body, in particular the belly and the back; tightening of the belt, and also of the band which they usually wear round the head; bandaging the diseased part; sprinkling or washing it with cold water in case of fever or inflammation. Sores or wounds are generally left to take their course, or the utmost done is to tie something tight round it, or, if inflammation has ensued, to sprinkle cold water upon it. Bleeding of the lower arm they apply in cases of headache. In order to cure a headache, a woman had another woman scratch open her head with glass shards so that the blood oozed on all sides through the thick hair.

The cure by bleeding is often practised by the men during the hot season. They do not allow the blood to run on the ground, but upon the body of some other man, directing the arm in such a manner that the stream forms a number of small crosslines, in consequence of which the body assumes the appearance of being covered with a tight-fitting network of very small meshes. The object of this custom is partly to cure diseases but partly also to promote the growth of the young people and to preserve the strength of the aged ones.

The natives have also their regular doctors who are called *mintapas* and who pretend to be able to remove, by sucking, sickness out of the body. They put their lips to the pit of the stomach in case of general disease, and to the suffering part where confined to any fixed spot, and, after having sucked for some time, pull out of their mouths a small piece of wood or bone, pretending that this is the body of the disease, which had been communicated by some evil-disposed person, and had now been extracted by them. So superstitious are these ignorant children of nature, that they passionately defend them against any expression of doubt.

[*Here follows a description of spiritual beliefs.*]

The natives show strong feelings of sympathy in cases of illness, the women particularly so, who, under an abundance of tears, prove their interest and attention by frequently rubbing and pressing the affected parts; but the sick themselves, in desperate cases even, submit to their sufferings with a surprising stoicism and resignation.

A very peculiar circumstance, not to be met with perhaps in any other uncivilised community, is that these natives have no chief or individual of acknowledged authority among them. All the adult men are quite equal one to the other, yet the young people show no little respect towards the old ones, a tribute to advanced age or to greater experience perhaps; but this, no doubt, is increased and preserved by a superstitious and dreadful horror of certain secret rites known to the grown-up men only, into the knowledge of which the young lads are initiated by degrees.

[*Here follows a discussion of stages of initiation and initiation practices.*]

The views of the natives in reference to supernatural beings or influences are very peculiar and remarkable. They have as clear a conception of the unsubstantiality and immortality of the soul as can hardly be expected of them. In order to express the former quality, they represent the soul as being so small that it might pass through a crack. When a human dies, the soul retires to an island and continues to live without needing nourishment. Some represent that island as being in the east, others in the west. On its journey to this island the soul is accompanied by a redbill, a kind of sea-bird, notorious for its piercing shrill voice, audible during the night. It appears that since they have found out the existence of the race of white people, they have adopted the notion that their souls will hereafter appear in the bodies of such white people. The whites are regarded therefore as the reincarnated souls of their ancestors, and Europeans have often been addressed by the names of dead natives. To von Blandowski it has occurred that an old 'lubra' (black woman), supposing him to be her former husband resuscitated, has most tenderly embraced and kissed him. It appears correspondingly that that 'island' is considered merely a temporary place of residence.

There do not appear to be clear views on morality, yet in rare instances one regards a misfortune as the result of previously committed wrongdoings.

> [Here follows a description of beliefs related to particular spiritual beings.]

Singing and dancing are the favourite and almost the sole amusements of the natives of this region. They are in the possession of a number of songs, each one consisting of two, or at most three lines, such as the following: -

La pirrá mirrána.	Iyurrá tyurra tyurra tyurráru
Iyíndo Katutyála.	Paltá paltá paltárni
Kauwirrá wirrána.	Ninna kutyu nyangkáli.

In the singing of this and other songs of the same kind, each verse is repeated twice, and when the last line is finished, they begin again at the first. They do not seem to give much attention to the meaning of the words, so long as the necessary measure and the proper number of the accented syllables are observed. The greater number of these kind of songs which exist among them are regarded as belonging to distant tribes, for they are not acquainted with the meaning of any of the words. Their songs are in different measures, some being slow and serious, others quick and lively. These, songs, however, do not offend the ear, but they are monotonous, and require that the voice should be raised and lowered with regularity. The singers are exceedingly accurate as regards the time, and, to prevent any mistake in this respect, they beat the time with their clubs. The end of the song is indicated by singing the last line in a low tone, sinking the voice gradually so that the last note is scarcely audible.

The mild summer evenings are generally chosen for dancing. If there should be a moon shining at this time, so much the better, but if not, they make up for the lack of light with bright burning fire.

[Here follows a description of cultural ceremonies.]

These evening amusements often last till long past midnight, especially should the number of dancers be great, or should two different tribes be present, in which case they do their best to amuse each other by the number and different kinds of dances. On these occasions joy and cheerfulness are depicted on each countenance, and it can scarcely be credited that these good-natured faces could assume the distorted traits of profound wrath, or that the mild behaviour could transform into the gestures of wild passion. This is all too often the case, especially during the hot season.

Their battles can be divided into two classes, namely the ones beginning suddenly, and arising from some paltry cause, the others being the fruit of deep premeditation, and proceeding from an earnest, sometimes from a true, and still more often from an imaginary cause. Although the behaviour of the Aborigines towards each other is generally characterised by good-nature, mildness, and even politeness, still it happens that friends go their different ways.

The most common causes of discord are that women do not always deport themselves as is becoming to their sex, that the children quarrel among themselves and do each other bodily injury, or that one or other of the men is neglected or forgotten in the distribution of food. An angry word or an offensive action in respect of any of the before-named cases acts like an electric spark. Each one springs up, grasps his weapons, and is ready to retaliate upon any verbal or actual insult offered to himself or to his friends. Abuse, often hurled by the women and seldom leading to any nasty consequences, is rarely used by men without it leading to a brawl. The friends of the insulted person often endeavour to appease him, and even use force in order to hold him back, but generally with little success.

First clubs are thrown, and then they rush upon each other, beating each other with the *middla*, which inflicts such severe wounds that the blood flows in streams, and the injured person falls senseless to the ground. Finally, should the fight become still more furious, spears are thrown, whereupon the women and children flee shrieking to watch from a distance the men's fervour. Should one of the combatants be dangerously wounded, the groans and lamentations of his friends and the women bring the fight to an end. After peace has been restored, each one seems sorry for having caused the momentary interruption, and whoever has wounded his antagonist severely feels for him as truly and as sincerely as any of the others. Should loss of life or serious hurt be the result of the fight, this is expiated by another conflict. On the other hand, if little damage has been done nothing more is said about it, and the parties that yesterday fell upon each other with a fury that could not be satisfied by anything other than the death of their opponent are today the best possible friends in the world.

Those battles which are the fruit of premeditation and deliberation are known to the natives weeks, even months, before they take place. A suitable place is sought by one side, and then messages are sent inviting the enemy.

The causes of such battles are generally abduction, murder, or attempted murder. The last of these generally has its ground in the superstitious beliefs that the targeted individual has brought about the death of a person who was perhaps recently deceased by supernatural but evil means. In such cases the next of kin to the murdered or dead man chooses some of his friends and traverses the country with them, with the firm resolution to kill the suspected person wherever they may discover him. In earlier years two fights took place here, one on account of a murder committed, the other on account of an attempted murder. In the first case the murderer and the brother of the murdered man were present, in both cases supported by a mass of friends. They were unanimous that the last-named person, as the avenger of the murder, should throw two spears at the perpetrator, and that if he should fail to hit his mark the quarrel should be regarded as forgotten. To judge from the violent and wild gestures of the warriors, the running about, the jumping, the biting of the beards and the weapons, the noise and the grimaces, a bloody conflict was expected. But this was not the case. The antagonists stepped from their own side into the foreground, and the avenger threw just one spear, which the other skilfully parried, whereupon the combat was brought to a close.

The second fight, on account of attempted murder, took place in Port Lincoln, and the party about to be attacked were invited by messengers to attend the combat. All upon their arrival were painted with a white colour and wore little peeled sticks which looked like plumes in their hair. They marched in a long line, three deep, stopping here and there, and with one voice poured forth with loud cries. As soon as they had completed these moves, the other party, who were rather surprised, set to work to answer the salutation. After having hastily painted themselves, and arranging themselves in single file, they marched in a regular quick short step towards the enemy, who had in the meantime formed a camp. After they had walked around the enemy's camp a few times, they formed themselves into a dense mass, bowed their heads, and uttered a piercing cry. After they had repeated these movements two or three times, they marched back to their own camp in the same order they had observed upon leaving it. That evening and the greater part of the night were spent in singing and dancing, and with sunrise of the next day the fight commenced. Eight men advanced from each side, making use of mimical gestures, although the most profound silence was observed. They formed into a row, two deep, about twenty paces from each other, so that they came to stand two to two. Each warrior stretched his legs apart and planted his feet firmly on the ground, holding a spear and sling in the right hand and their *katta* together with other spears in the left. They pushed forward their chests, and moved their bodies from side to side, as a sort of challenge. Each one fixed his eyes upon his especial antagonist and seemed to have no concern about any of the others, as if he had nothing to fear at their hands.

Not a sound was to be heard. Many spears were thrown on either side and were avoided by moving the upper part of the body to one side or were parried by giving the spears a blow with the *katta* or other spears held in the left hand so that the spears of the opponents missed their mark. This continued until some of the party who sent the challenge went over into the ranks of the enemy to show that they wished to put an end to the combat. One quarrelsome old man, however, who had struck the first blow, did not seem to be content to stay his arm without having spilled a drop of blood. He stood opposed to a young man of not more than twenty years of age, and he threw several spears at him after the youth had ceased fighting. The old rascal made use of the most insulting and provoking language and was paid back in his own coin. At length some of the old man's friends intervened and sought to calm him and knock his throwing-stick when he placed a spear on it, so that the weapon fell useless on the ground.

The skilful manner in which the natives avoid or parry the spears is truly astonishing. Schürmann saw the old man, who was renowned as a good marksman, take such good aim that it seemed almost a certainty that he would hit his adversary; nevertheless, each spear was met, and glided off the young man's *katta* and shot over his shoulder, passing in close proximity to his ear. This can only be accomplished by a sure eye and a firm glance, which are amongst the Aborigines looked upon as the highest virtues of which they can boast, and of which they are proud.

It has been said that the Aborigines of this country are possessed of a cowardly disposition, and it may be that, when opposed to the whites, who are better armed and generally mounted, they have been found wanting in courage. Anyone who has been an eye-witness to one of their own fights will have to concede that, when stirred up by passion, they will brave any danger. That little blood is spilled in these contests is to be ascribed either to their skill, or to the fact that they are by no means bloodthirsty.

Although, on the one side, the Aborigines possess a fierce and hostile spirit, still, on the other, it must be observed that they are capable of the more noble feelings of pity and compassion, for example in the case of serious wounds, severe illness, or at the death of their friends. Their loud lamentations upon the death of a relation or friend may perhaps be a custom inherited from their forefathers, for they always weep together and simultaneously and use other means to produce tears, for example by rubbing the eyes and scratching the nose, if their own frame of mind should not suffice. For weeks and months they bemoan their deaths, especially in the evenings when they are assembled for rest. One of them is accustomed to break out suddenly into a long, protracted, plaintive tone, and gradually his example is followed by the others. After this lamentation, a profound silence is observed, and in truth their behaviour is such as belongs to persons oppressed by great grief. For years the name of the dead person is not mentioned, not from superstition, but because 'they do not wish to weep so much'.

At the dead person's burial a roughly 1.6 metre deep and 1.3 metre long grave is dug, a little dry grass is strewn over the ground, and the body is laid in it with the legs bent upwards, as the hole is too short to stretch them out. The head is placed at the western end, a peculiarity based on their belief that the soul goes to an island in the east. The body is then covered with a kangaroo skin, and sticks are driven immediately above it lengthwise into the sides of the grave, leaving a vacant space between the sticks and the body, and then the grave is filled up with earth. At the conclusion of this simple proceeding, some branches or bushes are collected round the grave, presumably to prevent stray cattle and horses from trampling upon it. Deep graves are dug only when tools can be obtained from the Europeans; in the interior one digs with the *katta* only deep enough to cover the body. However, the insertion of the sticks above the body is observed everywhere, no doubt also to prevent the wild dogs from scraping up the body.

The natives inhabiting the triangular peninsula of Port Lincoln are divided into several tribes, namely the Nauo or Nawo, and the Parnkalla. In addition to these, the natives mention three other tribes, as known to them, namely the Pukunna in the north-east, the Kukata in the north-west, and the Ngannityddi in the north between both aforementioned tribes, some of whom occasionally visit the settlement. All these tribes seem upon the whole to entertain a friendly intercourse with each other.

The chief difference among the various tribes is the variety of language and dialect. This, however, causes no great inconvenience to those living on the border of their territories, as each native understands, at least, the language of the adjoining district; thus, they frequently keep up their conversations in two different languages, in the same manner as if a German and Englishman were to talk together, each in his own language, but both understanding that of the other party. This peculiarity frequently occurs in families intermarrying in the neighbouring tribe, for none of the members ever think of attempting to speak the language of the other party.

In conclusion, it should be observed that these interesting children of nature unfortunately are heading rapidly toward their demise. No matter where civilisation makes its way, the original inhabitants of all lands are disappearing. What an enormous reduction in the natives of Australia I have observed during my twenty-year stay in Australia! Where previously hundreds hunted their game, fought their wars, one now finds only a few wandering around who need to beg the intruders to support their existence. In various parts of the interior of this country the government has employed protectors of natives, and with every new moon a small quantity of flour, sugar, tea and woollen blankets is distributed as compensation for the lands taken away from them. In this way their lives are miserably limited. Herds of cattle and sheep scare away their game, eat or trample the plants and roots that once provided their food source. If they wander further into the interior, they are killed by hostile tribes, and thus they hasten toward their demise.

Georg von Neumayer, 'On the Intellectual and Moral Characteristics of the Natives of Australia'

Born on 21 June 1826, Georg von Neumayer studied in Munich and became a physicist researching the earth's magnetism, oceanography and hydrography. Leaving behind his chair in physics at Hamburg University, he came to Australia in 1852, working as a miner, a sailor and conducting research in Hobart. Returning to Germany in 1854, he secured backing from Alexander von Humboldt, the King of Bavaria and the British Royal Society to set up an observatory at Melbourne's Flagstaff Hill in 1858 and in the Melbourne Botanic Gardens in 1863.

As a member of the Royal Society of Victoria's Exploration Committee in the 1860s he joined the ill-fated expedition of Robert O'Hara Burke and Neumayer's good friend William John Wills from September until December 1860 as part of his broader magnetic survey of Victoria. He then headed south along the Murray, reaching Murray Bridge in mid-December 1861, travelling along the Coorong before returning to Melbourne via Mount Gambier and Ararat in January 1862.

Neumayer returned to Germany in 1864, where he was appointed hydrographer to the German Admiralty in Berlin in 1872, before moving to Hamburg in 1876 to continue his hydrographic work. In the German scientific community and beyond he became widely recognised for his work assembling all three editions of the Anleitung zu wissenschaftlichen Beobachtungen auf Reisen (Guide to scientific observations on travels), which provided instructions to German travellers on the collection of scientific data, including anthropological data. He died on 24 May 1909.*

Source:
Georg von Neumayer, 'Über die intellektuellen und moralischen Eigenschaften der Eingeborenen Australiens', *Berliner Gesellschaft für Anthropologie, Ethnologie und Urgeschichte*, 1871, 3–13.
Translation: Harald and Aileen Ohlendorf.

Mr Neumayer shares his experiences of the intellectual and moral qualities of the natives of Australia.

The term Australian is associated with the epitome of incomplete physical development and intellectual weakness, if one believes that one may still speak of an intellect in these creatures. It was with some trepidation that I accepted the invitation to speak about them, because my lack of scholarly education in regard to the matter under discussion hardly allows me to present what I have to say in an academic way. However, guided by the conviction that, in the current state of our knowledge of races and the whole direction of anthropological research, it is important to determine more precisely the mental powers, the impulses of more highly developed feelings among the various peoples and to prove how the limit of intellect can be defined in one or the other tribe, I nevertheless believed that I would be able to talk about many things that would be of interest to you. Observations in this sense require no extensive apparatus, no detailed knowledge of anatomy and physiology, but only an openness to all things human

---

* *Further reading:* R.A. Swan, 'Neumayer, Georg Balthasar von (1826–1909)' *Australian Dictionary of Biography* 5, 1974, https://adb.anu.edu.au/biography/neumayer-georg-balthasar-von-4290; 'Death of Professor Dr von Neumayer', *Evening News* (Sydney) 3 July 1909, 12; 'Zum Gedächtnis Georg von Neumayer' *Die Brücke* 26 May 1934, 18, 27; Peter Monteath, 'German Anthropology, Nationalism and Imperialism: Georg von Neumayer's 'Anleitung zu wissenschaftlichen Beobachtungen auf Reisen', *History and Anthropology* 31 (4) 2020, 1–22; Douglas Morrison 'Georg von Neumayer's Magnetic Survey of the Colony of Victoria 1858–1864', *Transactions of the Royal Society of Victoria* 123(1), 2011, 48–61.

and a gift of observation, which one cannot well do without when dealing with human beings. It is from this point of view that I would like you to judge the little I have to say, as I merely follow the urge to present to you the experiences and views I have acquired in my dealings with Australian Aborigines and thereby perhaps to contribute something to a more correct assessment of that race, which is usually placed on the border between humans and animals.

After these introductory words, it goes without saying that I will not entertain you here in an unnecessary and unprofessional manner about the characterisation of the dolichocephalic and prognathous nature, about the shape and size of the body of the Australians; rather, I have set myself the task of contributing to the delineation of the intellectual and moral character of the blacks of Australia. In this assessment, one must above all never forget that the island continent we are talking about here is completely isolated and has probably never had contact with India or other parts of Asia. Just as the animal world of this strange island continent differs considerably from that of other parts of the world in external appearance and habits, and even in anatomical structure, and only here and there offers points of connection, the same applies to human beings, who only here and there, and in any case at a much later stage on the northern coasts, came into contact with the inhabitants of more highly developed states, such as India and China. The deep oceanic channel between Borneo and New Guinea probably formed the dividing line for the direct influence of development, and thus we recognise the Papuans and the Australians proper as being separate from the Malays, with whom they indeed have little in common, as far as appearance and character are concerned. It has been pointed out by some quarters how the inhabitants of the Australian continent are related to the Dravidas of India, and that one should also look for a connection between them and the South American continent. But for the most part these are only assumptions that must be confirmed by further observations, which is why we have to consider them as isolated for the time being. The Tasmanians, whose curly hair makes them more like the real

Papuans and thus closer to the peoples of Africa, are less isolated. For me, this fact only means that the Aborigines of Australia could not be elevated and intellectually developed during constant contact with foreign peoples, but that they were on their own from the beginning.

Added to this is the peculiar physical structure of this continent, which is so mysterious in many respects. The lack of a perfectly sculptured surface was bound to be highly detrimental to the development of the sparsely distributed population. No mountain ranges rising high into the clouds regulate the meteorological precipitation here, as it were, and no developed river systems with more regular water levels promoted the traffic of the dispersed natives by spreading over the greater part of the country a certain uniformity in terms of habitability. A country almost as large as Europe offers enormous areas which cannot be at all conducive to the sustenance of the people or to their connection with each other, given the barrenness of all conditions of life in these areas. As a result, the Australians had to break up into an infinite number of small groups, which were almost exclusively dependent on themselves for their further advancement and development. Such isolation, due to the nature of the country alone, had to have an infinitely inhibiting effect on this development. Long coasts with few bays were not conducive to this development either. In view of this, I do not regard the present Aborigines of Australia as being at the lowest stage of human development, but rather as a race degenerated by complete isolation. My endeavour in this brief lecture is to throw light on a number of facts which aim to prove this assertion and to advocate that the character of the Aborigines, who are so often despised, is in many respects better.

In judging them, one very often forgets these determining influences given here in fleeting outlines: one considers a state of mind and feelings to be very close to the animal instinct and builds on this one's reasons for the transition from both kinds of beings, which, however, should decidedly, be attributed only to the degenerating effect of physical conditions. This is already expressed unequivocally in the population. If one were to make a generous estimate of the population before the European settlement of Australia, numbers would hardly have exceeded 70,000 souls, so that for the whole continent, each Aborigine had on average 32 English square miles at his disposal. This is certainly an astonishingly sparse population, which has hardly any equal on our earth's surface, if for the time being one does not take into account the population conditions of the Arctic regions.

In the areas where the ocean cuts deepest into this compact island mass: at the Gulf of Carpentaria and Van Diemen Gulf, it was here that the Australians first of all and probably only came into contact with peoples of other tribes. Malay and Chinese praus visited their shores annually to fish for the trepang snail, a holothuria prized as a delicacy. The coastal inhabitants were not normally very eager to fight but when defending themselves against the invaders and fighting for their survival, their courage increased. It is precisely for this reason that we find the most battle-hardened and wildest tribes in those areas, which still offer the greatest resistance to the settlers today. They often oppose the encroachment of their rights on their native soil with a ferocity that has given them a reputation for cruelty and treachery in comparison with their southern tribal kinsmen. Indeed, in the south, the expulsion of the more docile and less warlike blacks and the seizure of the land has always been made easy for the colonists. But instead of being determined to judge this docility favourably, one is only inclined to attribute it to the complete incapacity and the low degree of intelligence of the original inhabitants of New South Wales, Victoria and South Australia. While their northern tribesmen are accused of incorrigible savagery, not to say bestiality, because they do not know that milder docility which calmly consecrates its victims to destruction, they fare no better for that reason in regard to the classification of their powers of intellect. Thus, in both cases, the sophistical mind of the European is only able to recognise one and the same thing: *man at the lowest level.*

I could never agree with this logic but made it my business to make my own observations about it, which led me to an essentially different conclusion. An examination of the expressions of feeling and intellect of this unfortunate race, according to the same norms that we generally apply to the human race, convinced me that some of the noblest qualities, which we are wont to praise in ordinary life, are nevertheless undoubtedly inherent in these wild children of nature, even if they are unrefined and not clearly expressed. It always seemed to me as if the main reason for the differing, mostly unfavourable assessment of blacks lay in the different standard which was considered appropriate in this respect. What was recognised as noble in a white person without education was attributed to other motives and other causes in the case of the black person. I have seen Europeans, educated as well as uneducated, laugh at the blacks' expressions of intellect and feeling, as one is wont to be amused by expressions of a certain intelligence or affection in animals, and to my astonishment I found quite often that those ridiculed in this way were not at all insensitive to such insults, but on the contrary openly expressed that they did not like this or that person, since he was only laughing at their expressions. Indeed, on one occasion I heard a black man say that one of my companions was 'big one stupid' because he could only laugh when talking to him.

If I confine my remarks to the Aborigines of the southern part, starting at the Tropic of Capricorn, I think all those who have had any experience will agree with me when I say that their general character is peaceful and even benevolent. Many conversations on this subject which I have had with settlers of the first period of settlement have on the whole led to the same conclusion. The Australian savage is not, and never has been, of a bloodthirsty nature. Any hardships inflicted upon them were met by fighting, and these hardships were truly likely to provoke the utmost, bloodiest resistance on the part of the unfortunate individuals. To make this immediately obvious, consider from which class of our European population those people came with whom the blacks first came into contact. The fact that criminals were first let loose on the doomed population had the most decisive, even pernicious influence on their future.

How could the savages, to mention only one instance, be filled with anything but repugnance by the greed and rapacity of these people, who were in truth at the lowest level of humanity, since it is well known that a fundamental law among the Aborigines is the distribution of means for the maintenance of a free life based on complete equality! It was erroneously assumed that Australians are incapable of making such distinctions in customs and traditions. Without education and weak by nature, they soon overcame the aversion they had originally felt and fell into the vices and infirmities of their oppressors and would soon be ruined physically as well. The class of people I have just referred to, were, of course, incapable of judging the intellectual and emotional powers of the unfortunate race. What in my opinion is important in anthropological investigations in this respect is to distinguish between the positive intellect and what we are accustomed to call instinct. This is what even the more educated of the first colonists were not able to do, perhaps because they did not seriously want to – and this is how the highly unfavourable judgements came about. I have spoken to noble and highly educated men who lived through those initial periods of contact between the Europeans and the original inhabitants and who, even after 40 years, reported with veritable disgust the devastation often wrought among the natives by a 'gang' of 8 or 10 convicts. These mowed down the natives like wild animals because they thought the latter were interfering with the herds, or probably for no other reason than the bestiality of the persecutors. But who thought of testing the mental capacity of the unfortunate victims!? In the struggle for existence, the physically stronger and intellectually skilled Europeans displaced the original owners of this, for the most part, wonderful soil, the cultivation of which, however, leads to higher yields and a great future.

When I travelled through the colonies, the number of indigenous people had already dwindled considerably in the districts I visited, and those that were still there were no longer completely untouched by the influences of culture. My travels extended over the eastern, south-eastern and southern coasts of the continent, over the regions of the Brisbane, Darling, Murray and Murrumbidgee Rivers; but it is perhaps of the greatest interest from the general anthropological point of view to trace the first impressions of another world of ideas on the otherwise still untouched minds, and to recognise therein the peculiarity of their natural disposition.

Individual traits, which I can vouch for in every respect, will serve better than the most extensive treatises to illuminate the peculiarity of this natural disposition. When I travelled on the Lower Murray in 1861, I had to cross this river at a point where it was 450 feet wide. But how to manage this without a bridge and without a boat? Ten or twelve blacks of handsome, strong build were camped on the riverbanks, and when they saw what this was all about, they offered their services for a small sum of money. The frail canoes were to be used to transport the people and instruments. The deal was close to being concluded when two Europeans, who had apparently found refuge from the arm of justice in this wasteland, interfered in the negotiations and succeeded in persuading me to accept their services and to break off the negotiations with the blacks. Silently, but grudgingly and obviously hurt by this defeat, the blacks withdrew. The two Europeans made all the arrangements for the following morning to transport the wagon across the river by means of a barrel and to let the horses swim across. It turned out, however, that we needed the help of the Australians, because there was no other boat available, with which the people, the instruments and the rope for steering the wagon, could have been brought across. Silently, but conscientiously, they provided their assistance. Finally, the moment came when I had to entrust myself and all my instruments to a black man in one of these wretched canoes made of tree bark. A strong, handsome man scowled and told me to sit quietly in the boat so that everything would go well. There I was, sitting in the most fragile of all vessels, with a most valuable collection of mathematical instruments, drifting down the raging river. Any careless rocking movement could plunge us to our doom. My guide watched me steadfastly so that he could counterbalance any move I might make. I did not think of myself and my safety – I feared only for my instruments. But this was completely unnecessary, for after a few minutes my ferryman landed me and, having brought the instruments to shore, departed – not without a touch of disdain on his broad face. The whites had taken it upon themselves to pay the Australians for their efforts, which, let it be said in passing, constituted the main part of the whole enterprise; for in regard to the white men, I soon gained the conviction, which the blacks tried to teach me at the very beginning, by calling them 'Gammon'. Now, according to the Europeans' assurances, we had come ashore with our party in such a way that we could continue our journey without difficulty; as soon as they received their payment, they hurried to get out of our vicinity, and for good reason. We soon found that we were in the middle of the flood plain of the river, and that it was impossible to continue our journey through the countless creeks and swamps. What were we to do? After we had been cheated by the Europeans in this way, there was nothing left for us to do, but to seek assistance from the blacks, whom we had severely insulted. This was granted without a word of protest or even a mention of any payment. The good fellows helped us all day long to bring our wagons and effects over and across the water. It wasn't until the sun had set that we were in complete safety, and thereafter we found that we could continue our journey without encountering any further difficulties. Now it was time to pay the men. I had promised my blacks, 6 men who had worked hard, 10 pounds of flour and some money; however, to my astonishment, as I was measuring out the flour, I realised that it would hardly be enough to go round. When I had reached the sixth pound, the leader of the blacks indicated that I should stop, as I had nothing left for myself. Then I took my purse and gave them the few shillings I still had on me. Then one of my black friends tapped me on the shoulder and said with obvious joy: 'You good fellow' and gave me to understand that I should keep some of what little was left. We parted with the warmest handshake, and I can say that I felt some shame about my initial behaviour, which was dictated by the assumption that we were dealing with a group of men, incapable of any better understanding. This lesson was very salutary for me for the future; I also took the first opportunity to send the blacks an appropriate reward for their unselfish treatment of us.

On another occasion – some years later and hundreds of miles from the place where the incident just described took place – I was again able to make my observations about the reliability of the blacks. It involved crossing a fairly wide lake, and again there was only a simple bark canoe available for this purpose. I expressed my concerns to the owner whether it would be possible to use this boat successfully. At the same time, I told him that I was wearing a timepiece on each side of my upper chest, which would have to be protected from getting wet. These were my two precious timepieces for observations. The black man gave me to understand that I only needed to have confidence and take my seat in the back of the canoe. To my horror, he also let his two boys, aged 8 to 10, get in the boat, and now we were heading towards the far shore against a fresh breeze from the south-east. Soon it was clear that the boat was rapidly taking on water; all efforts to scoop out the water were in vain. Then, at a given signal, the two children jumped overboard like frogs and swam towards the shore. The boat, thus lightened, rose again a little, but not enough to carry us further. One mighty push and the light craft was only 10 to 12 paces from the shore – but it sank beneath our feet. But before I knew it, the black man had lifted me onto his shoulders and carried me ashore in such a way that at least the water did not come up to my two timepieces, thus keeping his promise perfectly.

Gentlemen, I could continue to entertain you for a long time with accounts of my dealings with the Aborigines, all of which would prove the same thing, namely, that they are reliable when treated fairly, and that their intelligence is also by no means as low as one always finds portrayed by inexperienced travellers. But I would be afraid of tiring you and will therefore confine myself to a few other encounters that throw light on the abilities of the blacks.

During the last months of 1861 there was a great movement among the native population on the Lower Murray; they were moving up the river in large numbers to a place where a great 'corrobboree' was to take place. I often passed small groups, but on one day, I met a large number of men and women, whom I had to ask for information about my future route. They pointed to a completely naked black man, sitting among the others with a certain look of authority on his face, as being the most suitable to give the desired information. When I told him my request in English, he answered me perfectly correctly in the same language that he could draw me the route if I gave him my notebook. This was done and in a few strokes this man sketched out the route and wrote the names beside the main locations in legible handwriting. When I asked him, he told me that he was now 24 years old and had, as a boy, spent two years learning to read and write in a missionary institution in Adelaide. He had later returned to his relatives and had not read or written anything for years now, and yet he was still quite able to do so. I think this is a testimony to a considerable degree of talent ... for just consider how many people you will find, even in Germany, who, with such a deficient education and after a long interruption in any opportunity to practise, would have achieved the same. I was so pleased about this that I took off my jacket and gave it to the black man as a present. His comrades understood at once that I wanted to honour him with this and said in their peculiar way of speaking, half of which was borrowed from their own language and the other from corrupted English words, that Jimmy, now that he was wearing a jacket and could write, was just as good as a white man.

There cannot be a more telling proof of the qualities of the Aborigines of Australia than the treatment meted out to King, the only surviving member of the great Victorian expedition. As is well known, Burke and Wills died at Cooper's Creek after twice crossing the Australian continent on foot. King, having lost everything and without his friends, decided to give himself over to the mercy of the blacks. A tribe kindly took him in, nursed him until he had regained his strength and willingly shared their fish and nardoo (*marsilea hirsuta*) with him, until at last, after three months, he was rescued by the Europeans who followed. He could never speak of the kindness of these natives without emotion. But when one knows how meagrely nature metes out sustenance to these people, one will know how to value this kindness more highly than if they had shared their surplus with their protégé.

Anyone who has had to employ the help of the Aborigines in Australia for purposes of exploration or settlement, will and must do justice to their loyalty (I can only point to the death of Kennedy), their dexterity in all activities in the bush. They are willing, obedient and frugal. One should only be careful not to treat them harshly and unjustly, or to forfeit their respect and affection by using certain forms of violence. Only in cases where, in their opinion, they are unnecessarily called upon to work, where their judgement tells them that to do this or that is completely superfluous, can they become unwilling and recalcitrant. I remember such cases from my own experience and, if I am to be frank, I must confess that the outcome often proved them right. On a journey over a rugged mountain range never before trodden by horses, for days in the most terrible weather in dense bush, alone with only my black companions, I was busy clearing a path for our party. They worked hard on the task set for them, but in some places, I thought the path was not wide enough for the heavily packed horses and I asked them to cut down yet another tree. One of them kindly explained to me that this was completely unnecessary, as the horses would have enough room to pass. I became angry and would not tolerate any argument; but in vain, I was told that the tree in question would not be felled, so that I, alone as I was, had to give in. The following day I had the opportunity to convince myself of the correctness of their judgement, and with visible joy they showed me that the tree in question was not in the way at all. As a rule, one may calmly trust their judgement and their sensory awareness in the bush. It is quite superfluous to point out here the high degree of all those qualities in the black man that make him a perfect bushman, for to him they are self-evident. With a condescending kindness we are always ready to acknowledge the excellent 'instinct' of the savage, who never gets embarrassed and behaves calmly and efficiently in danger! –

Before I say anything else about the mind of the Australian, I would like to expand on these fleeting remarks, which further refer to their good nature and sense of justice. Everything I have said so far, as well as what follows below, relates particularly to experiences I have had with men. My impression of the women is decidedly unfavourable. The position they occupy in relation to men, their seemingly physical subordination, are what give rise to this impression. I would just like to mention here in passing that various circumstances seem to work together to hardly permit an improvement in the situation of the women.

Above all, their apparent weakness and apathy is certainly due to the fact that they bear children too young and then they have to breastfeed them for too long. It is not uncommon to see women nursing babies who have already reached their fourth year. Add to this the carrying of heavy loads and I believe I have explained sufficiently their poor physical development. In fact, we can hardly assume that the spiritual powers of women should indeed be so much lower than those of men. Moreover, I can say with certainty that girls under the age of 10 show no difference either physically or mentally compared to boys of the same age. It is only in later years, under the pressure of the conditions I have mentioned above, that a difference between the two sexes becomes apparent.

While the woman, carrying heavy loads and visibly run down, drags herself along, the man, on the other hand, strides along in a manner unforgettable to anyone who has had the opportunity to observe these naked natives in the wild and untouched by culture. Australian men move lightly, firmly and with a certain dignity, and I once heard an excellent artist say of their gait that it was unmatched and reminiscent of the movements depicted in the statues of classical antiquity. But are we not in the habit of saying that there is much in a man's walk that expresses the vigour and nobility of the soul?

It cannot go unmentioned here that in relation to sexual intercourse, according to general experience, the Australian is moderate. A violation of morals on the part of the sober native, not yet touched by the vices of society, has hardly ever been reported. I have camped many a night near the camps of the blacks and would often have been in a position to observe any violence and indecency in this respect; but I cannot remember a single instance where the perceptions I have made could have offended my sense of morality.

Let us now turn our attention to a contrasting example. I once had a black man as a guide, whom they called Warreka or Wakeda Charley, which means the wild, unruly Charley, because he led a hermit's life in the bush and kept away from people, even from the other blacks. The man, by the way, was quite reliable; I could not perceive the least wild and unruly thing about him. But in the evening, after dark, he became restless from time to time and went off to the bush. I put this down to his hermit tendencies. One evening, while we were camped around a large fire near a creek, I suddenly heard something like a fleeting scurry from the neighbouring sand hill, and by the dim illumination of our fire I thought I recognised a figure in a hurry. Immediately our 'Warreka' was gone and it was not until the following morning that I had the opportunity to question him about it, as the inexplicable apparition had worried me to some extent. Now he confessed to me that it was his lubra (wife), who had run over the sand hills; she was no longer permitted to show herself to any white man, lest she suffer the same fate as his first wife, who had been 'seized by the burning fire' as a result of contact with whites, so that he had been forced to cast her out. A few days later I saw his unfortunate first wife and immediately recognised the cause of her separation from her husband: She was disfigured by syphilis in a truly horrifying way.

I now come to a section of my lecture which I would rather not have touched upon, but which I feel I must do so in order to solve the task set me.

It has always been a matter of special interest to me to examine the position of missionary work in relation to these poor, doomed human beings; whether this work is equal to its task, whether it understands the task at all, and in what sense. I said that I would rather not have touched on this question, for the reason that I could hardly agree with the way in which missionary work proceeded right from its beginnings, and yet on the other hand I was convinced that in most cases the missionaries tried to perform their work with the most honest intention and the greatest zeal. Later, their tactics changed and improved; but this change came much too late to be of any advantage to the tribes that were on the verge of extinction. From this follows the sad truth that, if good comes from missionary efforts, this can only apply to the present – it will probably not be a task for the future, since after all we have learned about it, the demise of the Australian indigenous population can hardly be prevented.

As I was walking through most of the Australian settlements 18 years ago, I had already begun to realise that the missions had made the mistake of starting to develop these unfortunate human beings and make them into better citizens of the world by preaching to them about the highest teachings of religion and trying to make them receptive to these, whereas it would certainly have been more beneficial if they had tried to improve their physical and social condition. Instead of pressuring adults in schools with the teaching of religion and other things, they should have been introduced to order and discipline in classes for gymnastics and wrestling and at the same time taught an understanding of the advantages of an orderly life and agricultural methods. Surely more would have been achieved in this way than by them sitting in school and church, both of which were completely alien to these children of nature. Thus, it happened that missionaries were often of the opinion that there was nothing to be done with the blacks and that missionary work among them could therefore be abandoned. The standard and criterion here was the acceptance of the truths and teachings of the Gospel. When the Aborigines were driven away from their best hunting and fishing grounds without recompense, we often saw them openly rebel against the missions and their protests degenerate into cruelty. This was the case, for example, in Queensland, when the German mission in Ebenezer on the Brisbane River tried to operate in dangerous circumstances with great sacrifices, finally as far as I know, gave up the cause as a hopeless case. Of course, this only happened when the majority of the original inhabitants had long since ceased to exist.

I have had many opportunities to see for myself how little was done to improve the material situation of the savages at the beginning of the missionary work. It is possible that this is partly due to the lack of sufficient means, but it is certain that the influence on the blacks in relation to the improvement of their material situation, which is what is most important, has not been beneficial, in spite of all the sacrifice and perseverance on the part of the missionaries.

One thing, however, was learned by these latest disciples of the Gospel: a certain sophistical reasoning when they set out to pursue their goal. Since the examples that serve to prove this at the same time provide evidence of the powers of reason of these savages, I do not think I can withhold them from you.

The mission provided the blacks with as much flour, sugar, tea and woollen blankets as they could. Of course, this distribution was on the condition that the blacks who had been given these items as gifts had to live according to the aims and regulations of the mission. Often, I met blacks who displayed a certain zeal in religious practices in order for their needs to be met, because the provisions they received had already become indispensable to them. I remember one such black zealot in particular, who locally was simply called the pastor, because he always carried a Bible under his arm and occasionally pretended to be reading in it. I asked him the reason for his piety, whereupon he told me with a certain cunning that if he read this book a great deal, he would always get sugar, flour and tobacco in abundance, but reading was out of the question for him, as he was not able to do so.

On one of my journeys, I was accompanied by two blacks, who belonged to a mission, and I had every reason to regard them as particularly skilful and alert. While climbing a mountain ridge for several days, we went through such a dense area of scrub and bush that it was dangerous to venture far from the camp without experienced guidance, since it was often difficult to find the way back. My young assistant, a brave sailor, was no particular hero in finding the paths again and for that reason was not at all courageous in the bush, however intrepidly he may have braved the waves. When

I returned to my camp one evening and found no tea ready, which is such a necessary comfort in the Australian bush, I learnt that my young assistant had not gone to fetch water from the spring, which was only a short distance from the camp, fearing that he might get lost. One of my blacks also heard this and said that the whites, if they were so scared, should never go into the 'bush' at all and concluded his speech, shaking his head, with the words 'white fellow big one stupid'. I then ordered him to go with my assistant to the spring, which he did, repeating what he had just said. After some time, we were sitting at our supper, each thinking his own thoughts, when Tommy, a bow-legged fellow, suddenly turned to my assistant and asked: Why don't you take a Bible with you into the woods? Because you see, he said, turning to me, if Mr. Gr ... (missionary) goes into the bush, he always takes a large Bible with him. Suppose he can't find his way, then he takes the Bible in his hand and prays to 'that big one up there', who immediately tells him all the things that can save him – then he added with a touch of irony and a certain triumph in his face, I have to go and 'fetch him out'.

One evening I arrived with my party at a deserted station, and as we had had no meat to eat for some days, I was delighted to hear the crowing of some stray cockerels in the early morning. I immediately asked one of my guides to shoot one of these birds for our meal, but he pretended that he could not do so, as the bird did not belong to him and he did not want to commit theft. I saw that this was only an excuse to persuade me to make a concession, so I said: You will get a shilling for the cockerel if you get it for me; this did not fail to have an effect. He explained to me that the cockerel belonged to a black man who had once taken one of his. Therefore, he could do what I asked with a clear conscience and a few minutes later we had an excellent bird in our pot.

All the various traits of character and intellect that I have told you about here certainly do not testify to the absolute inability of Australian savages to form concepts and to assimilate ideas of the most diverse kind. As noted above, their insensitivity to the teachings of Christianity has often been taken as proof of this inability, but no thought has been given to the fact that the untrained minds of these poor human beings are expected to grasp concepts which, after thousands of years of culture, we still grapple with and cannot quite come to terms with. If, of course, such a standard is applied, then the verdict on the powers of understanding, the correct definitions of which we are now concerned with, cannot for a moment be doubted in the case of exact scientific research in anthropology. If, on the other hand, the powers of the mind of the Australian Aborigines are considered merely from the point of view of their capacity for education in general, I do not hesitate for a moment to say that, if serious attempts were made and the right procedure followed, corresponding successes could be achieved and civilisation could be made accessible to these tribes. Unfortunately, however, this question, after what I have already referred to above, is from the practical point of view apparently completely superfluous and has only one value for the anthropologist, in that the individual tribes will not resist the influences of civilisation, and probably sooner or later no more will be left of them, as is already the case with their tribal brothers in Tasmania: only the memory of them.

It is not relevant to the purpose of my lecture to investigate the causes of the extinction of the Australian race, in order to deduce the means of remedying it; these matters, if they can still have any purpose at all, at least for the south of Australia, may be left to better and more practised observers in this field. As I said at the beginning, my only objective was to give a picture of this highly peculiar, so much maligned and so lowly placed race from my experiences in an intellectual, if you like, in a moral respect, which may perhaps help to give a more correct idea of the position of the Australians among rational beings. If I have succeeded in this, and even if I have perhaps given the impetus for a more competent force among you to examine the matter on scientific grounds before it is too late and the whole tribe recedes into oblivion, then I have achieved more than I dared to hope. But I find my satisfaction especially in the fact that, before an assembly so competent in questions of the physical and intellectual condition of mankind, I became an advocate for a race which has proved useful and faithful to me on many occasions, about whom I have been able to report no significant complaints, but only positive things.

Anthropologists and Ethnographers

Wilhelm Krause, 'Anthropological Journey to Australia'

Wilhelm Krause was born on 12 July 1833. The son of the anatomist Karl Friedrich Theodor Krause, he studied medicine and took his doctorate before working for a number of years in hospitals in Hannover. In 1860 he took up a position teaching and researching anatomy at the University of Göttingen. He moved to the Anatomical Institute at the University of Berlin in January 1892, working with Wilhelm Waldeyer, and in May of the same year he completed his habilitation and became Professor of Anatomy.

In his mid-60s, Krause travelled to Australia in 1897 to undertake, according to the Adelaide Advertiser, *anatomical research that focused on the craniology of Indigenous Australians. While in Adelaide and elsewhere in Australia he collected numerous Indigenous remains and sent them back to the Anatomical Institute in Berlin. Many of these remains have since been repatriated. Krause arrived in Adelaide on 24 May 1897 and quickly enmeshed himself in the scientific life of the colony. He was shown the Adelaide Museum by his compatriot Amandus Heinrich Zietz, who had arrived in Adelaide in 1883, and visited the Adelaide Zoo to study Australian marsupials. He also studied fossils that had been collected at Lake Callabonna and was reunited with his former student and Adelaide's Professor of Anatomy (on Krause's recommendation), Archibald Watson.*

Krause died in Berlin on 4 February 1910.*

---

* *Further reading:* Andreas Winkelmann, 'Wilhelm Krause's Collections: Journeys between Australia and Germany', in Cressida Fforde, C. Timothy McKeown, Honor Keeler (eds.), *The Routledge Companion to Indigenous Repatriation: Return Reconcile, Renew,* London, Routledge, 2020; 'Professor Krause' *The Advertiser* 31 July 1897, 6; 'Current Topics' *The Advertiser* 7 August 1897, 12.

Source:
Extract from 'Hr. Wilhelm Krause berichtet über seine anthropologische Reise nach Australien', *Zeitschrift für Ethnologie*, 29 (1897), 508–511.
Translation: Harald and Aileen Ohlendorf

Mr. Wilhelm Krause reports about his anthropological journey to Australia, during which the previously constructed travelling microscope made of aluminium (*Verhandl.* 1894, Vol. XXVI, 98) proved very useful, presents various objects that were brought back, among others those relating to the Ice Age in Hallett's Cove (South Australia), and the following treatise:

Australian Skulls
During my stay in Australia in the summer of 1897 I examined somewhat more than 200 skulls of Australian natives. This was conducted in June 1897 in accordance with the Frankfurt Agreement, to which the numbers of the first horizontal row in the tables refer. The skulls Nos. 1–17 and 24 were provided by the Professor of Anatomy, Mr. Allen, Melbourne, from the anatomical collection of the University; also from Melbourne are Nos. 18–23, the private property of Professor B. Spencer, No. 25, a gift from Dr. Peipers, and No. 26 from Dr. Ch. Ryan. The skulls Nos. 27–103 were examined in Sydney. Nos. 27–33 belong to the Anatomical Department in Sydney under its Director, Professor Wilson. Nos. 34–36 and 38–46 are in the McLeay Museum in Sydney; No. 37 I received from Mr. MacDowall, medical student in Sydney; Nos. 47–89 belong to the Australian Museum in Sydney; No. 90 is in the possession of Professor Liversidge also in Sydney; I received Nos. 91–103 from a private collection through Professor Wilson in Sydney. Nos. 104–187 I received courtesy of the directors of the South Australian Museum in Adelaide, Mr. Stirling and Mr. Zietz sen., with the exception of skull No. 135 from the Anatomical Department in Adelaide under Professor Watson. Furthermore, No. 151 is a gift from Dr. Lendon in Adelaide, No. 152–154 from Dr. Marten in Adelaide and No. 155 from Mr. Minchin, Director of the Zoological Garden in Adelaide. Skull No. 188 belongs to Mr. Mallor in Adelaide.

The following were sent directly to Berlin: a complete skeleton and another skull from Mr. Martin, Professor of Physiology in Melbourne, and 4 particularly beautiful skeletons, for which I owe thanks to my dear friend Professor Watson in Adelaide, as well as a skeleton from the Solomon Islands.

I would like to express my sincere thanks to all these gentlemen and especially to Professor Watson, who has supported me with many recommendations.

So far, about 150 Australian skulls have been documented, cf. the statistics of Virchow (*Zeitschr. f. Ethnol.* 1880, vol. XII, 1) and Turner (*The comparative osteology of races of man. Reports of the voyage of H.M.S. Challenger.* Edinburgh 1884, Vol. X, Pl. XXIX); few have been added since then. Wilson (Fraser, The Aborigines of New South Wales, Sydney 1892, 96–99, and 'Report of the Horn Expedition to Central Australia,' T. IV. *Anthropology*, 1896) measured 9 skulls, Halford (Brough Smyth, *On the Aborigines of South Victoria* 1878, Vol. II, 340–378) earlier measured 5 skulls.

Of the above-mentioned 200 Australian skulls, 187 were measured in accordance with the Frankfurt Agreement. In calculating the mean averages, 15 can be eliminated because they proved to be female; 4 because they were certainly or very probably half-castes, descended from a white father and a black mother. Furthermore, 10 are excluded because they were incompletely preserved and in parts only in fragments or were pathological; 6 because they were sent directly to Berlin with the associated skeletons; 10 because of their young age; 5 were still being macerated in Adelaide; 1 belonged to a giant; 1 skull was still in its burial shroud, and 4 could not be examined more closely due to the lack of time. Of the remaining 155, 21 are certainly male, except for the giant; 134, which are here called 'mixed', are to be included with the male skeletons for the establishment of mean numbers, for they are without doubt for the most part male, but there is no direct proof of this.

Taking the male and the mixed skulls together, the following results: The Australian skull is dolichocephalic (L.-B. = 69.7); almost hypsicephalic (L.-H. = 74.6); prognathous, for the profile angle is

78.6°; narrow-faced (facial index, according to Virchow = 119.4); with a narrow upper face (upper facial index = 70.0); leptoprosopic (zygomatic arch facial index =91.8); with leptoprosopic upper face (zygomatic arch upper facial height index = 53.6); chamaeconch (orbital index= 79.0); hyperplatyrrhine (nasal index= 64.0) and leptostaphyline (palatal index= 68.2).

The female skull is also dolichocephalic (L.–B. = 71.2) and hypsicephalic (L.–H. = 76.2), prognathous (79.7°), narrow-faced (116.8), with narrow upper face (70.7), leptoprosopic (90.9), with leptoprosopic upper face (54.7), but in contrast to the male mesoconch (83.8), platyrrhine (52.7) and leptostaphyline (63.7).

The general characters of the Australian skull are compiled here so that they need not be repeated in the discussion of each individual skull. The skull is very dolichocephalic and at the same time high, i.e., hypsidolichocephalic. The *arcus superciliares* are very prominent, the nasal root is depressed, the nasal bones are narrow in their upper half, all *cristae* (crests) and muscle attachments are very prominent. There is often a transverse occipital *torus* or a median frontal *torus* extending in the region of the obliterated frontal sutures. The forehead is narrow and receding, the width of the forehead is very small.

The zygomatic bones are rather oblique, with their lower edge laterally deviating. In the *norma verticalis* one can see through between the frontal bone and the zygomatic arches, due to the small width of the forehead. In the temporal fontanel, wormian bones are frequent, which tend to fuse with the neighbouring bones at one of their edges and then, depending on the circumstances, represent a frontal process of the *squama temporalis* or a long *processus sphenoidalis oss. parietalis*, or enlarge the ala magna, namely by widening its upper end.

Sometimes, but by no means always, the *ossa parietalia* are laterally flattened, so that the skull in the *norma occipitalis* resembles the roof of a house and is pentagonal. There is also sometimes a drop from the vertex to the back.

The *processus styloides* are thin, slender, often as if broken off, indicating a composition of several pieces, but their *vaginae* are usually very strongly developed. The *processus mastoides* are small, short, the *incisurae mastoideae* very often double. Very often *spinae supra meatum* are present, the *cristae supramastoideae* are usually very strongly developed, the *lineae temporales superiores* often extend across the *tubera parietalia*. Sometimes the *condyli occipitales* are separated into two halves by a transverse dividing line; very common are *processus paramastoidei*, furthermore deep pits between the lineae *nuchae inferiores* and the posterior margin of the *foramen occipitale magnum*.

All holes and openings on the skull are very wide. This phenomenon is most interesting in the auditory organ; the width of the *meatus acusticus internus* is probably related to a greater thickness of the acoustic nerve, the width of the external auditory canal to the extension of the tympanic membrane over a larger space, and both to the excellent hearing acuity of the natives.

The f*oramina ovalia* are sometimes very wide, more roundish than longitudinally oval (e.g., No. 179).

As for the face, the orbital rims bulge. This is by no means so significant as to resemble opera glasses, as Virchow characterized this formation in the apes, but more so than in European races. Furthermore, the usually very considerable depth and size of the *fossae caninae* is striking, and not infrequently *fossae praenasales* are present. Prognathism is very significant, which is not so obvious in the figures of the profile angle. Prognathism is mainly caused by the oblique position of the alveolar processes. The rows of teeth fit together at the front, in contrast to the races in which one row, usually the lower one, recedes behind the other. The teeth were ground down at an early age, which is a consequence of chewing uncooked roots or plant fibres for making nets; this is, of course, not the case in the civilised Australian natives.

Behind the wisdom tooth the *processus alveolaris* of the upper jaw extends backwards, sometimes containing a small cavity, and in any case providing room for a fourth molar tooth; the palatal end width is usually somewhat more considerable than the palatal middle width, but the differences are only slight.

Despite the great absolute length of the skull, the length of the skull base does not usually exceed the norm; it averaged 101.5 mm on 30 skulls. This shortness causes the above-mentioned retraction of the nasal root, which gives the living natives such a characteristic appearance.

The characteristics described, the varieties of which are to be compared, are more or less prominent in every Australian skull. These characteristics are not random but are related to each other. Some of them are classified in anatomy as varieties, which occur in all races, but in very different frequencies. They are related to embryonic deviation, disorders in the development of the masseter muscles, the hyoid muscles, the neck muscles and are characterised by a stronger development of these muscles in contrast to others. The Australian shares some of these characteristics with other primitive races, but nowhere, as far as we can tell, are they so pronounced. Each of these characteristics has the tendency to give the skull a more childlike or even more animal character. Scientific anatomy regards the Aryan as the normal human being, and deviations from this type can most easily be subsumed as disorders. A native Australian anatomist, if there were one, would probably hold the opposite view. However, one can now say that there is a disorder, a retardation in the development of the forehead region. Characteristic of this are: the *processus frontales* of the *squama temporalis* or the wormian bones in the temporal fontanel, the short length of the base of the skull in comparison to the whole length, the retraction of the root of the nose, the narrow width of the forehead, while the *arcus zygomatici* protrude laterally, the frequency of a *torus frontalis medianus*, and so on. The retention of the frontal region is undoubtedly not dependent on the skull, but on the frontal lobe of the brain. It would therefore be necessary to refer to the embryonic stages of development, or first to the brain itself, which, according to Waldeyer's advice, should be prepared in a formaldehyde solution prior to being shipped.

The well-known sexual characteristics of the female skeleton also apply to the Australian female. The middle part of the sternum is almost twice as long in the male as the *manubrium*; in the female, including the Australian female, the latter is relatively longer. The clavicle is less curved, the lateral parts of the *sacrum* are broader, the *arcus pubis* not as angular as in the male. All bones are more delicate, slender, the muscle attachments and joint ends less pronounced.

The female skull is smaller, its bones thinner, the former therefore lighter in total, the length-height index and the orbital index larger. Its dimensions are somewhat smaller, all the characteristics of the male skull compared to other races are present, but less pronounced. Dolichocephaly is slightly reduced, the capacity significantly so, on average approximately 100 cc less. All *foramina* are smaller, the orbital entrances more rounded, their rims not so bulging, the root of the nose not so significantly depressed, the muscle attachments and cristae less developed. However, it would be difficult to identify a female skull with certainty based on these characteristics [...].

Erhard Eylmann, 'Journey to Point McLeay'

Paul Erhard Andreas Eylmann remains one of the most enigmatic German travellers in Australia. His Australophilia manifested in three epic journeys to the continent and in a major publication, to this day barely known to an Australian readership.

Born on the island of Krautsand in the Elbe River in northern Germany, Eylmann studied botany, physics, chemistry and comparative anatomy in Leipzig. By the middle of 1884 he was studying medicine at the University of Freiburg, in his spare time pursuing a fascination with zoology and graduating with a doctorate in that area. He finally finished his medical studies in Würzburg, opening the path to a career as a doctor. For reasons likely to be connected with his wife's lung condition, Eylmann practised in the warm, dry climate of Cairo, at least until his wife's death, an event which seems to have persuaded Eylmann to abandon medicine and devote himself to a discipline in which he had no formal training, namely ethnography.

It is not clear why Eylmann directed his ethnographic interest almost exclusively to Australia. His three visits occurred in the period 1896 to 1913; any prospect of further visits was scotched by war, Germany's – and Eylmann's own – postwar economic crisis, and finally his death in 1926. Unlike many of his contemporaries, Eylmann eschewed the collective scientific expedition, travelling either alone or, at times, with a single fellow-traveller. His major achievement as a traveller took place over the period from March 1896 to the end of 1898, during which he made his *way from Adelaide to Darwin and back, largely on horseback and on foot, following the Overland Telegraph Line and taking detours to points of interest to the line's east and west. His preparations in Adelaide included discussions with a number of countrymen, among them the visiting physical anthropologist Wilhelm Krause. Later travels in June 1900 and again in 1912/1913 were confined to South Australia and western Victoria.*

The extract below is not from Eylmann's 1908 book Die Eingeborenen der Kolonie Südaustralien *(The Natives of the Colony of South Australia) but rather from the journal he kept during his travels on his second visit to Australia. While Eylmann was critical of missionaries and their efforts to understand Australians – he developed a strained relationship with Carl Strehlow during his stay at Hermannsburg – he nonetheless relied heavily on the hospitality of the missionaries and their local knowledge. In the extract below he travels from Adelaide to the mission station founded by the Aborigines' Friends' Association at Raukkan (Eylmann refers to it as Point McLeay) in Ngarrindjeri territory 80 kilometres south-east of Adelaide. Unlike the missionaries, Eylmann did not live long enough with any group to learn its language and culture in any depth; his contacts with Indigenous people, his interests and his publications were wide-ranging, and for all his scientific training and keenness of observation, he replicated many of the prejudices of his contemporaries. His overall assessment of the people he encountered was that they represented an early stage of cultural development, which however was not to be interpreted as an indication of biological or intellectual inferiority.**

Source:
Personal papers of Erhard Eylmann, held at the Übersee-Museum, Bremen. Translated and reproduced with permission.
Translation: Harald and Aileen Ohlendorf.

---

* *Further reading:* Peter Monteath, 'Globalising German Anthropology: Erhard Eylmann in Australia', *Itinerario*, 37 (1), 2013, 29–42; Peter Monteath, 'Erhard Eylmann's Missionary Position', *Anthropological Forum*, 27 (3), 2017, 240–255; Peter Monteath, 'Erhard Eylmann in South Australia', *Journal of the Historical Society of South Australia*, 41, 2013, 89–103; Wilfried Schröder, *Ich reiste wie ein Buschmann: zum Leben und Wirken des Australienforschers Erhard Eylmann* (Darmstadt, W.P. Druck & Verlag, 2002).

Milang (at Lake Alexandrina) Monday, 18 June 1900
In the morning I went by train to Milang, 64½ miles from Adelaide. During the first half of the journey, through the Mount Lofty Range, we were presented with the typical picture of a hilly landscape of the south coast of this colony, covered with sparse gum tree forests. At some points the view was over the hilltops and the flat coastal area to the distant sea. We then reached the plain between the Mount Lofty Range and Lake Alexandrina. From Strathalbyn to Sandgrove [Sandergrove] we drove through dense mallee scrub. Between the afore-mentioned station, where the railway track divides, and Milang, a treeless lowland stretches out. This is used for cattle grazing.

Milang is a small town on the western shore of Lake Alexandrina. The buildings do not form continuous rows but are scattered along wide tracks similar to tree-lined country roads [in Germany].

The present shore of the lake is flat and marshy. Sometimes closer, sometimes further from it runs another shore, which now and then slopes somewhat steeply. In any case, the water of the lake reaches this far in rainy seasons. Shipping is of no importance. Apart from two small steamers and a few fishing boats, I did not notice any ships. On the other hand, the water surface is populated by numerous aquatic birds, such as: waterfowl, ducks, pelicans, gulls, black swans etc. In the afternoon, I paid a visit to two black couples living together in a tent made of old sacks near the jetty at the foot of a steeply sloping bank. When I arrived, I had to announce myself by shouting, as they had covered the entrance due to the cold weather. One of the occupants then lifted up the corner of one of the sacks and invited me to enter the tent through the resulting opening. Crawling on all fours, I accepted his invitation. The two couples were sitting on old blankets around a fire in the middle of this tent, leisurely smoking their pipes. I was told to sit between the two men, and so that I would not dirty my clothes, the younger man spread an old jacket on the floor and put a greasy pillow on it.

The older man has white hair; he may well be 60 years old. The younger one, about 30 years of age, caught my eye because of his strikingly strong bushy eyebrows. Both have a half-length full beard.

The women are not stout, especially the younger one. The oldest is the ugliest woman I have ever seen. She has a moustache and a half-moon shaped beard on her chin. Like the hair on her head, the whiskers are partly grey and 2 cm long. The stature of the four is below the average height of a Southern German. The colour of the skin can be described as coffee brown, while that of the natives in the Australian interior is chocolate brown. In exchange for a gift of tobacco, I learned the following from these natives about their customs, habits, weapons, etc. They belong to the Narringeri tribe.

After death, the soul goes to a beautiful place far to the west (sunset), beyond the sea, which is particularly distinguished by its abundance of fish. Only one entrance leads to it. The younger man told me and the others that years ago a man from the region of Euchuka [Echuca] on the Murray had reported to him that a dead man had once returned with a large fish from this dwelling place of the souls of the deceased and had told him many things about this afterlife of the blacks, but after a week this man had to start his journey again, back to the realm of the dead.

Polygamy is common. The bad men, however, have or rather had to be content with one woman as punishment. As soon as the boys reached manhood, their beards were torn out and they were given a lubra. I would like to mention that each man had to undergo this operation only once. And that after the operation he let his beard grow to its full length.

Circumcision and subincision were not common. The dead were first laid on a 2–3 m high scaffold with their arms spread out 'like Christ' and a strongly smoking fire was kept burning underneath until the body was more or less smoked and then they were buried. Men and women used to carry a kangaroo bone in their nasal septum. Of the four I talked to, only the younger woman had a hole in her septum. When I asked them why they had given up this custom, they said that they could not obtain a kangaroo.

Fish were caught in a net made of rushes.

They had three forms of spear: a wooden spear with numerous barbs, a simple stick-shaped spear whose shaft at the bottom was made of the flower stalk of the xanthorrhoea plant, and a spear whose tip was armed with 22 rows of stone chips. These were not fixed with the gum of xanthorrhoea, but with the resin of the pine tree.

The younger brother-in-law made the sketches below of the usual cutting and short throwing weapons, as well as of the two shields. The wider of these was made from the bark of the redgum. The narrower one was only owned by a few.

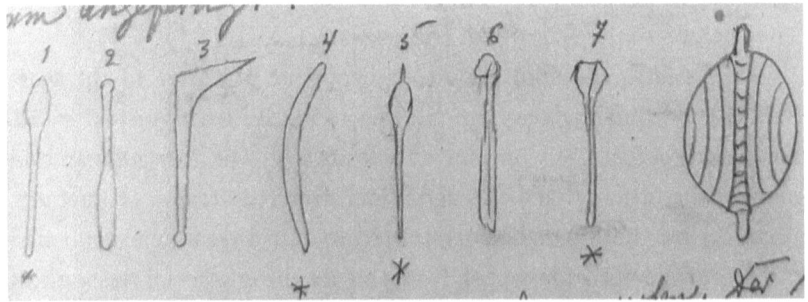

The weapons marked with * were thrown.
The boomerang – Fig. 4 – could be thrown so that it returned to the thrower.

Before leaving the blacks, I took some photographs of them.

Mission Station Point Mac Leay [Point McLeay], Tuesday, 19 June
I spent the night at the Pier Hotel. Here I developed the negatives of the photographs I had taken yesterday, which took me the first half of the night.

Around noon I left Milang on the steamer bound for Point McLeay and Meningie. My intention was to visit the first place mentioned, where the mission station of the same name is located. After a two-hour trip, our old paddle steamer docked at a small landing stage in Albert Passage, a narrow canal connecting Lake Alexandrina with Lake Albert. Here the passengers destined for Point McLeay had to disembark. On the shore was a young black man who was collecting the station's mail. When I told him I wanted to visit the missionaries, he offered me a seat in his two-wheeled cart. I gratefully accepted his offer, of course, as the station is 3 miles from the landing stage, and I had to carry a tin suitcase in addition to my photographic apparatus. After a quick ride over hilly terrain with a few casuarinas, we landed at the station. The superintendent of the station, Mr Garnedt [Garnett], and the warden joined us on our arrival. I introduced myself to the missionary and immediately told him the purpose of my visit. The reception was an extremely friendly one. When I had taken some refreshments at Mr Garnett's residence, I was asked not to leave the next day, but to return to Milang by steamer on Saturday when he would be back from his second trip to Meningie. Of course, I did not say no to their suggestion, as I always had an excellent opportunity to study the customs, traditions etc. of the natives at the mission stations. Towards evening I visited the native Daniel Wilson, who promised to send me a copy of each of the weapons used by the natives to my home in Adelaide within a month. This is the only black man who still makes weapons, and only to order, while the other men no longer have anything to do with them. In his room Wilson keeps a set of throwing and cutting weapons and a narrow shield, which had been ordered by an Englishman in Murray Bridge. I made sketches of these weapons below.

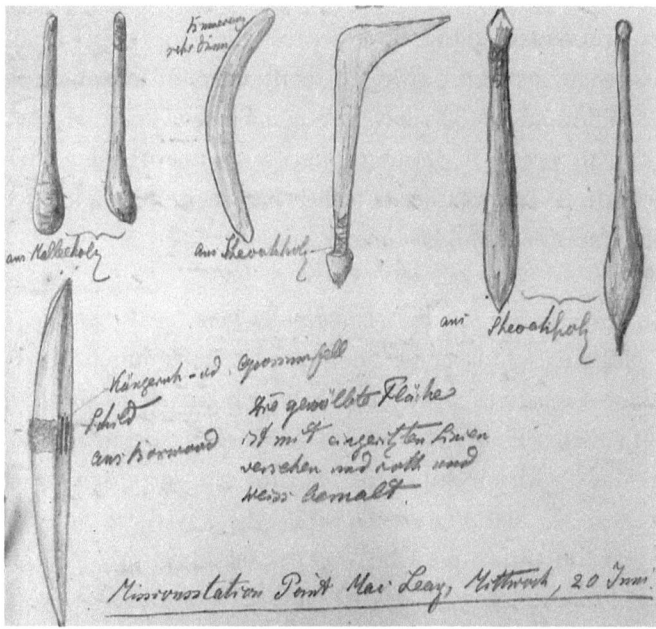

Pictures 1 + 2: of mallee wood, 3 + 4: Boomerang very thin, of sheoak wood, 5 + 6: of sheoak wood, 7: Shield made of box wood, kangaroo or possum skin. The curved surface has incised lines and is painted red and white.

Point McLeay Mission Station, Wednesday, 20 June
In the morning, with Mr Garnett, I visited a number of the tents near the building complex of the station. All the tents are quite similar to those of the four natives in Milang. On this occasion I saw a lubra who was sick with liver and spleen disease and a 40-year-old half-caste with partial paralysis of the lower extremities and bladder and a walnut-sized bone growth on the middle of his spine. Later we went to the school building and had the children perform a round dance accompanied by singing. The missionaries, in fact, intend to put on a kind of concert in Adelaide performed by the school children. An elderly half-caste, who is the first gardener at the station, claimed that the bones of the skull do not become thick by wearing a head covering, and that if a black man who never used to protect his head from the rays of the sun and the inclemency of the weather by covering it from the weather, were to start covering it, he would develop thinner skull bones. In the course of the conversation, he showed me an old scar on his head, which was supposed to have come from a blow with a waddy, and remarked that now, because the bones of his head would have lost their resistance through many years of wearing a hat, the wound would undoubtedly have brought about his end.

In the afternoon I photographed a group of old women and schoolchildren. The weather is bad. It has been raining for five days, and sometimes the wind becomes a gale.

Point McLeay Mission Station, Thursday, 21 June
In the morning I took some photographs. After lunch Mr. Garnett showed me the natives' workshop. Only ordinary shoes are made here, a pair of which sells for five to eight shillings in Adelaide. Most of the work is done with machines, i.e., cutting the soles, sewing etc. We then went to the station's vineyard. On the way there we passed the lonely grave of the native who was first baptised by Mr Taplin, the founder of the station.

Ringworm (*herpes tonsurans*), according to Mr Garnett, is a common disease among the natives and half-castes of the station. I believe that this skin disease is spread here especially by the dogs, which, as in the interior, also live with the people in their camps. The water in Lake Alexandrina is somewhat brackish. The natives get their drinking water from small wells on the shore of the lake and from a pump next to the vegetable garden, but this water is also quite rich in salts. Living hedges of buckthorn and [illegible] are often used to enclose gardens, pastures, etc.

The magpies and crows are said to cause so much damage when the fruit is ripe that the missionaries are forced to have them hunted.

Mission Station, Point McLeay, Friday, 22 June
I observed the following birds here: *gymnorhina leuconota* [Australian magpie] (common, gregarious in pastures, vegetable gardens and clearings), *corvus coronoides* [Australian raven] (rare), *hirundo neoxena* [welcome swallow] (common), *xema jamesonii* [Jameson's gull] (fairly common), *spatula rhynchotis* [Australian shoveler], *cygnus atratus* [black swan], *petroica multicolor* [Norfolk Island (scarlet) robin], *pelecanus conspicillatus* [Australian pelican], *gallinula tenebrosa* [dusky moorhen], (very common, gregarious), *phalacrocorax hypoleucus* [pied cormorant], *sauloprocta motacilloideo* [wagtail], *iliaticula ruficapilla* [dottrel].

Europeans are currently not allowed to shoot the aquatic birds, but the natives are allowed to shoot the game found here at any time of the year.

Mr Garnett told me that the two lakes are not rich in fish, as neither the saltwater nor the freshwater fish are able to live for long in the slightly salty water.

At Milang as well as in the vicinity of the mission station, there are outcrops of the travertine-like limestone of the Southeast in many places. In the vicinity of Lake Alexandrina, the soil consists of a dark humus sand, which often contains freshwater mussels in the lowlands. The water of Lake Alexandrina is coloured grey by silt. In all likelihood, the lake is becoming shallower and smaller due to the deposition of silt entering it from the Murray and will probably eventually disappear altogether over the ages.

Mr Garnett told me a few days ago that a loud noise was sometimes heard coming from the lake, and that the natives believed it was made by a spirit. This morning I went to some of the tents on the beach and got an old man to tell me the following about the noise mentioned, the customs, habits etc. of these natives. God Nurrundurie, when he is on the move from east to west, indicates his presence by the sound. The same has been heard from time to time since the beginning of the world. It is to be expected whenever 'the two little milk-white spots on the other side of the southern cross' do not appear. Just before the noise, small rainbows are seen around sunrise.

Nurrundurie is eternal, (*lulupuntkuli?* = no end). Long ago the natives saw him, and it is said that he was shaped like a tall man. When he passes by here, he orders the Njarringerie to honour magic. Corrobborees are then held to celebrate him [description redacted].

When a person dies, Nurrundurie leads his spirit to the dwelling place of the dead. Their migration goes first westwards through the Backstairs Passage and past Kangaroo Island, and finally turns upwards. There, where a table-shaped rock is washed by the ocean waves, they leave the mainland of Australia.

When I asked if there were any good or bad spirits apart from Nurrundurie, the native replied that the Njarringerie had only one god, Nurrundurie.

Nurrundurie once speared a large fish on his journey from east to west at Dorellar [not clearly legible], then cut it up and threw the pieces into the water. The fish whose descendants now live in the lakes developed from these pieces.

The dead are buried in a reclining position with their heads facing west, and an arbour is erected over the grave on four fork-shaped poles of leafy branches for protection. Men (*nörröggie*), whom the warriors had to obey as leaders in their feuds, are not buried, but at Nurrundurie's command a scaffold is erected for them, on which they are placed with their legs folded underneath, and so that the torso remains in an upright position, their hands are tied to two sticks projecting above the scaffold in such a way that the arms are spread out. Then a strongly smoking fire is kept burning under the grate on which the corpse is placed until the corpse is dry. In this state, the corpse is fastened to two long sticks after being wrapped in a soft mat of mallee bast (*tulongie*, 'as soft as a blanket'). The poles are placed in the ground at the camp site. When the corpse is moved, it is carried on the poles.

After 2–4 days, however, the dead person is finally laid to rest in the branches of a sheoak tree (casuarina). If the bones fall to the ground later, they are left there.

In the afternoon I went to see William, an old native, in his cottage. He told me that when the first white people came to this area, he had been a youngster. One day, while his relatives were sitting around the fire, some whites had suddenly appeared, and the natives' fear of them was so great that all the adults had thrown themselves into the lake and tried to save themselves by swimming ('like ducks'). He had been left behind and had rolled into the fire, which had caused a large burn on his leg, the scar of which could still be seen today.

William must therefore be at least 70 years old. His beard is white, but the hair on his head is only mottled grey. Despite his advanced age, his facial features are not yet aged. One would estimate his age at 60 at the most.

I owe the description of the chisel, the woomera and the four spear forms to him.

Their chisel consists of a long shaft and a rock splinter, which is fixed in a crevice of the shaft with resin.

The woomera forms a rod about 80 cm long, which has a spindle-shaped thickening in the middle. At one end there is a large hook (forming a whole weapon together with the rod) and at the other end there is a button-shaped thickening. The thickening in the middle and the end with the hook are flattened in one place. The button-shaped thickening serves, as William told me, to prevent the woomera from slipping out of the hand when the spear is being hurled.

The Njarrindjerie have four spear shapes. I made the sketches under the eyes of old William and his son-in-law according to their

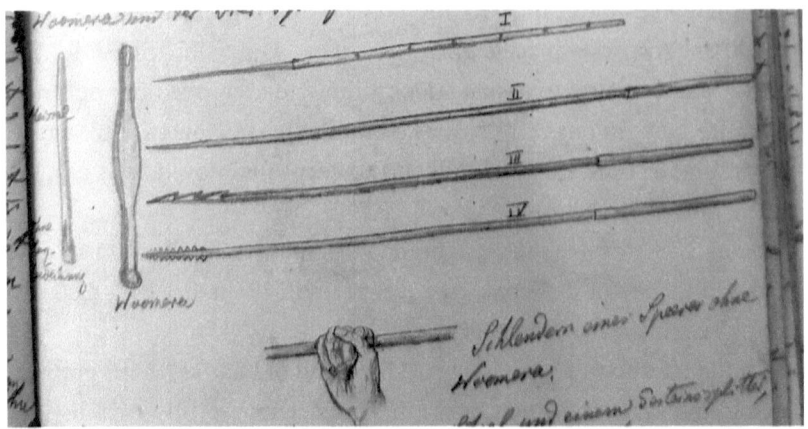

Images – Chisel without resin cover – Spears I, II, III, IV
Woomera
Picture – Hurling a spear without a woomera.

descriptions. No. 1 is the smallest of the spears. It has a shaft of cane (*phragmites communis*) and a simple tip of mallee wood. However, on my journey from the landing stage to the station, Abel Rankine [not clearly legible], my black coachman, had a bundle of cane stalks on the wagon that was intended for the boss. The cane stalks were not quite the thickness of a little finger.

Spears number 2, 3 and 4 have a wooden tip carved out of the top of the shaft. The tip of number 2 is barbed (a spear of this type in the Adelaide Museum, donated by Taplin, has three hooks) and the tip of number 3 is armed with rock splinters. The splinters form two rows and are attached to the wood with pine tree resin. The last third of the shaft is formed by the flower stalk of the xanthorrhoea plant. If the shaft of the three larger forms consists entirely of wood, it is hurled by hand. Sticks that were to be used as spear shafts were bent straight after they had been strongly heated in hot ashes.

Hatchets and knives were not made. Larger or smaller rock chips were used for cutting. The natives on the Coorong, on the other hand, are said by some authors to have had hatchets.

In the evening, a company of ten men (consisting of quadroons, half-castes and full-blooded negroes) entertained the people of the station in the church by singing solos and giving comic skits. The teacher accompanied the songs with music on the harmonium. The blacks distinguished themselves advantageously by their gesticulations and gestures. Blackmore, one of the singers, stood out to me because of his dark skin colour, shiny black hair and strong bushy eyebrows. The black audience gave their applause by clapping their hands and shouting.

After the concert, if I may call it that, I went back to old William and his son-in-law and asked them to tell me the following:

Nurrundurie, the name of the god, means the eternal one ('everlasting') and Njarringjerie means the ones who speak clearly ('plain speaking').

Nurrundurie once chased a large fish downstream. When it entered the lake and the god feared it would escape, he ordered a native to kill it and cut it into pieces. The pieces were then thrown into the lake, and from them the ancestors of the present fish developed.

Once two women ran away from their husband. The husband pursued them for a long time, and when the women finally reached the border of another tribal area and the husband feared that they might succeed in escaping, he called upon a higher power for help in his distress. Since he was a great sorcerer, his request was fulfilled when suddenly great masses of water rushed towards the women, forcing them to turn back. As punishment, they were turned into two rocks, which today are called the two pages. A similar legend is told about a rock in Lake Albert. A woman was turned into this rock because she was disobedient.

Long before the natives possessed fire, they had a strong desire to make use of it. When the need for fire grew very strong, a large meeting was called to find some ways of getting it. Among the crowd was a man whose height and appearance attracted everyone's attention. Through him they hoped to get possession of the fire. At a large corroboree he also danced and every time he bent his legs sideways, he pissed and with the urine numerous sparks always fell on the ground. The others now conspired to kill him so that the fire could be kept in his body.

A small but very clever man then lured the big one out of the crowd. Everyone wanted to spear him. Finally, however, it was agreed that the small, clever man had to kill him.

He then made the giant dance again and speared the giant's head from behind. Immediately, sparks flew out of the giant's body. Two people now tried to take possession of the fire by lighting flammable objects with the sparks, but they were so careless that the fire caused enormous grass and forest fires. When the giant was injured, he threw himself and his followers into the sea. He was transformed into a whale, and the spear wound served him to throw up the water that had entered his mouth while he was catching his breath. His companions became fish. But a similar fate befell all those who were present at the treacherous attack. The two who had started the huge bushfire flew away as robin red breast (*petroica*) and the others were transformed partly into plants and partly into animals of all kinds.

In earlier times the natives obtained fire using two flower stalks of the xanthorrhoea plant, by placing one vertically in a small hole of the other one, which was laid on the ground. By rolling the vertical stalk rapidly and persistently between the flat of the hands they finally produced some smouldering at the point of friction. Old William could not quite relate this method of extracting fire to the legends told just before. According to him, flints ('flint') were formed during the great bush fire. By striking two of these flint stones against each other (William spoke of 'friction'), sparks were obtained, and as a result two flower stalks of xanthorrhoea were made to smoulder by friction.

Leonhard Adam, 'On the Customs and Law of Some Australian Tribes: Personal First-hand Accounts from Two Natives'

Leonhard Adam was born in Berlin in 1891. He studied ethnology, law, economics and sinology in Berlin and in Greifswald. Although his passion remained ethnology, he made a career as a lawyer, after the First World War becoming an assistant judge and later district judge in Berlin. His passion and his career intersected in his particular interest in ethnological jurisprudence; he was the editor of the Zeitschrift für vergleichende Rechtswissenschaft (Journal of Comparative Jurisprudence) from 1919 to 1938. In the early 1930s Adam lectured in ethnological jurisprudence and primitive law and was a member of the board of experts of Berlin's Ethnographic Museum.

An early opportunity to apply his ethnographic skills came during the First World War, when German authorities permitted scientists, including ethnologists and linguists, to visit Prisoner of War camps detaining prisoners from the Entente Powers, including those from various parts of their colonial empires. In the course of his fieldwork in German POW camps, Adam studied two Indigenous Australians, Douglas Grant and Roland Carter, the latter a Ngarrindjeri man.

The encounter between Carter and Adam in a German POW camp in the First World War had a sequel many years later. Adam's own mixed heritage – he was part Jewish – persuaded him to seek refuge in Great Britain in 1938. As an 'enemy alien' he was detained in 1940 and sent to Australia along with some 2000 other German Jews aboard the Dunera. *After a period of internment in Victoria, Adam taught at the University of*

Melbourne and built up an ethnographic collection there. After the war he renewed his contact with Carter, by this time living back at Raukkan on Ngarrindjeri country. Both men died in 1960.*

Source:
Extract from Leonhard Adam, 'Über Sitte und Recht einiger australischer Stämme: persönliche Originalberichte zweier Eingeborener', *Zeitschrift für vergleichende Rechtswissenschaft*, 44 (1/3) 1928–29, 1–30.
Translation: Harald and Aileen Ohlendorf.

[...] Initially I did not think to include the second Australian, Roland Carter, in the study, since this tall and handsome young man, while possessing the unmistakable racial characteristics of the Australian natives, although with a lighter brown skin tone than Douglas Grant, was a half-caste. A horse-trainer by trade, he certainly demonstrated the lifestyle of one devoted to sport as a youth, who would play football with his friends from morning until night. But in his case I was pleasantly surprised in a different way. Having listened to a few of my conversations with Grant, Roland Carter offered, of his own accord, to give accounts of the natives at Lake Alexandrina. As I began to take down his personal details, the feeling of expectation had already started to grow that I would experience something meaningful. Indeed, what followed consisted not only of the confirmation of things already known to us, but also there were things which, at least to my knowledge, have been unknown until now, or at least have not been published. I would not, however, wish to overestimate the value of this interesting account. Even if my joyous surprise was indeed great when Carter suddenly began to speak of totemic things, what I have

---

* *Further reading:* Mary-Clare Adam and Robyn Sloggett, 'Roland Carter and Leonhard Adam: Friendship in the Preservation of Ngarrindjeri Knowledge and Cultural Heritage', *Australian Historical Studies* 49 (1) 2018; Aaron Pegram, 'Under the Kaiser's Crescent Moon', *Wartime: Official Magazine of the Australian War Memorial* (76) 2016, 32–37; Greg Dening, 'Adam, Leonhard (1891–1960)', *Australian Dictionary of Biography*, National Centre of Biography, Australian National University, https://adb.anu.edu.au/biography/adam-leonhard-9962/text17651, published first in hardcopy 1993, accessed online 27 May 2022.

collected is nevertheless too sparse to justify the enthusiasm which Josef Kohler and I felt when I brought these papers home in early 1918. Indeed, South Australia is no longer a *terra incognita* and has not been so for a long time; the ethnographic study of the area is relatively complete. All of us who were involved with the work in the prison-camps, Kohler, Dr Ernst Ubach, and I, knew that the interviews we conducted there could be no more than substitutes; further particulars on this point can be found in my introduction to the complete work cited above. However, a slight distinction has to be made: a) whether a missionary or a doctor makes observations in their spare time, without any comprehensive ethnological background, or b) whether an ethnologist builds his own theories through comprehensive studies of literature, or c) whether the latter, who knows his subject matter well, has the opportunity to stand in front of a person, who has grown up amongst totemic notions, and, in a carefully investigative manner steers the conversation almost imperceptibly to the point of discussing things that Europeans typically know only from outward appearances or from books. It is correct that the essence of totemism should not be judged in the way that the natives themselves have done, and especially as the natives themselves do today. One cannot dismiss the views of primitive people as completely insignificant. This is not the place to discuss the matter further. Roland Carter, as we shall see, makes absolutely no attempt to interpret, instead he provides us only with facts, which are much more important to us. His report, as I have said, ought not to be overvalued, but equally it should not be underappreciated. Whoever hears this lively, unspoiled child-of-nature speak, who certainly has never read an ethnographic book, nor done any ethnographic studies, must come to an understanding of the relative value of his untainted account. One must not imagine, however, that questions and answers simply followed one another, nor that Carter delivered his report without interruption. Rather, the conversation often went haltingly, extending over numerous days, lasting for several hours; some matters were described by the young man only when a memory was evoked by the context.

I have attempted in this account to represent the course of this ethnographic record as transparently as possible. On the whole, the primary source in the literature as a control for the ethnographic study with Roland Carter is Erhard Eylmann's work, *The Natives of the Colony of South Australia* (Berlin 1908, Dietrich Reimer [Ernst Vohsen]). The tribe about which Carter speaks – which he himself, however, does not name – is the Narrinyeri. I have reproduced some of Eylmann's significant findings as further explanations accompanying the record in footnotes.

III Roland Carter's report on the 'Lake Tribe' at Lake Alexandrina (South Australia)
(This ethnographic study was recorded in the English language, i.e. the transcribed conversation, which consisted of questions and responses, was held in English. A formal transcription of everything that was spoken could not be achieved, however, since there was nobody available who could have acted as stenographer. Therefore, as with most of the records of conversations with Indians, I wrote down the results of the interview in the German language. This admittedly was not philologically correct, but the danger of linguistic errors is as good as impossible, since both of the interlocutors were speaking a language they had mastered.

As I have incidentally remarked here, in the case of the Indian records, I later went back over the questions and answers, putting the appropriate Indian dialect into writing. This method would not have been possible for the Australians given the lack of time. It follows from the above that the following report contains many complete sentences in which Carter answered my questions with only a 'yes' or 'no'. The report therefore is in general an analogous reproduction in the German language of the results of the interview.)

Roland Carter first gave us his personal details. He stated (this was in March 1918) that he was 25 years old and described himself as half-caste. Together with him, I drew up the following sketch of his family tree:

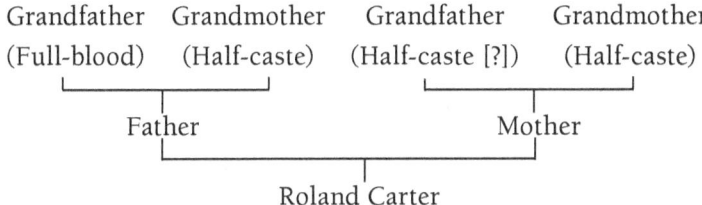

The name of his mother's tribe was apparently unknown to him. He could only say that it was located by Lake Alexandrina in South Australia and that he was born in Goolwa at Lake Alexandrina and lived in Point McLeay on the same lake. He works there as a horse-trainer. He speaks only English. He seemingly does not speak the native language, but he understands it when spoken by others. He went to the English school up until the age of 14. He says that he is a Christian. He claims to have always lived close to the natives. His mother and father live together. His grandfather on his mother's side is reputed to have been a great warrior.

1. Tribal Organisation, Leadership and Tribal Management.

The tribe has approximately 3000 members (men, women and children included).[1] The tribe is separated into groups, which are 2–3 miles distant from each other and each has approximately 500 souls.[2] The tribe has a leader, who resides in one of the tribal groups by the lake. He is also the leader in wars, which are often fought with other tribes. The leader fights from the front line. Roland Carter has experienced such battles. He says: Today they are forbidden by the English police.

Each of the subgroups of the tribe has a leader, too. This leader is not always an old man. The leader's successor is his son. If he proves incapable, then the most capable man in the tribe will become leader. This is also the case when there is no existing son. The brother of the leader is not entitled to succession. The election of a leader only occurs when no son capable of succeeding is available. This is done by the council. Here, the individual, whose election is being planned, is absent. The council consists of the male elders of the tribe. Its responsibilities include making decisions about official matters.

If the leader wished to wage war against another tribe, he would consult with the council assembly of elders and inform them of his plan. The assembly then decided to go to war and sent a messenger to the enemy tribe with a wooden pole of about 1 foot in length with carved signs, containing an invitation to fight on a particular hunting ground and at a particular time. The other tribe was not allowed to kill the messenger, but instead had to answer the message. Should the requested tribe refuse to come to battle, or simply did not appear, the other tribe attacked and spared no one. If someone had previously been insulted by a man of another tribe, he would tell his leader about it, who would then engage in war with the other tribe. Today, now that wars have been forbidden, the offended man demands a duel with the offender, which is carried out in the English manner by means of boxing or with native weapons.

The leader of a tribe's subgroup has to refer to the tribe's leader everything that he cannot determine for himself, or which cannot be dealt with to the satisfaction of the group's members. The leader is not a judge. Anyone who has been insulted or harmed by another, personally demands a duel with the offender, thus achieving satisfaction for himself.[3] The leader is clothed no better than other members of the tribe. Tribal costume is worn, which consists only of a covering of the genitalia.[4]

After the battle there was no formal peace agreement and each tribe returned home. There was no abduction of women or children. On the whole, only the warriors would meet, women and children stayed at home and did not come in contact with the enemy.

The natives live from hunting and fishing. The groups move around within the tribal region. They have huts, which are constructed from quite thin tree branches, the tips of which are tied together. The floor of the hut is round; its interior is only one room.[5] Each family lives in one home. The size of the hut is determined by the number of family members.

2. Family and Personal Law

The father is the head of the family. Each individual has a unique name. An example of a male name: Ngautaun, an example of a female name: Ngaulaun.

When a man dies, his widow assumes his property, e.g. animal furs, possessions. She decides what she wants to pass on to the children. In principle the children do not inherit anything. The father gives orders to his wife and children. If one of the spouses treats the other badly, then the leader will kill the perpetrator.[6]

Children are not sold. Children of either sex are treated well and are valued. The younger brother must obey an older one. Children must obey their mother. The family has all of their meals together.

There is no ceremony following the birth of a child. After approximately three days either the father or the mother gives the child a name. Particular behaviour of the father or of the mother following birth was not observed.[7]

The natives are Protestant Christians.

I proceeded at this stage to ask questions relating to totemism. At first Carter seemed not to understand what this was about. He responded in the negative to the question of whether among his tribe there was a belief in supernatural qualities of animals. This was perfectly justified, as is shown in the definition that he later provides of the *ngatji*. After that I changed the discussion to the topic of hunting, and Carter explained that the tribespeople had a great interest in hunting. I then asked whether in that case every animal could be killed. He thought for a while and then answered: 'No'.

For him killing a pelican would not be permitted. This prohibition was not generally applicable, only to his family. A closer examination produced the following:

The pelican is an animal considered to be a 'friend' by Roland Carter's family. He once wanted to shoot such an animal, but his mother forbade him: 'You must not kill that bird, because it is our *ngatji*!'[8, 9]

Other families also have animals as 'friends', such as birds and snakes, but not plants and stones.[10]

Ngatji are: wild goose, swan, *punkeree* (described by Carter as 'a kind of duck'); as well as a black water snake (up to 6 feet in length, dangerously venomous).[11]

This snake does not, for example, bite the members of its related totem family.

> [*Carter describes the following, which he witnessed with his own eyes in approximately the year 1905*]

A group of natives making their way to a Christmas celebration came across a large snake. Everyone fled in horror, but one old man asked what kind of snake it was. When he heard that it was a black snake, he took a piece of wood about as long as a forearm and moved towards the snake with the stick held high in his hand, addressing the snake in his native language. The snake raised itself up, its tongue darting out at him, and obeyed his command to leave, turning around and vanishing.

Another *ngatji* is a small black bird, which is never still, but always in motion. Its English name is not known to Carter, its Aboriginal name is: '*richeruckoree*'. This bird warns members of its *ngatji* group of possible danger, such as the approach of a snake, by appearing with its wings outstretched, fluttering back and forth and singing.

(Carter explains, after specific questioning:) The *ngatji* is not seen as a relative. Neither is a *ngatji* a 'god', rather, it is just a good friend who helps you. Carter cannot say in which particular way the pelican can help.

The members of a group, which has the same *ngatji*, all live in the same home. This constitutes a family. A woman has to have a different *ngatji* from a man, but after marriage she loses hers and takes on the *ngatji* of her husband. The children have the same *ngatji* as their father. Before her marriage Roland Carter's mother had the *ngatji* 'goose', his father had the pelican [sic]. This then became the mother's *ngatji* and later that of Roland Carter. There are many families with *ngatji*.

Individual families do not hold their own ceremonies; there are only corroborees of the whole tribe.

[Carter now describes the dances at corroborees. On multiple occasions he insisted on providing a description of these dances and looked forward to giving his report].

[Here follows a description of ceremonial dances.]

These dances do not take place at the same corroboree.

Carter does not know of other animal-dances. The dances take place at the beginning of each corroboree, at about 8 pm. This is followed by general dances involving both men and women. Dances by women only were not observed.

The Burial of the Dead: In former times, the dead would be smoked on a frame of wood. Four poles were driven into the ground, two of which stood at a shorter distance from each other, so that the four holes in which the poles were placed formed a long, narrow rectangle. The poles placed further apart from one another were connected by a crossbar. Shorter crossbars were placed above this. The dead body was then laid upon this, without any wrapping and the like, in a sitting position, with the legs crossed. The arms were crossed, and underneath a fire was lit with small green branches. The body, thoroughly smoked and thus preserved, remained for 1–2 years in the family's house in a corner. Then it would be placed in a tree canopy. This is now forbidden by the English police. It is believed that later the dead will be seen again.

[The following details from Carter amount to a case of trial by duel, modified due to totemistic notions.]

[Here follows a description of the practice to identify a murderer.]

The arrangement of the huts is not subject to any particular rules. One can build one's hut next to any other one that belongs to a different ngatji-group.

Kinship Relations: Carter knew only two kinds of these; he remarked that he was not aware of others. Their names: sister: *marrawee* and brother: *keelawee* (English pronunciation).

Laws of Marriage and Marriage Ceremonies: Carter does not know of any polygamy. It is stipulated that the wife must have a different *ngatji* to her husband. The age of marriage for men is at about 18 years, for women 16–17 years; however, marriage can also take place in later years. The bridal suitor is not the son himself, but his father; however, the son may point out a person of his choice to his father. Otherwise, the father chooses the bride. The mother must also agree. The father goes to the girl's parents. If they do not agree to the marriage, the marriage cannot take place. If an agreement is reached, then the sister or a female relative of the young man must be given as a wife to the brother or a male relative of the girl.

[*Here follows a description of beliefs related to weddings and marriage.*]

Property. Matrimonial Property Law: The natives bring the skins of animals they have hunted to the mission, teacher and the other few Europeans, and exchange these for foodstuffs, sugar, blankets and so on.

The husband owns all the belongings; the wife becomes the owner of all the presents she is given. After the death of the husband, the wife inherits everything. She can give items from the estate to their children if they would like certain things, for example, if a son wishes to have his father's rifle. After the death of the mother, the objects will be distributed amongst the children, according to what is suitable for each child. Weapons, for example, will only go to sons. Married children will also inherit.

There are also illegitimate children. The father of the unmarried mother asks her about the identity of the father of the child. Thereupon he approaches the parents of this man in order to arrange that the man and the girl marry. The child receives the *ngatji* of the father. An unmarried mother is not treated with scorn. Should the young man refuse to marry her, he will be killed.[12]

The Status of a Widow: The widow can stay on in the house or return to her parents. She is allowed to remarry but has to wait 12 months. Cases where a man might marry his brother's widow are not known. The man can marry any woman except the sister of his deceased first wife, just as the widow may not marry her brother-in-law.

Divorce: A man can leave his wife, and vice versa, if he or she does not like the other. The person who has been left is allowed to remarry. Roland Carter describes a case in which a man fell in love with a woman who arrived in the area, and disappeared with her, leaving his own wife and child behind. After one year, he returned with his new wife and a child, and lived in the same house as the first wife. This was a semi-detached house consisting of two separate rooms. The man was quite friendly to his first wife, but simply no longer lived together with her.

Slavery is unknown.

Naming: The father or the mother names their child a few days after the birth. Free choice is allowed in this regard. Sometimes the eldest son receives the name of his father, the eldest daughter that of her mother. Sometimes children will be named after deceased friends of their parents.

The belief in protective spirits is apparently unknown to Carter, with the exception of the *ngatji*. The killing or abandonment of children has not been observed.

Coming of Age Ceremony: The following custom was practised 10–11 years ago (going back from 1918): all the body-hair of young men aged 16–17 was ripped out by some older men of the tribe, and then they were rubbed with red ochre. In this way they would become men.

Nothing is known about young men's houses. Circumcision was not practised.

Some men and women paint their bodies at corroborees. White paint is used. No particular designs are known.

Tattooing is not practised.

Premarital Sexual Intercourse/Prostitution: Premarital sexual intercourse is an exception. A girl who engages in this, was or is not considered a prostitute. Professional prostitution was non-existent and was even strictly forbidden.

Animism: The Aborigines believed that souls go into another world, located above, which resembles this world. All souls go on the same journey.

Adoption: This occurs and was already practised before the European era. The adopted child had the same status as the biological children of the adoptive parents. Adopted children could not marry any children of their adoptive parents. Carter does not know whether the children received the *ngatji* of the adoptive parents.

Nothing is known about artificial brotherhood, or milk-kinship. It used to be that motherless children, or those of unwell mothers, would be nursed by unrelated women. These breastfed children would be seen as related and would not be allowed to marry the biological children of their wet nurse.

3. Property Law

Property: The land belonged to the whole tribe. One family had no particular rights to a piece of land. The house belonged to the family, but the father had full right of disposal; he was allowed to demolish the house and construct a new one anywhere.

Found Objects: The finder was obliged to look for the person who had lost the object. If he could not find him, he was allowed to keep the object. If he found him, then he had to return it. The person who had lost something was not obliged to reward the finder; instead he could offer a reward if he wished.

Hunting Law: The hunter was the owner of the hunted game. There was no general medium of exchange.

Goods were not purchased, instead they were only exchanged. According to Carter's statements, an exchange was irrevocable. It could not be reversed, and no party could subsequently demand a return because of any fault in the exchanged goods.

Giving of gifts: This was practised. Nothing is known regarding any obligation to give a reciprocal gift.

4. Penal Law and Criminal Prosecution
Theft did occur, but not often.

Murder: On this point, see above. There was an obligation to seek blood vengeance. This had to be carried out by any of the male relatives of the murdered individual; redemption from blood vengeance was not possible.

Personal Injury: Whoever suffered from this had to kill the perpetrator, if he was not hindered by the perpetrator's relatives from doing so. The person seeking blood vengeance was not punished.

Right to Asylum: A public place of refuge did not exist. The perpetrator could, however, flee to the house of friends, the pursuers then waited for him. If the perpetrator did not appear of his own accord, then the first member of the respective friends' household was seized. After one or two weeks, but without keeping him captive in the meantime, they dealt with him in the same way as the perpetrator had acted against the victim. Thus, the crime was avenged, and the perpetrator would no longer be pursued.

In the case of theft, there was no process for the victim to take matters into their own hands. The leader had to be called.

Whoever did not wish to take revenge themselves against an offender, took him to the leader, who had the right to impose any punishment which he deemed appropriate, including the killing of the perpetrator.

Punishments:
1. Death penalty. The leader ordered four to five chosen men to pierce the perpetrator with spears.
2. The binding of thieves to a tree for a week. Friends were allowed to bring the punished person food and water. Carter could not recall further punishments.

An unintentional misdeed would not be punished, according to Carter. Adultery supposedly did not take place at all.

The Identification of a Perpetrator: In former times, there were so called 'trackers' in the tribe. These were a type of detective, who had to search for and pursue perpetrators of punishable acts. If, for example, a murderer was being hunted down, one of about 20 trackers would go on the search for the culprit – young people of about 19 years of age – not armed but provided with a rod. The tracker only had to find the offender. It was not his responsibility to overpower and apprehend him. Instead, this was the responsibility of three to four warriors who accompanied him. The captured man would be brought before the leader. Nowadays, uniformed state police officers act instead of trackers.

Legal Procedure: There were no formal trials. There was also no negotiation before the leader, and equally no witness testimony. Sworn oaths were not known.

Carter knew nothing of magicians, or conjurers of spirits.

Notes

1. This figure is objectively incorrect. Eylmann, who stayed in Australia in 1896, wrote (1908) that the Narrinyeri were near to complete extinction; apart from half-castes they numbered only 100–120 people, most of whom lived on the Point McLeay [McLeay] mission station or in its neighbourhood. I consider it out of the question that Carter might have been consciously lying in his responses. Either he included the half-castes in his calculations and overestimated the number, which primitive people often do, or he meant times in the past, although he never said so.
2. This statement strengthens my supposition expressed in footnote 1, that Carter is referring to the past. According to Eylmann (p. 156) this tribal name means *'Die deutlich Sprechenden'* = plain speaking people. Eylmann attributes this interpretation to an old ward of the Point McLeay mission station.
   According to Taplin (*The Narrinyeri* p. 1) the name is an abbreviation of *Kornarrinyeri*, from *Kornar* = Man (Person) and *inyeri* = to belong, meaning 'belonging to the people'.
3. This statement is in contradiction with what Carter reports further under the section on penal law on p. 20.
4. This statement also proves that Carter is speaking of former times. The natives in his area wear only (unpleasant and unkempt) European clothing, the women partially covered in shawls (cf. table VIII in Eylmann p. 208/209). Incidentally, especially the natives at Lake Alexandrina originally had, by way of exception, warm clothing for bad weather, namely, the men wore coats made from the possum pelts and the women round rush mats.
5. C.f. Eylmann p. 313 ff. and table XIII.
6. Certainly, this is a wildly fantastic claim.
7. Carter could not report on circumcision or subincision. Rightly so, because the Narrinyeri do not know and have never known either of these. (cf. the list on p. 117 in Eylmann).
8. This is Roland Carter's pronunciation. In this text I use the German version *'ngatschi'*. Eylmann identified the same recording in Port McLeay, however, he wrote it as *'ngaitije'*. He explained the following: 'The totem becomes a friend, known as *ngaitije*. It may be hunted or caught by anyone if it is an animal. If a person kills an animal that is under their protection, the meat is given away; they may only eat any piece that is given back to them.' In war, all warriors carry a part of their *ngaitije*,

9   such as pelt, pieces of fur worn on the head, and sometimes placed on the spears, so that there is no confusion between 'foreign brothers' and enemies. One of my informants, a ward of the mission station, saw these ensigns as similar to the flags of European soldiers (Eylmann p. 164).
9   The pelican as a totemic animal is confirmed in the literature; according to Reverend Taplin (*The Narrinyeri* p. 2) this bird is the totem of the Tanganarin group, and Goolwa where they live is also the birthplace given by Carter (c.f. Eylmann p. 164).
10 This claim, that neither plants nor stones can be *ngatji*, coincides with the reports of Taplin and Eylmann.
11 Taplin's list is much longer, it encompasses those animals named by Carter, partially under other descriptions; it does not, however, include the wild goose. Carter indeed said to me that there were other *ngatji*, but he could not think of them at the time.
12 This claim can also be attributed to times long gone, if it is to be considered correct at all.

Index

A

Aboriginal: children 113; language 270; life 11; lore 12; nations 1; people ix, x, 3; rights 1; settlement 115; woman 145; *see also* Aborigines; Indigenous Australians

Aborigines 29, 32, 49, 68–9, 72–3, 92–3, 96–103, 108, 111, 115, 117–19, 122, 124–33, 135–6, 145–6, 148, 162–9, 174–5, 193, 211, 215, 218–19, 224–8, 231–3, 236, 239, 274; *see also* Indigenous Australians

Aborigines' Friends' Association 251

Adam, Leonhard 16, 263–4

Adelaide ix, 1–3, 5, 8, 10, 12, 23, 31, 35, 37, 46–7, 49, 58, 67–8, 76, 91–2, 95, 106–8, 113, 115–17, 121, 124, 128, 131, 134–5, 143–4, 146–8, 158, 161, 173–4, 184, 193–6, 232, 243–5, 251–2, 255–6; region 2; Town 24; tribes 24, 30, 33, 35–6, 101, 200–1, 204; *see also* Tarndanya

Adelaide Museum 243, 260

Adelaide, University of 76

Adelaide Zoo 243

Advertiser (Adelaide) 243

Afghan people 4

Africa 26, 32, 85, 197, 225

African Negroes 26–7

Albert, Lake 77, 108–9, 254, 261; Passage 254

Alcheringa time 162

Alexandrina, Lake 77, 85, 106, 108–10, 252, 254, 257, 264, 266–7

Allen, Harry Brookes 244

Altona 41

American languages 180–1

Americas the 49, 287 *see also* South America

Anatomical Department, Sydney 244

Anatomical Institute Berlin 243

anatomists 243, 248

anatomy 223–4, 243–4, 248, 250

Angas, George 119, 173

Anglobalisation 3–4

Anglophones 13

Anhalt-Cöthen 173

animism 274

anthropologists x, 3–5, 7, 12–17, 161, 239, 251; physical 15, 17, 251

anthropology 7, 11, 13–16, 223, 228–9, 239, 244; *Anthropologie* 15;

physical 15; *see also* ethnography; ethnology
Antipodes the 10, 50, 66
Arabs 180
Aranda people (Arrernte people, Arunta people) 12, 160, 162–6, 169
Ararat 222
Arctic the 226
Arrernte people *see* Aranda people
Arunta people *see* Aranda people
Aryan 248
Asia 224; East 181
assimilation x, 3
Atalana 165
Atlantic, the 23, 41
Aus allen Weltteilen: Illustriertes Familienblatt für Länder- und Völkerkunde 194
Auschwitz 8
Australasian, The 166
Australia ix-x, 1, 3–11, 13–17, 42, 46, 49, 62–3, 75–6, 86, 160–2, 173–4, 177, 179, 181–2, 184, 193–5, 206, 220, 222, 224, 226, 232–3, 236, 238–9, 243–4, 250–1, 253, 257–8, 263; Central 160, 162–4, 168, 245; Indigenous 15–16; Northwest 16; Southern 17; Western 77
Australian Alps 77
Australian Museum, Sydney 244
Austria-Hungary 77

B

Backstairs Passage, South Australia 258
Baltic Germans *see* Germans
Baptists 62
barbarism 11, 69; barbarians, 112, 174, 178
Barker, Collet Captain 46
Barngarla language 115
Barossa Valley 76, 147, 173
Barow (Barrow) Creek 165

Basedow, Herbert 66, 162, 169
Basel Missionary Society 91
Bass Strait 32
Batavia 180
Bates, Mrs. 166
Battara yurarri (Gumtree people) 136–7
Behr, Hans Hermann 173–4
Berlin 15–16, 91, 115, 147, 184, 222, 243, 245, 263
Berlin, University of 184, 243
Bethany 116
Bethesda (Killalpaninna) *see* missions
Bible 4, 60, 146, 237–8
biologists 161
biology 14, 251; biological racism 7, 16–17
Blacket, John Rev. 161, 165
'blacks' *see* Indigenous Australians
Blandowski, Johann Wilhelm Theodor von 184–5, 192, 214
Boas, Franz 14
Bonin, Lake 50
Borneo 224
Boston Bay 134
Boston Island 134
botanists 173, 194
botany 173, 250
Botocuden 27
Brahmins 180
Brandenburg 9, 41, 76, 160
Brisbane River 228, 236
Britain x, 1, 3, 4, 9, 16, 76; *see also* Great Britain; England
British 4, 6, 15, 17, 161; *see also* English
British Royal Society 222
Bugle Ranges 193
burials 43, 50, 52, 73, 100, 111–13, 118, 124, 191, 219, 245, 271
Burke, Robert O'Hara 222, 232

Index

C

Cairo 250
California 52
Callabonna, Lake 243
Cambunga Lagoon 176
cannibalism 79, 166–7
Cape Jervis 78
Carter, Roland 263–7, 269–76
Celle 23
Celts 183
ceremony 32–3, 83–4, 98, 105, 111–13, 118, 151, 165–6, 177, 191, 198, 202, 215, 269, 271, 272–3
chauvinism: cultural 13
chiefs 70, 82, 93, 163, 213
China 224
Chinese 4, 179–80, 226
Christ 60, 98, 113, 253; Gospel of Christ 168
Christianity 17, 62–3, 74, 102, 144, 161, 169, 239, 267; *see also* Baptists, Episcopalian; Lutheranism; Protestant Christians
civilisation 14, 17, 59, 60–1, 63, 69–70, 175, 179, 182, 185, 195, 220, 239
classical: antiquity 234; languages 76
Coffin Bay 134, 139, 203
colonial 3–4, 6–9, 16–17, 76; empires 76, 263
Colonial Association (*Kolonialverein*) 76
Colonial Secretary 113
colonialism 5, 17; *see also* settler colonialism
colonies 7, 16, 136, 228; British 76; German 17, 76; Portuguese 32
colony 9–10, 23, 66, 74, 97, 124, 134, 173, 184, 194, 243; British 4, 9, 76; South Australia 9, 185, 251–2, 266; Victoria 50, 185

colonisation ix, x, 1–4, 6, 9, 4–5, 14–16; colonisers 11
colonisation commissioners 1
colonists x, 1, 32, 35, 38, 67, 69, 106, 132, 176, 226, 228
Cooper Creek 160
Coorong 77–8, 184, 222, 260
Cordes, Heinrich 144
corroboree (korróbora) 34–6, 58, 72, 88, 163, 175–7, 261, 271, 273
cosmology 3
Country 3, 136
craniologists 15
craniology 243
Crusades 179
Cuxhaven 41

D

Dahme 91
Darling River 79, 184–6, 191, 228
Darwin 251; Darwinian: social ix
Denmark 41
dialects 24, 32, 75, 85, 121, 136, 148, 175, 177, 181, 220, 266
decolonisation 3
Dieri people 165; language 160
diffusionism: theory 14, 16
disease 39, 73, 84, 120, 146, 157–9, 169, 190, 212–13, 256–7
dispossession 2–3, 5, 7–8
doomed race theory 15
dream time 162–3
Dresden ix, 91–2, 143–4, 185, 194
Dresden Mission Society 91–2, 102, 115–16, 119, 125, 132, 136, 143–4, 147
Duncan, Elisabeth 143
Dunera 263

E

East India: islands 32
Ebenezer *see* missions

economics 9, 263
education 59, 63, 95–6, 123, 143, 151, 174, 223, 227–8, 232, 239
Elbe River 250
emigration 49, 67, 76, 164
emigrants 23, 41
empire 3, 13, 76, 263; *see also* German Empire 77
Encounter Bay 23, 46, 85, 92, 98, 106–7, 108–9, 111, 113, 115, 120–1, 136, 147–8, 177, 195; *see also* missions
England 74, 94, 145; *see also* Britain
English 25, 38, 42, 46, 48, 59, 67, 75, 98, 119; language 5, 15, 30, 32, 42, 44, 59–60, 63, 119, 121, 146, 148, 177, 185; sectarians 181; *see also* British
entanglements 4, 6, 17
Entente Powers 263
entomologists 173
entomology 173
Episcopalian 98
Ethiopians 24, 26, 59
ethnographers 12, 161
Ethnographic Museum, Berlin 263
ethnography 49, 161, 193–4, 250, 264–6; *Ethnographie* 15; *see also* anthropology; ethnology; *Völkerkunde*
ethnologists 15, 263, 265
ethnology 263; *Ethnologie* 15; *see also* ethnography; *Völkerkunde*
Europe x, 1, 3, 6–9, 13–14, 16–17, 43–4, 61, 63–4, 66–7, 73, 76, 85, 94–5, 122, 125, 144, 146, 154, 225–6, 274
Europeans 1, 5, 8–10, 25, 39, 44–5, 47, 64, 67, 73, 79, 86, 92, 96–7, 101, 103, 105–6, 110–11, 113, 117, 119, 123, 127, 144–5, 149, 151–2, 154, 176–9, 187–8, 196, 198–9, 203, 214, 220, 226–30, 232, 247, 257, 265, 272
evolution 163
Eylmann, Paul Erhard Andreas 14, 250–1, 266
Eyre, Lake 12, 165
Eyre Peninsula 77, 193–4

F

First Nations people 2–9, 17; *see also* Aboriginal: people; Aborigines; Australians; Indigenous Australians
First World War *see* World War One
Fischer, Eugen 17
Flagstaff Hill 222
Flores 32
Forty-Eighters 66, 173; *see also* revolutions of (1848)
Franconia 160
France 77
Francophones 13
Frankfurt 173
Frankfurt Agreement 244–5
Frankfurt Parliament 49, 173
Franklin Harbour 136
Fredersdorf 160
Freiburg, University of 250
Frobenius expedition 16

G

Gawler, George Governor 46, 91, 136
genocide ix, 7–8, 15
geographers 24
Geographical Society of Berlin 24, 174
geography 24, 62
geologists 116
German 11, 15, 42, 86, 146, 266
German-Hebrew 146

Index

Germanic 180; Indo-Germanic: civilisation 182
Germans 1, 4–7, 9–10, 13–17, 66, 76, 116, 184, 193, 220; Anglo-German 16; Baltic 11; emigrants 23, 41, 49; Jews 263; Lutherans 147; migrants 6; missionaries ix, 4, 6, 11, 16, 43, 49, 236; science 6, 222; settlers 4; sojourners 6; Southern 253; travellers 223, 250; *see also*
Germany 3–13, 17, 24, 49–50, 66, 76, 92, 94, 122, 161, 173–4, 185, 193–4, 222, 232, 250, 252, 263; Admiralty 222; Anglo-German relations 16; Empire (*Reich*) 9, 13, 77; Imperial 7; State 13; *see also* anthropology; prisoner of war camps; settlements
Gerstäcker, Friedrich 5, 10, 49–50, 173
Gleiwitz (Gliwice) 184
Glenelg 23
Godeffroy 193
Gold Rushes 9, 143, 184
Göttingen, University of 243
Government 64, 67–8, 115–16, 123–4, 143, 168, 184, 221; English 74
Government House 63
Graebner, Fritz 15–16
Grampians 203
Granite Island 46
Grant, Douglas 263–4
Great Britain 263; *see also* Britain
Great Migration the 179
Greek 164; mythology 165
Greifswald 263
Gross Machnow 76
Guichen Bay 184
Guinea 23
Gulf of Carpentaria 226

H

Hahn, Dirk Meinerts 10, 41–2
Hallett's Cove (South Australia) 244
Hamburg 23, 41, 49, 66, 222
Hamburg University 222
half-castes 167, 245, 256, 260
Hanover (Hannover) 1, 243
Happy Valley Congregational Church 143
Havana 41
Hawson, Frank 132–4
Hebrew 146
Hegel, Georg Wilhelm Friedrich 13
Herder, Gottfried 13–14
Hermannsburg (Ntaria) *see* missions
Hindu people 181, 183, 192
historians 7–8
Hobart 222
Holdfast Bay 23–4
Holocaust 7
Hope, Lake 165
Horseshoe Bend 161
horticulturalists 193
Humboldt, Alexander von 173, 222

I

Ice Age 244
Immanuel Synod 160
immigrants 23, 41, 179–81
immigration 161–2
India 224
Indian archipelago 180; islands 32
Indigenous Australians 1–8, 10–17, 49–50, 115, 143, 161, 174, 180, 193, 228, 236, 243, 251, 263; Australians 82, 87, 175–6, 179–81, 185–6, 192, 223–6, 228–30, 233–4, 236, 239, 248–9, 251, 266; Australian natives 69, 77, 179, 194–5, 209, 220, 223, 244, 247–8, 264; Australian savage 227, 238; blacks 25, 37, 44, 50–63, 68–9,

74, 78–9, 83, 85–6, 112, 121, 163, 166–9, 196, 203–4, 208, 224, 226–7, 229–238, 245, 252–6, 261; women 111, 214; blackfellows 67, 169 *See also* Aboriginal: Australians; Aborigines
Indigenous peoples x, 5, 8–9, 14, 92, 179
Indo-European language 181
infanticide 123, 149
invasion ix, x; invaders 11, 177, 226
Irish 27
Israel 181
Italy 41

J

Jänicke's Mission Institute, Berlin 91, 115
Japan 180
Java 49
Jehovah 113
Jews 167, 263
journalism 10
Jung, Emil 76, 78, 82, 84, 86; Inspector of Schools
jus talionis 169

K

Kangaroo Island 23, 134, 258; *Karta Pintingga* (Island of the Dead) 2
Kant, Immanuel 13
Karatinjeri people *80*
Karkarinjerar people
Kauo people 139
Kaurna country (land) 2, 9, 90, 115; language ix-x, 2, 91–2; people ix-x, 1–2, 33
Kaurna Miyurna 1 *see also* Kaurna
Keysser, Frieda 160
Killalpaninna *see* Bethesda
King, John 232
King George's Sound 32
Kingscote 23

Klaatsch, Hermann 7
Klose, Samuel Gottlieb 112, 115, 143
Koeler, Hermann 10, 23–4, 39
Kohler, Josef 265
Köthen 173
Krause, Karl Friedrich Theodor 243
Krause, Wilhelm, 15, 243–4, 251, 261
Krefft, Gerard 184
Kukata 220
Kulturvölker ('peoples of culture')13–15; *Halbkulturvölker* 14

L

Lacepede Bay 78
Lampinjerar people 148
language ix, x, 1, 3–4, 11, 14–17, 23, 29–32, 59–60, 75, 91, 85–7, 91–2, 95–7, 100, 104, 107–9, 112–13, 115, 117, 119–21, 125–6, 131, 134, 144, 146–8, 160–1, 163–5, 169, 176, 178, 180–1, 194–5, 220, 232, 251, 266–7, 270
Lathinjeri people *81*
Latin 119
law 1, 10, 263; Aboriginal 2, 169, 228, 269, 272, 274–5
Leipzig 76, 193, 250
liberalism 9–10, 173
liberals 4, 66
Light Pass 160
Lincoln Point 64
linguistics ix, 6, 85, 161
linguists 263
Listemann, Gustav 10, 66
Löhe, Wilhelm 160
London 23, 144
Loritja (Luricha) peoples 160, 162, 165, 169
Löwenberg (Lwówek) 143
Lutheranism 91; Lutheran Synod, Adelaide 12

Index

Lutherans ix, 10, 143, 147, 160; Old 4, 9, 41

M

Malay 180–1
Malays 32, 26, 59, 179–80, 224, 226
Malli 138, 140, 142
marriage 63–4, 82–3, 94, 98, 148, 151–2, 196, 199, 211, 270, 272
Martin, Charles James 244
Maschmedt, Wilhelmina Charlotte 116
massacre x, 2
Mauritius 144
Maximillian II, Joseph, King of Bavaria 222
McLeay Museum 244
medicine 10, 243, 250
medicine men 61, 63
Melbourne 184, 194, 222, 244–5
Melbourne, University of 263–4
Menge, Johannes
Meningie 254–5
Merkani, the 79
Methodists 62
Meyer, Heinrich August Eduard Rev. 59, 85, 106, 109, 111, 115, 143–4, 147, 194
migrants 6
migration 9, 180, 258; see also Great Migration, the 179
Milang 252, 254–7
military 139
Milmenrure people 108
Minchin, Alfred Corker 244
mission: schools 50, 74, 147; stations 85, 160, 168, 251, 254–5, 257
Mission Aid Society 91
Mission Institute, Berlin 91, 115
missionaries ix, x, 3–4, 6, 9, 11–12, 16, 43, 45, 49, 62–3, 78–9, 85, 88, 91, 93–4, 111, 115, 119, 125, 135, 141, 143, 160–1, 194–5, 235–8, 251, 254–7, 265; Adelaide 92, 116, 232; Dresden 92; Dresden Four 115, 143
missions 134, 144, 162, 168–9, 236–7, 272; Bethesda (Killalpaninna) 12, 160; Ebenezer 92, 236; Encounter Bay 115, 147; Hermannsburg (Ntaria) 160–1, 251; Point McLeay (Raukkan) 81, 85, 251, 254, 256–7, 267; see also Basel Missionary Society 91; Dresden Mission Society
modern languages 76
Mongolians 181
Moorhouse, Matthew 2, 49, 58, 65, 106, 145
Mount Barker 41
Mount Gambier 184, 194, 222
Mount Lofty Range 252
Müller (Mueller), Ferdinand 193–4
Munich 222
Mura, Lake 165
Murondee 176
Murray Bridge 222, 255
Murray River (River Murray) 32, 46–7, 59, 64, 69, 79, 83, 87, 98, 107–8, 111, 115–16, 121, 125, 148, 154, 178, 184, 191, 193–4, 200, 222, 228, 253, 257; districts 196; Estuary 78, 85, 176; lower 79, 175, 193, 229, 231; mouth 43, 77–8
Murray tribes 196, 198, 200–1
Murray Valley 50
Murrumbidgee River 228
mythology: Greek 165
myths 81–2, 163, 179

N

Narrinjeri people 78–9, 81–2, 85–6, 88; see also Ngarrindjeri people
Narrinyeri people 266, 276
Narungga people ix

natural sciences 185
naturalists 184
Naturvölker ('natural' peoples) 13–15
Science Society ISIS (*Naturwissenschaftliche Gesellschaft ISIS*), Dresden 194
Nauro 136, 141, 220
Nazism 7, 16–17
Neuendettelsau 160
Neumayer, Georg von 222–3
New Guinea 164, 224
New Holland 24, 32, 118, 122, 175, 180, 182
New Hollanders 25, 29, 71, 180
New South Wales 32, 122, 226, 245
New Testament 60, 160
New York 41
New Zealanders 180
Ngadjuri people 2
Ngannityddi people 220
Ngarrindjeri: country, 264; language 86; people 2, 9, 82, 147, 263; territory 251; *see also* Narrinjeri, Narrinyeri; Njarringerie, Raminjeri
Njarringerie people 258
Nicholson, Margaret 92
Nordic 181
North Terrace, Adelaide 2
Northern Territory 14, 168

O

Oceania, people of 180; languages 181
Old Testament 146
Onkaparinga River 46
Ooldea 166
Overland Telegraph Line 251

P

Pacific, the 49, 173
Pankinjerar people 148

Papuans 67, 224–5
Parnkalla: language 115, 136; people 136, 220
Paul the Apostle 94; Romans 1 and 2
Peramangk people 9
Persian Wars 179
Pestanjee Bomanjee 91
Piltawodli (school) 91–2, 143
Philippines the 173
physicists 222
physics 222, 250
physiology 223, 245
Point McLeay *see* missions
Point Pass 160
Poland 184
politics 16, 173
polygamy 106, 118, 135, 190, 253, 272
Port Adelaide 24, 41–2, 66, 136
Port Lincoln 92, 115–16, 132, 134–6, 139, 141 194–5, 204, 210, 217, 220; natives of 136, 138–9, 141, 195–6, 200, 203–4, 208; *see also* missions
Portugal 41; Portuguese 32
Posen 9
Princess Louise 66
Prisoner of war camps (POW camps) 16, 263
Protector of Aborigines 2, 49, 106, 115, 119, 145, 193, 195; Adelaide Blacks 58
protectors: government 64, 74, 116, 123, 221
Protestant Christians 269
Prussia 4, 9–10, 184
Pukunna 220

Q

Quakers 136

Index

Queen Adelaide of the United Kingdom and Hanover *see* von Sachsen-Meiningen, Adelheid
Queensland 236

R

race 7, 13, 17, 24–6, 39, 42, 48, 73, 94–5, 119, 120, 136, 167, 177, 179, 183, 185, 192, 214, 223–5, 227–8, 240, 247–9, 264; Australian 239; Ethiopian 59; Malay 180; Malayan 59; *see also* doomed race theory
racism ix, 5–8, 13, 16–17
Ramindjeri language 115, 147; Raminjeri people 85, 115, 148–9, 155; *see also* Narrinjeri people; Ngarrindjeri
Ramong 125, 148
Raukkan *see* missions: Point McLeay
Reformation 119
religion 4, 9, 11, 41, 55, 63, 73, 81, 91, 97–8, 104, 121, 161–6, 175–6, 179, 182, 190, 236–7
reservations 67
Reuther, Johannes G. 12, 160
revolutions of (1848) 4; failed 9, 66; liberal 173; *see also* Forty-Eighters 66, 173
rights 1, 74, 226, 274
Royal Botanic Gardens, Melbourne, Victoria 193, 222
Royal Society of Victoria 194, 222
Rufus River 114
Rundle Mall, Adelaide 2
Russia 41
Ryan, Ch. Dr. 244

S

Saint Peter's College, Adelaide 76
Samaria 167
San Francisco 173
Sandgrove (Sandergrove) 252

'savages' 1, 29–30, 32–3, 35–7, 42, 44–8, 58–9, 62, 79, 174–6, 178, 227, 233, 237–8; savageness 198; savagery 26, 226
Saxony 91, 115
Sayce, Conrad 168
Schiller, Johann Christoph Friedrich von 175
Schürmann, Clamor Wilhelm ix, 4, 91, 95, 97, 99–100, 103, 115–16, 143–4, 146–7, 193–5, 197–8, 218
science 4, 7, 193
Semitic languages 181
settlements 1, 3, 8–10, 24, 33, 35, 41, 76, 105, 115, 120, 133, 136, 142, 220, 226–7, 233, 236; pre-settlement 3
settler colonialism 4, 8, 15; colonists 3; *see also* colonialism
settler colonies 8; British 1
settlers 1–4, 8, 10, 17, 46, 70, 74, 86, 132, 182, 226–7
Sicily 41
Siebert, Otto 161
Silesia (Śląski) 9, 143
sinology 263
skulls 245–6, 248
slavery 70–1, 273
Sleaford Bay 203
sojourn 10
sojourners 6
Solomon Islands 245
Solway 23
South America 27, 174, 224 *see also* Americas the
South Australia 1–14, 23–4, 42, 49–50, 66–7, 71, 76, 91–2, 115–16, 120, 122, 125, 143, 147–8, 173–5, 185, 193, 226, 244, 251, 265–7; language 30; *see also* Northern Territory

South Australians 2, 24–30, 40, 174; natives 205; 207; see also Aborigines; Indigenous Australians
South Australian Company 23
South Australian Gazette 100
South Australia Illustrated 173
South Australian Museum, Adelaide 244
Southern Australia 114
Southern Ocean 77
Spain 41
Spanish American 38
Spencer, Baldwin 161–2, 244
Spencer Gulf 77, 175
Stansbury 92
Sternicke, Friedericke Wilhelmine 147
Strathalbyn 252
Strehlow, Carl 12, 15, 160–1, 251
Swan River 32
Switzerland 91
Sydney 47, 49, 62, 103, 113, 122, 244
Sylt 41

T

Taganarin people 80
Tandanja (Tandanje) tribe (Adelaide)121, 125; see also Tarndanya
Tanunda 59, 76
Taplin, George Rev. 85, 87–8, 256, 260
Tarndanya 1, 3; see also Tandanja
Tasmania 23, 239
Tasmanians 224
Teichelmann, Christian Gottlob ix, 4, 91–2, 95, 111, 115, 126–8, 143, 146–7
Teutons 50, 183
Third Reich 14
Timor 32
Torrens River 38, 50, 68, 91

Torrens Weir 143
totemism 265, 269
Tranquebar 144
travel literature 49, 222–3
Tropic of Capricorn 227
Tunapapa 165

U

Ubach, Ernst 265
Uluru Statement from the Heart 6
Unaipon, James 81
United Kingdom 1
United States 41

V

Van Diemen Gulf 226
Van Diemen's Land 24, 32
Vedas 192
Victoria 50, 116, 143, 184–5, 193–4, 222, 226, 251, 263
Victoria, Lake 50
Victoria Ranges 203
violence 3, 7–8, 11, 15, 27, 59, 115, 233, 235
Virchow, Rudolf 245–7
Volk 14
Völkerkunde (cultural or social anthropology) 15, 194; see also ethnography; ethnology
von Anrep-Elmpt, Reinhold 10
von Sachsen-Meiningen, Adelheid 1

W

Walkerville 143
Waldeyer, Wilhelm 243
Wambirri yurarri (Coast people) 136
war 42, 45, 82, 148, 176, 188, 250, 268
warfare 55, 188, 200
warriors 33–6, 72, 105, 192, 217–18, 267–8, 258, 267–8, 276

Watson, Archibald 243–5
Wilhelmi, Johann Friedrich Carl (Charles) 193–4
William 23
Wills, William John 222, 232
Willunga 106
Wirramu 120
World War One 4, 11, 16, 161, 263
Würzburg 250

Y
Yorke Peninsula 92, 115

Z
Zebra 41–2
Zeitschrift für vergleichende Rechtswissenschaft 263
Zietz, Amandus Heinrich 243
Zoological Garden, Adelaide 244–4
zoologists 184
zoology 250

Wakefield Press is an independent publishing and distribution company based in Adelaide, South Australia.

We love good stories and publish beautiful books.

To see our full range of books, please visit our website at
www.wakefieldpress.com.au
where all titles are available for purchase.

To keep up with our latest releases, news and events, subscribe to our monthly newsletter.

Find us!

Facebook: www.facebook.com/wakefield.press
Twitter: www.twitter.com/wakefieldpress
Instagram: www.instagram.com/wakefieldpress

www.ingramcontent.com/pod-product-compliance
Lightning Source LLC
Chambersburg PA
CBHW021347300426
44114CB00012B/1122